Digressions on Some Poems by Frank O'Hara

JOE LESUEUR
DIGRESSIONS ON

Farrar, Straus and Giroux : New York

SOME POEMS BY
FRANK O'HARA

Farrar, Straus and Giroux

19 UNION SQUARE WEST, NEW YORK 10003

COPYRIGHT © 2003 BY THE ESTATE OF JOE LESUEUR

DISTRIBUTED IN CANADA BY DOUGLAS & MCINTYRE LTD.

PRINTED IN THE UNITED STATES OF AMERICA

FIRST EDITION, 2003

GRATEFUL ACKNOWLEDGMENT IS MADE TO ALFRED A. KNOPF, INC., FOR PERMISSION

TO REPRINT POEMS AND EXCERPTS FROM THE COMPLETE POEMS OF FRANK O'HARA,

EDITED BY DON ALLEN, COPYRIGHT © 1971 BY MAUREEN GRANVILLE SMITH,

ADMINISTRATRIX OF THE ESTATE OF FRANK O'HARA. PERMISSION SHOULD NOT BE

CONSTRUED AS AN ENDORSEMENT BY THE O'HARA ESTATE OF ANY INTERPRETATION

OR OPINION SET FORTH IN THIS WORK.

LIBRARY OF CONGRESS CATALOGING-IN-PUBLICATION DATA

LESUEUR, JOE.

DIGRESSIONS ON SOME POEMS BY FRANK O'HARA : A MEMOIR / JOE LESUEUR— 1ST ED.

P.   CM.

ISBN 0-374-13980-6 (HC : ALK. PAPER)

1. O'HARA, FRANK.   2. NEW YORK (N.Y.)—INTELLECTUAL LIFE—20TH CENTURY.

3. POETS, AMERICAN—20TH CENTURY—BIOGRAPHY.   4. ART CRITICS—UNITED

STATES—BIOGRAPHY.   5. GAY MEN—UNITED STATES—BIOGRAPHY.   6. O'HARA,

FRANK—RELATIONS WITH MEN.   7. LESUEUR, JOE.   I. TITLE.

PS3529.H28 Z7 2003

811'.54—DC21

[B]

2002033880

DESIGNED BY QUEMADURA

WWW.FSGBOOKS.COM

1   3   5   7   9   10   8   6   4   2

Contents

Contents · ix

Preface

Because I lived with Frank O'Hara for nine and a half years, from the summer of 1955 until January 1965, and because his poetry tends to be autobiographical, I am inundated with memories of our life together when I read certain works of his from that period and just before. The four apartments we shared, the people we saw, the events large and small that shaped our lives—all of this is brought to mind. Thus, in the present work, it was my intention to explore these aspects of Frank's poems, the evocation of old memories; and in doing so, I was discursive and disposed to going off on wild tangents. Also, since I thought it important that the reader have some idea of who I am and where I am coming from, I added extensive background material about myself—so much, in fact, that I had the uncomfortable feeling I was upstaging Frank. But what could I do? The book wrote itself, just as its title was automatic. These personal notes on Frank's poems are indeed digressions, and I make no claim for their value.

EAST HAMPTON, NEW YORK, 2001

Introduction: Four Apartments[*]

We met on New Year's Eve 1951, at a party John Ashbery gave in a one-room apartment in the Village. Paul Goodman said, "There's a poet named Frank O'Hara I think you'll like," and led me across the room to him. Tchaikovsky's Third Piano Concerto was playing at full volume on John's portable phonograph, and almost immediately Frank and I began dreaming up a frivolous ballet scenario.

The rest of the party is a blur to me. I don't know what happened to Paul after he introduced us, and the Tchaikovsky is the only piece John played that sticks in my memory. Also, I don't remember anything else Frank and I talked about that evening. But before we parted we learned that we lived near each other, only a block apart in the East Forties. And very soon we began to see a lot of each other.

In June 1955, when I moved back to New York after living out of town for a couple of years, Frank said he'd put me up until I found a place of my own. But come to think of it, I'm not at all sure that anything was said in a formal way. I often stayed with Frank on my weekends in town, and he always made me feel at home. So that was probably how we began living together: I just came for the weekend and stayed longer than I usually did.

---

[*] First published by the St. Mark's Poetry Project in the March 1969 issue of the mimeographed magazine *The World*. Since Joe LeSueur often refers to "Four Apartments" in his memoir, it is placed here as an introduction.

DIGRESSIONS ON SOME POEMS BY FRANK O'HARA

326 East Forty-ninth Street

On good days so much sunlight flooded the place that it woke you in the morning, and when you got up you could look out and see the new UN building, a fair amount of blue sky, and pigeons on the next-door roof. Inside, the view wasn't so good. It was a perfectly decent tenement apartment, a sixth-floor walk-up spacious enough for the two of us. The trouble was, it never had a really thorough cleaning, and just about anything you could think of was strewn through its four rooms. Then there was the cockroach problem. But Frank said, "The cockroach and the ginkgo tree are the oldest things on earth," as though that made everything all right. And the place needed a paint job so badly that it was a good thing you could hardly notice the walls for the paintings. By the time I moved in with Frank—he'd previously shared the place with Hal Fondren, who actually had it first, and then with Jimmy Schuyler—he already had a number of things by Joan Mitchell, Larry Rivers, Mike Goldberg, Grace Hartigan, Al Leslie, and other friends, as well as a very beautiful de Kooning from the mid-forties that really belonged to Fairfield Porter. Rudy Burckhardt said he wanted to photograph the place, it looked so great; but he never got around to it. Jane Freilicher, on the other hand, agreed with us that we needed somebody to clean the apartment, and she put us on to Mildred, a blasé cleaning woman who chain-smoked while she worked. So once a week for about two months—she simply didn't show up one Tuesday and we never heard from her again—Mildred would drop by and leave a trail of ashes through the apartment that testified to her thoroughness. On one of her visits, just as she was leaving, she looked over at the rows of empty beer bottles that were accumulating in the kitchen and said, "Boys, you'll never have to worry about getting up carfare so long as you've got those bottles." But in those days we didn't worry about anything, not really.

I guess that's why this is the apartment I'm nostalgic about, because later on we didn't lead such easygoing, uncomplicated lives. Frank ran the information desk at the Museum of Modern Art and I worked at the Holliday Bookshop on East Fifty-fourth Street. We could walk to work and meet for lunch, and at the end of the day we could forget about our jobs. Most important of all, Frank—unknown as a poet and not yet officially involved in the art world—had no demands made on his time. Going to parties, movies, and the New York City Ballet; drinking at the San Remo and the Cedar Street Tavern; sitting around with friends at home—that was how we filled so many of our nights. And as far as I could tell, writing poetry was something Frank did in his spare time. He didn't make a big deal about it, he just sat down and wrote when the spirit moved him. For that reason, I didn't realize right away that if you took poetry as much for granted as you did breathing it might mean you felt it was essential to your life. But I think Frank's attitude toward poetry, or toward life in general, was merely consistent with the way he lived. As important as art was to him, it was after all only part of life and not separate from it so that he had to shift into high gear to get ready for an aesthetic experience. He was in high gear all the time, high on himself, and his every waking minute, regardless of what he was doing, was vital, super-charged, never boring if he could help it. Two weeks before his death, during a weekend at Larry Rivers's place in Southampton, a particularly exhausting all-night session of drinking, talking, and listening to music prompted J. J. Mitchell to ask Frank, as dawn was breaking, "Don't you ever get tired and want to sleep?" Frank said, "If I had my way I'd go on and on and on and never go to sleep."

Maybe he didn't have his way, but he came awfully close. Sometimes he'd come home at three or four in the morning and charge into my bedroom. "Getting your beauty sleep?" he'd say caustically. Or: "Joe, would you mind getting up and having a drink with me? I have something I want to talk to you about." Other times, instead of waking me he'd write a note, which he'd leave on the kitchen table. One stands out in my memory: *Wake me up if you have to kill me. XXX F.* And the next morning—I'm talking about the later years now—he'd cough his lungs out, light a Camel, read a little Gertrude Stein, have a cup of coffee, sip an orange juice laced with bourbon while he shaved, get on the phone for fifteen or twenty minutes, then go off to the museum, where he'd work with extraordinary efficiency for a couple of hours before going out for a two-hour lunch preceded by at least one (but usually more than one) martini or negrone. If inspired, he'd also manage to squeeze in enough time to knock off a poem after lunch. Back home at six or seven, he was ready for whatever was on the agenda that night. Though he loved parties, he was relieved if nothing was happening and he could stay home, which meant watching Clint Walker in *Cheyenne,* talking on the phone with Bill Berkson for an hour, having a late dinner after lots of drinks, reading anything from *Harlow* to Pasternak for two or three hours, and ending up with a thirties movie on *The Late Late Show.* He was seldom ill; when he was, he didn't complain or indulge himself, and by the end of the day he'd be so restless that he'd drag himself out of bed, have a stiff drink, and by sheer will get back into the swing of things. I couldn't keep up with him, hardly anybody could. I think he exhausted everybody except Patsy Southgate, Joan Mitchell, and Barbara Guest, who stayed up with him longer than any of his men friends. Never the three or four of them together, of course; tête-à-tête until dawn was Frank's specialty.

Yet he always found time to write during the years we lived together, the last year or so excepted. Not that he needed much time, because he usually got what he was after in one draft, and he could type very fast, hunt-and-peck fashion. From the very beginning it seemed to me that he never tried to get a poem going, never forced himself to write; he either had an idea or he didn't, and that was all there was to it. Of course it's possible that any number of his things were written in that wonderful, generous hand of his, apart from his collaborations with painters. But I know of one or two non-typewriter works: his poem about James Dean "written in the sand at Water Island and remembered" and his "Lana Turner has collapsed" poem, which he wrote on the Staten Island ferry on the way out to a reading at Wagner College.(I might add that he opened his reading with the Lana Turner poem, got a good laugh, and was followed by Robert Lowell, who wryly apologized for not having written a poem for the occasion.) But ordinarily Frank was lost without his typewriter. I remember he wanted to write something one weekend at Morris Golde's Water Island beach house (not the same weekend as the James Dean poem). He said he wished he'd brought his typewriter and I suggested that he try writing without it. He took my suggestion, but what he wrote, or tried to write, was by his own admission pretty bad, and I think he threw it away without showing it to anyone.

The first time I observed Frank in action came early on, about a month after I moved in with him. Over coffee one Saturday morning he said he had an idea for a play. He began writing it a little before noon, and by cocktail time, which rolled around early on Saturdays, he'd finished it. What he wrote turned out to be a fairly long one-act play. He called it *The Thirties;* and John Ashbery liked it so much that Frank said he'd dedicate it to him. But like the play itself, this story has an unhappy ending. A couple of weeks later, after spending a week or so in Maine with Fairfield Porter and his family, Frank lost the original and only draft at Penn Station, along with his suitcase and typewriter.* John Button took up a collection from some of Frank's friends and bought him a new Royal portable, but Frank said he couldn't reconstruct what he'd written that day. And while the few of us who'd read the play found its loss sad and distressing, Frank characteristically took what happened in stride and never talked about it again. He had the same reaction when still another play, *The Houses at Falling Hanging,*† was lost after he'd given the only copy to the Living Theatre. He cared all right, but he couldn't waste time and energy fretting.

---

* I recently asked Alvin Novak what he remembered about the play. He told me he thought it was inspired by an Ernst Lubitsch drawing-room comedy from the thirties that Frank had seen that week at the museum. (That would figure, and the movie was probably *Trouble in Paradise,* which he described in his only movie criticism, an unsigned piece in *Kulchur,* as "the greatest drawing room comedy ever made.") But Frank's play was a drawing-room comedy with a difference, namely its tragic denouement. It was set in a European capital during the thirties, and it was all very lighthearted and sophisticated, somewhat in the manner of Noël Coward and, as Alvin says, reminiscent of a Lubitsch movie. But I think Frank was making a comment on the period. At its climactic moment— and this is about all either Alvin or I can remember, as we'd read the play only once through quickly and its plot was awfully slight to begin with—the leading lady, whose part was written with Lotte Lenya in mind, throws herself in front of a diplomat or general to shield him from an assassin's bullet. As she dies, she explains (this was the play's curtain line): "I was afraid it would mean war."

† This play I never read, and I've been unable to find anyone who remembers much about it. John Bernard Myers tells me it was inspired by an unusual house and household in Sneden's Landing, New York, where Frank went for drinks circa 1954. The house, an architectural nightmare, spilled precariously over the side of a ravine, and the hostess was a bigger-than-life creature who'd had the doors removed from the johns. From what I gather, the play had absolutely no line of action.

DIGRESSIONS ON SOME POEMS BY FRANK O'HARA

In January 1956, Frank took a six-month leave of absence from the museum—the only one he had from 1955 on—when he accepted a grant from the Poets' Theatre in Cambridge, Massachusetts, where he was presumably expected to write a play. But he hated being away from New York and all of his friends and returning to the scene of his college years, and while he was up there he wrote no play and only a few poems. When he could manage it he stormed back to New York, drank more than I ever saw him drink, and talked about how provincial and boring Cambridge was. The grant enabled him to see a lot of Bunny Lang and George Montgomery, his two great Cambridge friends, and he met and became friendly with John Wieners and Don Berry. Otherwise, the leave was sheer hell for him. Frank clearly wasn't cut out for grants, which he never applied for, or for places like Yaddo, where he never went; they created what I think he viewed as artificial writing situations. But it seemed to me the museum setup worked for him. Not that he liked the routine and the paperwork, which in fact frequently drove him to the point of despair; it was simply that he must have needed the reality and discipline of the workaday world. Renée Neu, who worked closely with him from 1960 on, helped him get through it. "I wouldn't be able to do it without her," he told me once when I asked him how he stood the routine. And finally, he believed in what he was doing. It wasn't just a job to him, it was a vital part of his life's work. And at the time of his death, with the Pollock and de Kooning shows on his agenda and a full curatorship in the offing, he was at last being put into a position that would draw upon his full resources.

90 University Place

This was a fair-sized loft apartment, and we moved here in February 1957, mainly because we wanted to live downtown. Its disadvantages were manifold: a thin partition between our two rooms that allowed no real privacy, a two-burner stove without an oven that made cooking a more exasperating chore than it already was, and a downstairs door that mysteriously stuck at night and forced us on more than one occasion to take refuge at Joan Mitchell's for the night. The apartment's one advantage, apart from good wall space for hanging pictures, was of course its location, which put us within walking distance of most of our friends' places and just down the street from the Cedar, where Frank could slip in for a talk with the painters he was so crazy about. Franz Kline was one of his favorites, and out of their Cedar-based friendship came the interview "Franz Kline Talking," which Frank conducted in our apartment. But "one of his favorites" is perhaps a little misleading, because he seemed to be inspired and exhilarated by all his painter friends, from Bill de Kooning, whom he idolized, to certain painters who appeared in the sixties, such as Allan d'Arcangelo. He devoted so much time to looking at and thinking about their work you'd have thought he had a vested interest in their development as artists. But I don't entirely go along with the idea, as suggested by several of Frank's friends, that his generosity took him away from his own work. That wasn't exactly what happened. He offered them encouragement, inspired them with his insights and his passion; they impinged upon and entered his poetry, which would not have been the same and probably not as good without them. And if he was generous with his time, it naturally never occurred to him; he was too busy enjoying their company, too stimulated by them to stop and wonder what was in it for him. Besides, Frank needed people—all kinds of people and not necessarily artists—and right to the end he always had room for someone new in his life.

All of this isn't to say that he wasn't generous to a fault. I remember his borrowing money from Larry Rivers so he could lend it to a friend, then paying Larry back and forgetting all about the money the friend owed him. And while he valued the works his artist friends showered on him, he never kept one of his lithograph collaborations with Larry, Jasper Johns, and Franz Kline that had been presented to him in recompense for the part he played. They all became gifts to friends. I guess his attitude toward those works wasn't any different from the way he felt about his only solo art effort: a charming collage featuring a photograph of Rimbaud he gave to Edwin Denby. Then there was the inordinate amount of time he devoted to helping friends who turned to him with their troubles. It was while we were on University Place that he really came into his own as a sort of confidant-confessor—except Frank, unlike an analyst or priest, did most of the talking.

DIGRESSIONS ON SOME POEMS BY FRANK O'HARA

He was a born talker, and he especially liked giving advice, which often came down to nothing more than encouragement: *You can do it, all you have to do is make up your mind; You've got lots of talent, so what's stopping you?* etc., etc. But it wasn't what he said that counted; it was his authority and passion, along with his marvelous understanding of a friend's needs, that made the difference. And there were times when I thought he was in love with at least half of his friends, for it was possible for him to get so emotionally involved that it wasn't unusual for him to end up in bed with one of them and then, with no apparent difficulty, to go right back to being friends again afterward. That was always his way in the years I lived with him. He didn't make distinctions, he mixed everything up: life and art, friends and lovers—what was the difference between them?

I've probably given the impression that life with Frank was a bit chaotic—and I guess it was by ordinary standards, whatever those are. But we also lived simply, made few demands on each other, and had a relaxed attitude when it came to household chores, which we'd tacitly divided up by the time we were on University Place. Frank supplied the liquor and always made sure the ice trays were full, and I bought the groceries and did most of the cooking. Economically, the arrangement put me ahead, for the liquor bills must have come to at least twice the amount I spent on food. But we never argued about money or about who was doing more around the house. We saved our energy for arguing about important things, like the merits of a new Balanchine ballet or what movie to see.

By now Frank was assistant curator in the museum's international program, which handled traveling exhibitions. This meant that he had bigger responsibilities, and as a result he was sometimes distracted from his writing. He realized what was happening and worried about it. But he never seriously considered giving up his museum job, because his passion for painting could only be answered by playing an active role in the art world. A line from one of his poems tells it all: "Sometimes I think I'm 'in love' with painting." He also began to have occasional dry spells, but all he could do was go on living and hope that out of his life another poem would emerge. At times like that he drank more than usual and made life hell for his friends, mercilessly took them to task or got difficult at parties. We all put up with this side of Frank, who was ordinarily more thoughtful and gracious than anybody around. Then, too, he usually touched on the truth, and we were grateful.

But Frank could get away with murder, and that wasn't just because his friends were afraid of tangling with him. At a large party given by Arthur Gold and Bobby Fizdale after an Alice Esty recital, Frank lost his temper when a former friend, an art critic, pursued him all evening in an effort to get back in his good graces. "Listen," Frank finally exploded, his voice loud enough so that half of the party heard him, "there are eight million people in New York and I like about ten of them and you're not one of them." The thorn in Frank's side was promptly removed by Arthur. "But, Arthur," I protested in amusement after the poor guy had been shown to the door, "he wasn't doing anything. If anybody was out of line it was Frank." Arthur couldn't have been less interested. "Frank can do what he wants in my house and if somebody's bothering him they've got to go." That was the kind of affection Frank inspired in his friends.

Besides the Kline interview, a number of other things Frank wrote at this time come to mind as I think back on our University Place days. And, not at all surprising, the works I remember almost inevitably grew out of an experience I shared with him. There was the weekend John Wieners stayed with us in the fall of 1957. Saturday afternoon John went to do some sort of research at the Forty-second Street public library while we went to see *The Curse of Frankenstein* at Loew's Sheridan. That evening John, high on benzedrine, came home and told us about the horrifying, hallucinatory experience he'd had at the library. Later, I said to Frank, "Isn't it funny, we go to a horror movie and don't feel a thing and John just goes to the library and is scared out of his wits." Over the next few weeks Frank wrote "A Young Poet," with its reference to our seeing *The Curse of Frankenstein* juxtaposed with an evocation of John's life. But sometimes it works the other way around: the details in a poem will remind me of a day I would otherwise have forgotten. Mother's Day 1958, for example. Frank was struck by the title of a *Times* book review, "The Arrow That Flieth by Day," and said he'd like to appropriate it for a poem. I agreed that the phrase had a nice ring and asked him for the second time what I should do about Mother's Day, which I'd forgotten all about. "Oh, send your mother a telegram," he said. But I couldn't hit upon a combination of words that didn't revolt me and Western Union's prepared messages sounded too maudlin even for my mother. "You think of a message for my mother and I'll think of one for yours," I suggested. We then proceeded to try to top each other with apposite messages that would have made Philip Wylie applaud. Then it was time to go hear a performance of Aaron Copland's Piano Fantasy by Noel Lee. "It's raining, I don't want to go," Frank said. So he stayed home and wrote "Ode on the Arrow That Flieth by Day," which refers to the Fantasy, Western Union, the rain, and Mother's Day. I couldn't have pieced together this memoir without Frank's poems before me.

441 East Ninth Street

We heard about the place from Larry Rivers and Howard Kanovitz. There were two small bedrooms on opposite sides of the apartment, and I saw this as an ideal arrangement that would give each of us privacy and allow me to get the sleep Frank so disparaged. Also, I liked the idea of the apartment being only one flight up and just off Tompkins Square Park. Frank, though never enthusiastic about the place, was eventually won over, and with Al Held's help we made the move. But by early summer 1959, when we'd been living there only a few months, we realized we'd made a terrible mistake. "Well, it was your idea to move here," Frank reminded me when I complained about the street noises and the alcoholic super who bothered us all the time and the cockroaches (the kind that don't necessarily restrict themselves to the kitchen) and a black rat the size of a well-fed cat, which appeared one morning. Even the park turned out to be a disappointment; in those pre-hippie days it was a bleak and forbidding place frequented by disgruntled old people. The apartment's low rent was its only asset, but what we saved in rent money was spent on cabs, as the place was terribly inaccessible.

Yet it was here that Frank probably reached the high point in his writing, both in productivity and quality. The reason isn't hard to find. He was indifferent about his surroundings: it was people who mattered to him. For in the summer of 1959 Vincent Warren entered his life, and right after that began the invasion of younger poets, spearheaded by Bill Berkson, who became his collaborator and great friend. Frank Lima, Tony Towle, Ted Berrigan, Jim Brodey, Kathy Fraser, Allan Kaplan, Ron Padgett, Aram Saroyan, Peter Schjeldahl, Steve Holden, Joe Ceravolo, David Shapiro—some of them found their way to Frank via Kenneth Koch's poetry workshop classes at the New School; a few had been in Frank's own workshop, which he ran only one semester; others simply looked him up on their own and came around. He never treated them as students or disciples but always as colleagues and friends, and his extraordinary rapport with them rivaled his deep friendship with painters.

It's no wonder that Frank accomplished so much at this time. Still, when I look back on our Ninth Street days, I don't understand how he managed not to be distracted from his writing. Despite new and more demanding responsibilities at the museum, he somehow found time to step up his social life, increase his circle of intimate friends, and galvanize those friends of his—myself included—who needed a little prodding. To get me going, for instance, he went so far as to collaborate with me on a three-act play and two teleplays, none of which turned out too well; but eventually, with his encouragement and show of interest, I wrote a play that was produced on *The Play-of-the-Week* television series.* Meanwhile, he was turning out one poem after another as well as occasional prose pieces. But as I've already indicated, Frank didn't need a great deal of time to do his writing, any more

---

* The three-act play I wrote with Frank, called *The Heat of the Night,* dealt with the problems encountered by a young black man and a pretty blonde who decide to marry. The girl's Quaker parents have no objection to the marriage, but the guy's proud, middle-class mother isn't sure the girl's good enough for her son. One teleplay, called *Stay Out of the Rain,* concerned a more conventional couple whose only problem was too much happiness, of all things, while the other one (untitled) had to do with the marital and financial problems of still another couple, a struggling New York painter and his ambitious wife. All three works had some good lines, most of them Frank's, but they also lacked genuine dramatic conflict.

than he needed ideal working conditions. I remember in particular how two works from this period were written.

One night after dinner—the manuscript carries the date September 3, 1959—Frank mentioned that Don Allen was coming by for a piece on poetics he'd promised for Don's anthology, *New American Poetry*.* It was already long overdue and he hadn't so much as jotted down an idea, though the piece must have been in the back of his mind for weeks. He poured himself a bourbon and water, thought for a moment, then went quickly to the typewriter. I asked him if he wanted me to turn off the radio. "No, turn it up," he said. "They're playing Rachmaninoff's Third next." I said, "But you might end up writing another poem to Rachmaninoff." He liked the idea. "If only I could be so lucky," he said. Then the concerto began and Frank was off. Less than an hour later—in fact, about the time it took for the concerto—he got up from the typewriter and let me see what he'd written. "Do you think it's too silly?" he said when I'd finished reading it. "No, I think it's great," I said. The only thing I didn't like or wasn't sure of, I told him, was the title, which was "Personalism: A Manifesto." "'Personalism' is the name of a dopey philosophy founded in southern California," I explained. "Oh, then I'll call it 'Personism,'" he said.

A month later we were planning to meet Norman Bluhm for lunch at Larré's. Norman was flying to Paris that night and I thought it would be nice if Frank wrote a little something for the occasion. I guess, as precedent, I was thinking of such off-the-cuff occasional poems as the one he wrote for John Button's thirtieth birthday and the one celebrating Jane Freilicher's marriage to Joe Hazan. So I called him at the museum and told him my idea. "Are you crazy?" he said. "We're meeting him in less than an hour and I've got piles of work to do." But at lunch he gave Norman a poem, the one called "Adieu to Norman, Bon Jour to Joan and Jean-Paul" and beginning "It is 12:10 in New York and I am wondering / if I will finish this in time to meet Norman for lunch." (Joan Mitchell and Jean-Paul Riopelle were flying to

*As it turned out, Don eventually used another statement by Frank in his anthology, and "Personism" first appeared in LeRoi Jones's magazine *Yugen*.

New York from Paris at about the same time, so the poem was written for them as well.) Come to think of it, I wonder if this story contradicts what I said earlier about never trying to get a poem going. Well, it's all speculation anyway. Maybe it's an example of action writing or spontaneous poetry. In any event, it's probably the only of his *Lunch Poems* written *before* lunch.

Frank may have written in a casual, offhand way, but he also took his work seriously and had a high regard for it. By that I mean he had enormous confidence, and that was why he was so indifferent about being published, so free of envy, and so generous in the support of poets he admired. When an attack was leveled against Allen Ginsberg at a Wagner College symposium in 1962, Frank came to Allen's defense with an argument that was both persuasive and impassioned. As I recall, it was implied by someone in the audience that Allen's poetry didn't merit the attention it received. But Frank wasn't bothered by Allen's fame any more than he was by his own lack of it. At the same time he rarely put down poetry he didn't like, and this attitude held for the work of the poets who won all the prizes. "It'll slip into oblivion without my help," he said once, then immediately began praising several poets whose recent work he admired. "But what about *your* work?" I asked at length. He looked at me as though he didn't understand the question. "What about it?" he said. "I mean," I said, "how do you think it stacks up against their stuff?" Very simply and without elaborating, he said, "There's nobody writing better poetry than I am." That was in 1961, if memory serves. But earlier than that, not too long after I met him, his confidence was so great that Paul Goodman interpreted it as downright arrogance. That was funny coming from Paul, though he may have had a point. But Frank's arrogance, if indeed it existed, was free of smugness, vanity, and petty ambition.

791 *Broadway*

Now, at last, in the spring of 1963, we found ourselves ensconced in a clean, comfortable, cockroach-free, eminently handsome apartment. A floor-through loft converted into a two-bedroom apartment, it looked directly out on Grace Church and had enough wall space to accommodate big-scale paintings by Helen Frankenthaler, Alex Katz, and Mike Goldberg. But we made the move from Ninth Street with considerable reluctance, as it wasn't our style to devote time, money, and energy to fixing up any of the places we lived in. Also, had it not been for Donald Droll, who occupied the second floor of the Broadway building, we would never have made such an ambitious move. Backed up by all of our friends, who seemed more depressed by Ninth Street than we were, Donald convinced us that we owed it to ourselves to live in a decent place.

It worked out beautifully—the apartment, I mean; Frank and I couldn't have been happier with the place. We had bigger and better parties, we filled the place with plants, we even managed to keep it reasonably neat. Beyond that, I find there's not much I can say about this final phase of our life together. It's still too close to me. Right now I attach some significance to the fact that lovely old Grace Church—as opposed to Joe's Deli and Garfinkel's Pharmaceutical Supply Company on Ninth Street—never found its way into Frank's poetry. But later on, I might see things in a different light. Frank, after all, was as energetic and involved in life as he'd ever been. He kept up almost all of his old friendships and constantly added new ones; the last readings he gave, at the Loeb and the New School, were well-attended, particularly by the younger poets; his trips abroad for the museum were, I gathered from the way he talked, among the happiest and most enriching experiences of his life. And in 1965 and 1966, respectively, he organized and selected the Robert Motherwell and Reuben Nakian shows. There was an engaging, semiprofessional production of *The General Returns from One Place to Another* in 1964, and the year before his death *Lunch Poems* and *Love Poems (Tentative Title)* finally appeared. But I have no memories of, no stories to tell about, Frank's writing anything while I was living with him on Broadway. He didn't write a great deal then, and if he had I'm not sure I would have known about it. Gradually, our lives had become separate; he went his way and I went my way. And in a sense Frank's life, though no more hectic, had become less private, for it was more involved with his museum work than with his writing.

Yet the less we saw of each other, the more we got on each other's nerves.

DIGRESSIONS ON SOME POEMS BY FRANK O'HARA

At Christmastime 1964, we had a series of long discussions and came to the conclusion that it was time to part. If we weren't going to share each other's lives the way we always had, we couldn't very well share the same apartment. We realized, too, that by separating we could go on being good friends. So in January 1965, I got a place of my own.

1968

WHO I AM AND WHERE I AM COMING FROM

According to "Four Apartments," Frank and I met on New Year's Eve 1951, at a party John Ashbery gave in his Greenwich Village apartment. Not so, it turns out, and it was John who set me straight—John, who has always been known for his infallible memory and for never being wrong about anything. But I had a more compelling reason for accepting his account of how Frank and I met. For when, in the spring of 1969, not long after my memoir appeared in *The World*, he sidled up to me at a party downtown and asserted in that cool, confident manner of his, "Joe, you and Frank met earlier that fall at a concert," it was as if he had commanded, "Open, sesame!" Instantly, before he spoke another word, the door to the storehouse of my mind flew open and everything came back to me: my running into John during intermission at a Town Hall concert one Sunday afternoon in the fall of 1951, his introducing me to someone with whom I barely had eye contact, and, just as the warning bell sounded, my introducing them to the person who had come with me—no, we could not have had a conversation, because that, through the years, would have kept the afternoon alive in my memory.

And now, as John continued with his account of the concert, reminding me that it was a program of contemporary American music, I remembered the searing self-consciousness that had swept over me as we were exchanging introductions, my blushing as I was wont to do in those days, usually when I thought I was being admired or scrutinized, but on that occasion for an entirely different reason: I'd come to the concert with a black man who was physically unattractive, which could not have been said of any of the Negroes I went to bed with and was happy to be seen with. Was I aware how heinous it was of me to be ashamed of my companion? You bet, and I reproached myself even as I wondered what John and his friend made of him. Oddly, it didn't occur to me that John, being up on everything, would know him by name: he was Howard Swanson, whose Short Symphony had just won

· 3 ·

the Music Critics Circle Award, which meant that I, being vain and callow, could have taken pride in being seen with him, no matter that he was unprepossessing.

As for John's friend, as to how he figured in all of this—again, I wasn't thinking; after all, this might be the only time we'd ever see each other, so on top of everything else it was ludicrous to care what he thought. And that wasn't all. As I'd learn in a couple of years, Frank had a predilection for black men that was so great, so inclusive, there was no way he could have entertained the notion that my companion wasn't *sortable*—or, as tacky queens said back then (the only equivalent for that Gallicism?), "not for streetwear."

No doubt about it, we met at that Town Hall concert in the fall of 1951, and I suppose I should leave it at that—except I can't resist adding a proviso of sorts about another concert, an earlier one, where I may have caught my first glimpse of Frank, a likelihood that came to Frank's and my attention because of, albeit indirectly, an inane line of dialogue spoken by Joan Crawford in a 1941 movie called *A Woman's Face*. We'd just seen it on *The Late Late Show* at one of John Button's TV evenings, probably in 1958, and as we were turning in, we began tittering over the line that earlier had John, Jimmy Schuyler, and the two of us roaring with laughter. Conrad Veidt is playing the piano for Joan Crawford—tossing off a Chopin nocturne, if memory serves. "Do you like music?" he inquires, as though the question is one of great subtlety. "Some symphonies," she answers grandly, "and all piano concertos." To us, that was camp of a high order, so I was a little surprised when now, at home, Frank seemed to have changed his mind: he abruptly stopped laughing and allowed, quite seriously, that he knew how the Crawford character felt. "I have yet to hear a piano concerto I don't like," he averred. I had no reason to disbelieve him, works like Paderewski's soupy Piano Concerto and Rachmaninoff's feeble Fourth being only two of the meretricious essays in the form I'd known him to sigh over. At the moment, however, I thought I knew of one piano concerto he wouldn't like. "What makes you think I haven't heard it?" he shot back when I proposed that possibility. "Because it can't have been played much since its first performance," I told him. "Which you heard," he put in. "Right," I said, "and I'll give you a hint. The pianist was the composer's wife." Frank said, straight off, "That could only have been Joanna Harris." "Very good," I said. "And Roy Harris gave his concerto the silliest title—" "The Pan-American Piano Concerto!" Frank broke in triumphantly. "It was played in Los Angeles in 1946, at the Wilshire-Ebell. And I loved it." "You were there?" I said in astonishment. "Just before my discharge from the navy," he said. "Wasn't Werner Janssen the conductor? He was married to Ann Harding, remember? Funny," he mused, "both of us being there before we knew each other." I thought a moment; I cast my mind back. "I remember seeing a sailor there that night," I said. "It was you, it had to be." Frank looked skeptical. "You were in the balcony," I continued, "three or four rows down from where I was sitting with a girlfriend from high school." He smiled, still unconvinced. "Of course I'd be in the balcony," he said. "It's all I could've afforded." As additional proof, I offered more details that admittedly may have come into my head through the power of suggestion. "You were alone, you arrived late, and you were the only sailor in the house," I told him. "Naturally, I'd be alone," he said. "It was hardly the sort of thing my buddies went to on leave." "I still think I saw you there that night," I insisted.

Whether I did or not seems unimportant to me now, because the picture I hold in my mind's eye, of a slightly built sailor slipping discreetly into his seat as the house lights dim and the conductor strides to the podium, is as vivid and indelible, and therefore as true, as anything I'll be writing about in these pages.

Let us go back to "Four Apartments" and its assertion that I met Frank on New Year's Eve 1951, at a party given by John Ashbery. *Paul Goodman said, "There's a poet named Frank O'Hara I think you'll like," and led me across the room to him.* And that, of course, was my real introduction to Frank, the one that took. It led somewhere and for that reason became etched in my memory.

At the time, Paul—the first intellectual, the first poet, and the first bohemian or nonconformist I ever got to know—was still in my life, still of some importance to me, and the hold he had over me, sporadic in the three years we'd known each other, came to an end once and for all when, by introducing me to Frank, he unwittingly turned me over to him. I don't mean to say I was a pickup with no will of my own, someone who was passed around, nor was I as deferential in my relations with Paul as might be inferred. Yet without question, I was unduly compliant and even submissive with friends I thought of, usually with justification, as superior to me in intelligence and accomplishment. Need it be added that I sought out exceptional people? I had since high school and I continued to do so through college and later, after I went to New York. While reflected glory was obviously what I sought, it could also be said that I was an intellectual climber, one with vague, pretentious notions about becoming a writer—which is to say, my desire to be a writer was not so much an ambition as a fantasy.

When Paul Goodman and I met, or introduced ourselves, under circumstances that might strike some readers as disreputable, I was due to graduate from the University of Southern California in a month and a half. Understandably, it was a period in my life fraught with uncertainty, so that my tendency to be acquiescent and susceptible to influence was more pronounced than ever—surely, an opportune moment for this messianic figure to enter my life. Yet Paul and I wouldn't have gotten together, I wouldn't have been drawn to him in the first place, had it not been for another desire, a desire far more compelling than my addled ambition to be a writer.

A classmate at school put his finger on it. "You're like Madame Bovary, languishing in the provinces," he kidded me, aware of my dissatisfaction with Los Angeles but not realizing his jest was no exaggeration. For just as poor Emma devoured sentimental novels, I was voracious since adolescence for anything that evoked New York—the gargantuan Sunday *New York Times* and the urbane *New Yorker,* which I pored over at the public library, and any book that had anything to do with New York. But at an even earlier age, when I was ten or eleven, I was having fantasies about big-city life that stemmed from movies set in Manhattan, most of them glossy M-G-M productions that so often seemed to feature a long-suffering, rags-to-riches Joan Crawford (yes, her again!), with whom I identified for the simple reason that, having read in *Photoplay* that her real name was Lucille LeSueur, I had become convinced we were related.

Before long, I deemed it my destiny to live in New York; there, and only there, would I find the glamorous and exciting life denied me in Highland Park, South Gate, Huntington Park, and Lynwood, the dreary communities of my childhood and adolescence. Why so many different places? Because my family, hard hit by the Depression, moved every two or three years in search of ever cheaper rentals. And with each move, my dissatisfaction grew along with my dreams of big-city life. But not until I was a senior in college did those dreams loom as an attainable reality—attainable because of the one-way, cross-country Greyhound Bus ticket I bought without telling anyone. I remember carrying it in my wallet; at odd moments, I'd take it out and look at it, simply look at it. It was my ticket to freedom and a new life. Its departure date: one month to the day after graduation.

"But why do you want to go to New York?" my mother cried, taken aback when apprised of my plans. "Let him go," said my father, who didn't care what I did. My mother, whose possessiveness more than matched his indifference, then wanted to know how long I'd be gone and what I'd do for money (yes, she treated me as though I were years younger and had never been away from home). "I've saved enough to see me through the first three or four months," I said evasively. Her litany of misgivings continued, but I stood firm; I had made up my mind.

Or had I? As graduation approached, nagging questions began to weigh on me: Did I have the courage to go someplace where I didn't know anyone? How would I support myself? What would I do? I had no vocation or skills, and I knew that my liberal arts degree was worthless. Plagued by second thoughts, I even entertained the notion that my mother might be right when she said I should stay put and get a job after graduation. But then, she didn't know me, the real me, for she was unaware of my dreams and aspirations, and had no inkling of my secret life, of its dire and shocking nature. So how could she advise me? She couldn't, of course she couldn't. Yet, no matter what I told myself, I became increasingly indecisive; and with time running out, I felt my resolve slipping away.

Enter Paul Goodman. The time: a Saturday night in the spring of 1949. The place: Maxwell's, a saloon right out of a Hollywood Western—rough-hewn, unadorned, with a high ceiling, exposed beams, and a rickety-looking staircase. Along with other respectable homosexuals, I was drawn to the place because of the trashy element that thronged its unlovely premises, riffraff of every stripe, an all-male assemblage of hustlers, drifters, rough trade, and transvestites kept in check by an indulgent, potbellied cop who appeared unruffled by his unusual beat. "It's so sordid," I remember purring in appreciation the first time I entered the place with two other thrill seek-ers from USC, "sordid" being a key word in our lexicon, the standard to which we held our libidinous experiences. But Maxwell's wasn't simply sordid, it was also the best queer bar in all of southern California in the years immediately after the war, not to mention the most notorious dive in the red-light district of downtown Los Angeles.

Socially, too, it was the place to be. I met Christopher Isherwood there one night, but the pandemonium of the place made conversation impossible; it wasn't until a number of years later, through Don Bachardy, that Christo-pher and I got to know each other. Paul, on the other hand, was unfazed by the turmoil and deafening din of Maxwell's; he singled me out, got me to talking, deftly drew me away from my companions. "You look like you go to college somewhere," he began, and with supreme confidence took it from there, plying me with questions about my studies at USC, where my major was English, and thereafter engaging me in a discussion of the present-day international literary scene, whose principal protagonists, I soon found out, were William Faulkner, Jean Genet, and the very person who was alternately holding forth and seeking my opinion, thereby impressing but not intimi-dating me.

Our improbable conversation must have gone on for close to an hour, during which I was flattered into thinking that I was as intellectual as I sometimes pretended to be—no doubt the desired effect of my wily interlocutor. I was being taken seriously, I was holding my own with a well-read and articulate writer who might be as important as he claimed. And my new friend was from the city of my dreams!

Suddenly, blinding lights flooded the place as last call was announced over a blaring loudspeaker: it was ten minutes to midnight, closing time for Los Angeles bars in those days. As always, there was an immediate stir in the crowd as frenzied queens clamored for one more drink while others, single-minded about finding a bed partner, tried to score at the last minute. To add to the commotion, a fight broke out when the potbellied cop, now out of patience, herded several troublemakers in the direction of the exit, prodding them with his billy club as if they were cattle, while at the same time, not far from where Paul and I stood, two johns began fighting over Ace, the star hustler of Maxwell's, a sullen youth whose extraordinary endowment was displayed through torn, tight-fitting Levi's. I remember thinking that it was the best night ever at Maxwell's.

Paul looked alarmed; it occurred to me that he'd never before been to a rough place like Maxwell's. "Let's go!" he shouted above the tumult. "Want to have coffee with us?" he added, taking my arm. By "us," he meant himself and three ordinary-looking men who, on cue, appeared at our side; and before I could respond to Paul's invitation, introductions were made with last names included, not the usual gay bar protocol that eschewed such formalities. Feeling as if I had nothing to say about what was happening—resigned, as well, to not making out that night—I drifted off with my new friends, pausing at the exit to wave a nonchalant goodbye to my erstwhile companions, whose jaws dropped in dismay over the company I was keeping.

Later, one of them—the same classmate, incidentally, who likened me to Madame Bovary—asked about Paul. In this instance, he was more baffled than amused. I don't remember how his question was put—it was along the lines of "Who the hell was that cruddy-looking guy you took up with at Maxwell's?"—but I remember my indignant reply: "That was Paul Goodman, an important avant-garde writer from New York." He roared with laughter, and rightly so, as I'd not read a word Paul had written nor did I even recognize his name when he identified himself. "Paul Goodman?" said my friend, who prided himself on being well-read. "Never heard of him." (In another part of the country, in Cambridge, Massachusetts, where he was in his third year at Harvard, Frank O'Hara had yet to meet Paul Goodman, whose cult following barely existed at the time, yet he was already reading things of Paul's—stories, poems, and critical pieces—that appeared with some regularity in the little magazines. Which I suppose says something about the disparity between the lives Frank and I were leading in 1949.)

I could hardly disagree with my classmate's assessment of Paul's appearance and physical attributes, for he was truly a sight, beginning with the way he dressed. Shabby and ill-fitting and in what I remember as dismal shades of gray and brown, his pathetic, makeshift wardrobe—he'd wear any old thing, I would soon learn—gave the impression that he had no regard for his appearance, while the overweening confidence he exuded gave a contradictory impression, one that bespoke complete satisfaction with what he was wearing, not to mention an unawareness that his was a face marked by nature's cruel indifference. His eyes were lackluster, his nose a misshapen hook, his mouth an unlovely orifice. In fairness, I suppose I could add that he had a head of thick brown hair; but it was matted, had no sheen, and appeared not to have been recently washed.

Afraid my classmate might draw the wrong conclusion about the night's activities, I explained that I only went to have coffee with Paul Goodman and his friends, omitting any mention of where I ended up—not, as I had expected, at the gathering place after Maxwell's closed, a sleazy, all-night cafeteria at Broadway and Third Street, but at a rambling, nondescript frame house on a street called Benton Way, a fifteen-minute drive from Maxwell's, where Paul's hosts lived and where he was being put up during his two-week stay in Los Angeles. Five people lived there, the three men I'd met at Maxwell's plus two other members of this unusual communal arrangement, a man who was described to me as a poet and a soft-spoken, middle-aged woman, "the resident fag hag," as I was informed later by one of their friends. All of the men, by the way, were between five and ten years younger than Paul, who was in his late thirties at the time.

I don't remember whether we actually had coffee, all I remember is that everyone talked a lot and that it was like nothing I'd ever heard—knotty, incisive, often with a psychoanalytic thrust. Except for the fag hag—in reality, an attractive woman who was a fanatic cat fancier and an inveterate reader of mystery stories—everyone was Jewish: that, I concluded, had a lot to do with the tenor of their conversation, its intensity and intellectual rigor. I seem to remember there was talk about poetry, *Partisan Review,* Wilhelm Reich, Wittgenstein, Marxism, Freud. Of course it was all a jumble to me as I gamely tried to grasp the gist of their abstruse discourse. I was hooked, nevertheless, so that by the time I made my exit, at about two in the morning, I knew I wanted to see more of Paul and his interesting friends.

Over the next couple of weeks before Paul's departure, I frequently got together with this spirited band of gay bohemians, which was how I thought of them—though, I might add, more bohemian than gay, since they weren't run-of-the-mill queers defined by their sexual orientation but fiercely independent intellectuals who happened to be homosexual; and to me, they constituted a new breed, an elite brotherhood whose ranks I instantly wanted to be part of, like a child who dreams of running away to join the circus.

As absurd as that last bit sounds, it was pretty much the way I felt—and how could it have been otherwise? I grew up in a large Mormon family from which, at an early age, I felt alienated. I knew I was different from my brothers and sisters and knew, too, by the time I was an adolescent, that the day would come when I'd have to carve out a life of my own, a deviant, subversive life that would also be intellectually stimulating—very much like the lives of Paul and the Benton Way crowd, though in my case I'd be saddled with something they knew nothing of: the burden of a strict religious upbringing. In order to be free I'd feel compelled to react against it by going to extremes, by leading a wild, dissolute life, by defiantly doing everything I was taught not to do, everything disapproved of by the Church of Jesus Christ of Latter-day Saints: drinking coffee, tea, and alcoholic beverages; smoking, masturbating, ignoring the Sabbath, taking the Lord's name in vain; having sexual relations outside marriage; and, most egregious of all, recognizing and acting upon what I knew was natural to me, a curse (that was how I thought of it) I acknowledged from the time I was eleven or twelve when my older brother, irritated with me over something, innocently called me a queer, a word I'd never heard before, causing our mother to stop what she was doing and admonish him, "Never call Joe a queer! It's the next worst thing to being a murderer." A *queer*! The word resonated, took hold; whatever it meant, I embraced it, I knew I was a queer—why else would Mama take on so, leap to my defense? And from that moment on, through adolescence and early youth, my conviction that I was an outsider and a pervert, along with the concomitant feelings of guilt and shame I experienced, colored my perception of myself and the world. How fortunate, then, that my lust should prove far more efficacious than any negative feelings thrust upon me, so that what I once thought of as a curse I came to regard as a blessing, a blessing that enabled me, year after year, until the advent of AIDS, to wallow in lusty, uninhibited gay sex.

Now an unpleasant development that I'm sure you saw coming: on Paul's last night in Los Angeles, I stayed over at Benton Way and wound up in bed with him—the last thing I wanted to happen, but what could I do? He was persuasive, not to say coercive, and, more important, I set great store by his offer of friendship, his insistence that I look him up when I came to New York. Still, though I had something to gain by not rejecting him, it might be wondered why I was so accommodating, then and on future occasions. Well, how often do attractive women endure sex with unattractive men, without anyone thinking twice about it? Isn't it what we expect? Such women are powerless, and through sex with repulsive but powerful men they appropriate power. To some extent I was like those women, since I sometimes played a comparable role with aggressive men who possessed none of the physical attributes I ordinarily sought in bed partners. Yet power wasn't what I was after, not exactly. It was something else, something undefined and therefore far more elusive.

I didn't finish telling you about the night of the New Year's Eve party at John Ashbery's, which was for cocktails, though I'm sure it dragged on until midnight or later, with martinis and Manhattans (very à la mode in those days) served along with a few bags of potato chips. From there, from John's modest, sparsely furnished apartment, I taxied uptown to Francesco Scavullo's townhouse and studio on East Sixty-third Street, where a large, lavishly catered New Year's celebration was already in full swing and where Gianni Bates, Scavullo's assistant and my lover, about whom you'll be reading more later, was impatiently awaiting my arrival. Without waiting to be introduced to the fashion model he was standing with, and without so much as an apology for being late, I shouted above the din, "I just met the most terrific person!" Those were my very words, not an approximation or paraphrase, for as I write this, an unbelievable five decades later, I remember sensing the importance of the occasion, that in Frank O'Hara I'd happened upon what I'd been searching, hoping, waiting for in my two and a half years in New York. But what, exactly? An opportunity, a way of life, an avatar? Perhaps all three, though not a new lover, not someone to replace Gianni—that was one thing I was sure about. Otherwise, what I felt was nebulous, purely instinctual, which means I didn't question or analyze what had happened between me and the warm, animated person I'd met that evening, someone to whom I was not, by the way, sexually attracted. Then, too, I felt so confident that he liked me and wanted me for a friend that I didn't stop to wonder if his interest in me extended to sex. Nor did I wonder why I had been drawn to him any more than I understood what had happened in the hour and a half I'd spent with him. All I knew was what I felt, an eagerness and a sense of security, the conviction that my life would be different now, and better.

I'd like to go back two and a half years, to the beginning of my New York adventure—to an early morning in mid-July 1949, right on schedule, just as I planned, exactly a month after I received my useless bachelor of arts degree.

Weary, scruffy, eager to put my ignominious cross-country experience behind me, I alighted at a place that was more like hell than the city of anyone's dreams: the old, now-defunct Greyhound terminal off Times Square, the acme, the crown jewel, of all the vile bus stations I'd been exposed to from Los Angeles to New York, and especially hellish now because of the foul air and stultifying heat of the city in midsummer. It was there I lingered until I thought it seemly, late enough in the morning, to turn up at Timothy Hobson's Murray Hill apartment, Timothy being the only person I knew in New York apart from Paul Goodman. They would never meet, I saw to that: to me, they represented incompatible worlds, in a sense what would prove to be my two lives, my superficial uptown life and my serious—pseudo-serious?—downtown life.

Paul had barely returned to New York when I met Timothy, whose appearance in my life seemed no less providential than Paul's. He'd come to the West Coast on a business trip with Herbert Jacoby, the nightclub and cabaret entrepreneur who employed Timothy as a troubleshooter at the Blue Angel on New York's posh East Side. I don't remember how or where Timothy and I met; all that comes to mind now is a steamy weekend at Laguna Beach and being told, before we parted, that I'd stay at his place when I came to New York and I'd spend the first two weeks of August with him in Provincetown, all of this stated in no uncertain terms, as though I had no choice in the matter—fine by me, since having Timothy as well as Paul awaiting my arrival in New York gave me double entrée to the city, not to mention the promise of an affair with an attractive guy who knew his way around.

A year younger than me, though he gave the impression of being several years older, partly because he smoked a pipe and spoke in peremptory tones, Timothy seemed ideal for a pleasure seeker plainly destined to muddle through life. But the person who loomed as a potential lover in the afterglow of Laguna Beach was someone I never got to know. Significantly, I was unaware that he was linked to the most sensational court trial of the day until one morning, a week after my arrival, I opened the *Times* and found his name emblazoned on the front page. *Found* it? It jumped up at me from a dense block of print, as forcefully as if it were my own name: Timothy, identified as Alger Hiss's stepson, was scheduled to testify that afternoon at the perjury trial that was tearing the country apart. So that was why he'd gotten up at dawn and taken an early-morning train to Washington! I was at once stunned, apprehensive, and titillated; yet when I saw Timothy late that night at the Blue Angel, where I sometimes joined him for a drink, I said nothing about the story, nor did I subsequently refer to it or bring up his relationship to Hiss. That was how close we were; there was nothing but sex between us, though I didn't fully admit it to myself at the time. Also, in retrospect, I realize that the curious way I dealt with the Alger Hiss situation—*didn't* deal with it—says a lot about my style at that time, my social and psychological disposition, if you will: I had the crazy notion that if I asked questions or confessed my ignorance about something, I'd appear gauche and unsophisticated, the last thing I wanted. At all costs, the impression I had to give was that nothing shocked, daunted, or touched me.

Meanwhile, amid all this Sturm und Drang, had I become so distracted that I was unmindful of what brought me three thousand miles across the country? Not at all. Map in hand, walking fifty, sixty blocks a day that first heart-pounding week, resorting to the subway only to get to far-flung parts of Manhattan, I eagerly surveyed the reaches of the island I'd so long ago decided would one day be my home. Yet the place I'd envisioned paled beside the reality—an understandable reaction for me to have, since all I ever knew, all I could compare the city of my dreams with, were dismal suburban sprawls where nobody walks because there's nothing to see, where there is no spring, summer, fall, or winter, only unchanging days of humdrum sunshine that lull you into thinking comfort is all that matters in life. Small wonder I was agog over what I instantly recognized as the cosmopolitan atmosphere of a true city, whose want of any hint of provincialism thrilled me to the quick and whose awesome scale, ceaseless roar, and pounding tempo at once stunned, stirred, and seduced me. God, how the place bustled with people and activity! And it was now my home, it was where I would live.

But what of the mesmerizing messiah who'd had me under his spell back in Los Angeles? (Did I make clear what a stimulating talker Paul was, how his overbearing confidence was matched by his perspicacity?) Anything but forgotten, he was seldom far from my thoughts, because more than ever I felt drawn to what he represented, the kind of life I knew I'd promptly pursue if and when Timothy gave the signal that we were not seriously committed to each other. And, indeed, the very day he made it known that he didn't expect us to spend every night together—it was right after our two weeks in Provincetown, a less than thrilling experience for both of us—I was on the phone to Paul and in no time was wending my way downtown to a tenement on Ninth Avenue off Twenty-eighth Street (I may not be entirely accurate about the location), where, in a fourth-floor walkup, what I soon learned was called a cold-water flat, he lived with Sally and their young son, Matthew.

Never had I seen a dwelling of its kind before. With a sinking sensation, I wondered if this was what lay in my future. There was no refrigerator, I remember, and only the barest necessities—a pinched, woebegone scene, to be sure. But because of the presence of books, hundreds of them, and an upright piano, it was inevitable that I would romanticize the whole thing, and that I'd do it in hackneyed, bohemian terms: the struggling artist, his humble garret, a life of high-principled sacrifice—actually, not far off the mark, however myopic my point of view. But it would be a while before I fully understood the unusual nature of Paul and Sally's relationship, which seemed to be determined as much by her permissiveness as by his insistence on self-gratification. At least it was my impression that she was as approving of his egocentricity and homosexual activities as she was of the radicalism he lived by, principles that kept him outside the system and prevented his making a decent living. True, he had published a score of books by then and his work appeared regularly in the little magazines, but the proceeds from his writing amounted to very little, certainly not enough to live on. Come to think of it, I don't know how he and Sally made out before the publication, eleven years later, of *Growing Up Absurd,* which brought him recognition and economic security.

Paul was admirable, no question of that; but without pretty, bespectacled, quiet-as-a-mouse Sally in his life, he would have been forced to change his ways. She made everything possible, including the small, brief role I played in the Goodman household—a role, incidentally, that involved my baby-sitting Matthew several times, naturally without remuneration from Paul. All of which might sound like a ménage à trois. Well, it wasn't—because Sally and I weren't close enough for such an arrangement. It was simply that this intelligent, private person, to all appearances oblivious of whatever might be going on between Paul and me, didn't make me feel unwelcome on those occasions when I dropped by and went off with her derelict mate, to whom, by the way, she wasn't legally married, since the state could not, in Paul's view, have anything to do with his private life.

A couple of months later, an old friend of Paul's congratulated me on passing the "Sally test"—indisputable evidence, I was given to understand, of the power wielded by this quiet, unassuming woman who was the mainstay in Paul's life. At the same time, in regard to her attitude toward Paul and me, it would be an exaggeration to say that our peregrinations had her blessing; I suspect she was indifferent, even relieved, to have him out of the house, as he could not have been easy to live with.

What, then, were her feelings toward Paul? Was she in love with him? Was she *ever* in love with him? It was my impression that she was somewhat in awe of him, as so many of us were; otherwise, I had no idea what she felt about him. And Paul? Well, one could see that he cared for Sally and needed her, and he clearly had great respect for her, his philandering notwithstanding. But did he love her in a more or less conventional, romantic sense? Somewhere he has been described as "ostentatiously homosexual and ostentatiously heterosexual at the same time," which must have come from Paul himself. (So struck was I by this brazen assertion that I made a note of it.) To me, it's a joke; I never knew him to show the slightest interest in women, and I can't believe he had an eye for them. Like all the self-proclaimed bisexuals I've ever known, he had a pronounced preference—in his case, for what can be described as the male shiksa. Sally I remember as more boyish than womanly, also as a prototypical shiksa. Maybe that tells us something about the soi-disant bisexuality of Paul Goodman.

None of these considerations crossed my mind at the time, doubtless because I was too busy thinking about myself; I don't even remember wondering how Sally felt about what was going on—that was how callow and self-absorbed I was. Thus, with Paul as my Virgil, I blithely set forth on a pilgrimage that put me in touch with what would form the nucleus of the downtown life I referred to earlier. And what comes to mind when I think of that phase of my New York adventure? Before anything else, one of three bars, the crypto-queer San Remo, the macho Cedar Street Tavern, and the blustering White Horse Tavern. A couple of times, Paul took me to a working-class bar on the waterfront where he sometimes sat at a table and wrote his stories and poems. Next, I remember down-and-out parties of cheese, crackers, and jug wine. At one such gathering I was asked, quite seriously, if I was a Stalinist or a Trotskyite; I guessed right and claimed allegiance to the Trotsky camp. And in a grim and dusty industrial loft on the Bowery, Anarchist Club meetings were held on Saturday afternoons; they were solemn, earnest, somehow touching to me—it was as though its downtrodden members (including a young poet named Irving Feldman) believed that their utopian flights of fancy might someday materialize. Less portentous but more amusing were the gatherings at the Gotham Book Mart, receptions for famous writers crowded with shabby literary types and freeloaders who had no compunctions about lifting first editions when the cranky, gray-haired proprietor, Frances Steloff, wasn't looking. The most notable book party of all was the one in honor of a sodden, bleary-eyed Dylan Thomas, who looked as though he wanted to be someplace else. I went to recitals of modern dance and recitals of experimental music that I pretended to like; at a storefront gallery on Third Avenue I saw—and didn't know what to make of—a group show of Abstract Expressionist paintings; I was present at the first productions of the tacky yet exciting Living Theatre (exciting, that is, unless they were mounting one of Paul's didactic, singularly undramatic plays); and then there were Cinema 16 screenings of grainy, amateurish "art" films in a cavernous auditorium in Chelsea, a cheerless experience that was not a bit like going to the movies.

It was all very heady, my having moved so abruptly into a world different from anything I'd ever known, beginning with its imposing dramatis personae, the people I met through Paul. A list of their names, when I reel them off, is for me like a mantra that magically evokes the essence, spirit, and soul of the downtown New York I knew in 1949 and on into the early fifties: Julian Beck, Judith Malina, Parker Tyler, John Ashbery, Willard Maas, Marie Menken, Dorothy Van Ghent, Edouard Roditi, John Bernard Myers, Harold Norse, David Sachs, John Button, Alvin Novak, Jean Garrigue, Marguerite Young, Oscar Williams, Gene Derwood, John Cage, Merce Cunningham,

DIGRESSIONS ON SOME POEMS BY FRANK O'HARA

Lou Harrison, Irving Feldman, José Garcia Villa, Anaïs Nin, Ned Rorem, Edwin Denby, Harold and May Rosenberg, Percival Goodman, Irving Howe, Dwight Macdonald, George Dennison, Fritz and Laura Perls, Isadore From, I. Rice Pereira, Robert Motherwell, Jackson Pollock, and, if we forget that prior meeting through John Ashbery, Frank O'Hara. Some of these names are now forgotten and will be recognized only by readers who were on the scene at that time. As for me, I remember each person as sui generis and equally consequential, each his or her own person. And because of Paul, because he made me feel at ease with these writers, artists, and intellectuals (he drew me out, brought me into their conversations, treated me as their peer), I felt that New York was where I belonged, a conviction he instilled in me and then, a couple of years later, gratuitously undermined—an ugly development I'll cover in due course, along with a rundown on Paul's brief, abortive friendship with Frank.

I did not stay with Timothy for long. Less than a week after our return from Provincetown, we parted amicably, without regret, and I moved directly from his place to the apartment of a window dresser with whom I'd struck up a conversation at one of the bird circuit bars—the Blue Parrot, I believe. We had nothing in common and we didn't especially like each other, but he needed a roommate to split the rent as much as I needed a place to stay. Down to my last few dollars by then, I was confronted with the necessity of finding work, any kind of work. No, I couldn't write home for money, because there was no money to write home for; my family was hand-to-mouth working class. And of course Paul was in no position to help, nor had I any other friends I could turn to. Yet I dragged my feet for weeks on end, slept around, had a good time, did nothing to improve my lot. I survived by accepting every dinner invitation that came my way, mostly from casual friends I made in Provincetown, and at other times by making a meal of hors d'oeuvres served at cocktail parties—on balance, as I look back, an exhilarating if somewhat trashy phase of my youth. Unquestionably, the initial excitement of being in New York had not worn off; it kept me enthralled, it fed the illusion that what I was doing had point, validity, meaning.

Then one morning, after resourcefully holding my anxiety at bay for close to a month, I awoke with a start and had no idea where I was until I glanced around and saw that I lay in bed next to a stranger whose apartment, I gradually remembered, was on the Upper West Side, some hundred blocks from the window dresser's downtown digs, a hike I did not look forward to on what I could see with a glance out the window was a blustery, rainy day (subway fare was only a dime, but the night before I'd foolishly chipped in my few pieces of change, all the money I had, for the taxi ride uptown). Only then did the full extent of my plight hit home and compel me to act. Without waking the cute guy at my side, foregoing the pleasure of another coupling, I eased myself out of bed, gathered my clothes and dressed as I tiptoed out of the apartment, carrying my shoes until I was in the hallway, at which point I buzzed for the elevator and finished dressing. I was on my way; I had already begun putting my life in order.

It was an endeavor that entailed a grim ritual. Beginning that very morning, and for the next week and a half, I started each day by scrounging through litter baskets in Washington Square Park until I found that morning's *New York Times,* which in 1949 went for the princely sum of three cents. On one such morning, around the beginning of October, I ran across what I was looking for, an ad in the help wanted section that seemed right up my alley. NO EXPERIENCE NECESSARY were the key words that caught my eye. Next thing I knew, I was applying for a clerical job in the garment district.

Never had I felt so dejected: the place turned out to be a sweatshop of what I imagined to be Dickensian squalor. But what could I do? I had no options, so I took my lumps—that is, I took the job when it was offered to me, at $30 a week before withholding taxes—and then, determined to save enough money for a Greyhound ticket back to Los Angeles, I showed my mettle by dutifully turning up for work through all of October and all of November and well into the month of December, until exactly one week before Christmas, which was when my days of woe, the misery and humiliation of punching a clock, of sorting, stamping, and filling orders, came to a screeching halt thanks to the sort of experience that befalls most carousing homosexuals: I had a chance encounter in a bar that altered the course of my life—

for a second time, now that I think of it, because meeting Paul at Maxwell's should also be counted as a turning point.

On this occasion, it was the now-defunct San Remo in the heart of Greenwich Village, at the corner of MacDougal and Bleecker Street, one of the places Paul had introduced me to, a dark, smoky, cramped establishment with a big espresso machine, loud jukebox, and crowded tables, whose patrons—seedy literary types, grubby bohemians, quiescent queers who shunned screaming gay bars—mainly drank fifteen-cent glasses of tasteless draft beer. The night in question was an unusually slow night in the middle of the week, when there was a lot of talk and no serious cruising, so that it could have been as early as half-past ten when I resignedly set my empty glass on the bar, shook my head as the bartender approached, then turned to leave—at which point, out of nowhere, a man in his early thirties, tall, square-jawed, with regular features, a face and demeanor out of an Arrow Shirt ad, magically materialized, smiled openly, and asked, as though he meant what he said and wanted an honest answer, "How're you doing?" And indeed that was the kind of person Humphrey Noyes—Reichian therapist, Yale man, scion of an Oregon lumber family—proved to be, decent, upfront, uncomplicated. And what did I say in reply? Perhaps feeling maudlin from too much beer, though I'm sure I also hoped to be provocative, I made this preposterous assertion: "I'm a failure." Humphrey said, "You're too young to be a failure," and took me home with him.

As so often in the past, I allowed myself to be swept along by what seemed an inexorable march of events. Actually, it was Humphrey who in this instance shaped the immediate course my life would take, and he did so from the outset when the usually obligatory "Your place or mine?" went unspoken—he simply hailed a cab and gave his address. Thus, the next morning, I was not terribly surprised when, over coffee, he suggested that I quit my job and move in with him. "Just call them up and quit," he said, handing me the phone. "All right," I said, relieved I'd never again have to set eyes on the place. And later the same day I carted my few belongings uptown to Humphrey's unimaginative but comfortable apartment. "Let's get away for a couple of weeks," he said as he watched me unpack. "It's hell in New York during Christmas." Before I knew what was happening, I was whisked off to Sea Island, Georgia, for a winter vacation.

I took these whirlwind developments in stride, as if I had never planned on returning home or knew all along I'd be rescued in time. Also, it was with great aplomb that I settled into and soon took for granted my cushy life. How cushy? Let me think. In the top drawer of his chiffonier, my benefactor-lover kept an ivory box stuffed with twenty- and fifty-dollar bills so that I need never ask for pocket money, and as a guideline he offered these words, which I interpreted as leave to indulge myself: "When in doubt about financial matters—say, you can't decide whether to take the subway or a cab—stop and ask yourself, 'What would Humphrey do?' " And that became the byword when I was with certain of my indigent friends: "What would Humphrey do?" I'd suddenly whoop when we seemed to be heading for a subway station; then, stopping in my tracks, I'd hail a cab with a flourish, gaily shouting, "Taxi!"

To my credit, something mattered more to me than taking cabs and throwing money around: the cultural advantages I could now enjoy, concerts and plays to my heart's content and afternoons whiled away in art galleries and museums and, to give my life structure, three graduate literature courses at Columbia University. As a concession to Humphrey, for that was how I thought of it, I also sat in his Orgone Box three times a week, twenty minutes each session, and tried to get through one of Wilhelm Reich's weighty tomes. I was not in love, but I was content.

Then disaster struck in the form of nightmares, nosebleeds, headaches, and, most distressing of all, a sleep paralysis that seized me afternoons when I lay down to read. Almost immediately, I'd grow drowsy and then, as I hovered between consciousness and a curious state of sleep wherein I knew I was dreaming but was unable to stir myself awake, it would happen. With my eyes wide open, staring at objects in the room, I would be riveted to Humphrey's sofa as a buzzing sound emanated from the ceiling, swiftly descended, and headed straight for the middle of my head where, instantly transformed into what seemed a dentist's drill, it would zip across my teeth, both upper and lower rows, before flitting off into space, from whence it came. Then and only then, with a spasmodic jerk, would I be released from the immobility that had gripped me moments earlier.

A strange phenomenon, indeed; and stranger still, it became my secret fetish, an experience I compulsively courted. For as much as I feared it, I desired it: I thought of it as my scourge, a retribution visited upon me; and somehow, along with my nightmares, nosebleeds, and headaches, it caused me to treat Humphrey wretchedly, as though he were to blame, which in a way he was, for in retrospect I realize that my life with him, its comfort and security, gave me the luxury to experience symptoms that pointed to my being repressed and in need of help.

At the time Humphrey understood better than I what was going on, and I'm sure he knew why I drank too much, slept around, was frequently sharp with him: I wasn't cut out to be a kept boy. So—no surprise, I knew he'd had it with me—he decided against taking me to Europe for the summer and proposed that I remain in New York, get a job, find a place of my own, and begin seeing a psychoanalyst. I assented to all four suggestions, with alacrity to the last, and not simply because I liked the idea of being analyzed (it seemed glamorous). I knew I needed help and I wanted it more than I wanted a trip abroad, because as sybaritic as I was, I clung to an idealistic notion that so far had not motivated me: I felt—I had to believe—that there was more to life than having a good time. Undergoing psychoanalysis was surely a step in the right direction.

It was not a Reichian Humphrey sent me to. "You need depth analysis," he said. "There's a Jungian I want you to see." Had his decision anything to do with my having had a number of ineffective, Reichian-derived sessions with Paul Goodman, who had recently become a lay therapist? (Lay therapist, indeed. Paul saw nothing unprofessional in being intimate with someone he was treating.) To this day, I don't know if Humphrey knew of those clandestine sessions or, for that matter, of my wretched ongoing liaison with Paul. In any event, it is interesting that Humphrey should have turned to a highly respected analyst trained in an entirely different discipline from the one he embraced. (Later—how labyrinthine it all became!—I learned that the group of Reichians he was working with took it upon themselves to investigate me and then, having concluded that I was a notorious Forty-second Street hustler who would surely undermine Humphrey's efforts to go straight, urged him to end his relationship with me. Instead, he terminated his affiliation with this particular group of Reichians.)

There is no point in my going into the menial job and the cheap apartment I found: what signifies is the treatment I underwent, and even there I am reluctant to go into detail, one's psychoanalysis being about as interesting to other people as one's dreams. But it's an important part of my story, so hang on.

My analyst was a woman named Assia Abel, who must have been in her late sixties when my sessions began in the spring of 1950. A taciturn, dwarfish Russian Jew lame from an automobile accident that took the lives of her husband and only child, she immediately made me think of Maria Ouspenskaya playing the part of a gypsy fortune-teller in—was it *The Wolf Man* starring Lon Chaney, Jr.? Yes, I think so; and a B movie at that. No matter; transference was immediate, and within a month my psychosomatic ailments vanished as mysteriously as they had appeared.

(Psychosomatic ailments? Since they were bound up with an anomalous period of two and a half years, a period that relates neither to what came before in my life nor to what came after, I feel it's appropriate that parentheses enclose and set apart my account of that time. Self-contained, irrelevant, surreal—that is how the experience strikes me now, as something that happened to someone else, a story I read or a movie I saw. Another odd aspect to it: for all the discomfort and misery of those years, what I mostly remember is the exhilaration I felt at being on my own for the first time in my life, with no family or church to stifle and constrain me. Young for my age, just out of high school, I should have been homesick but I wasn't, so thrilled was I to be living with men, exclusively men, one of whom—a beautiful Swede from Kenosha, Wisconsin, as straight as I was queer, at twenty-six an older man to me—not only returned my love but made the first move, drew me to him, kissed me on the mouth, so unlike the others who jerked off with me out of frustration, not out of love, and turned away afterward. Need it be added that these two and half years were the time I spent in the service?

Drafted into the army, I served as a medic attached to the mine platoon of an infantry antitank company that saw action at the tail end of the Second World War—specifically, during the last phase of the Italian campaign when Italy was known as the Forgotten Front and Allied troops were deployed in a holding action. Inevitably, my wartime experience came up early on in my sessions with Dr. Abel, who drew me out until I found myself describing an incident I'd never until then thought about or spoken of with anyone. It was immediately following my outfit's baptism of fire, in the summer of 1944, when we were stationed in a rest area awaiting further orders. Along with seven other medics, I was ordered on a detail about which we were told nothing except that a truck would pick us up and that we'd be separated for the day from our respective platoons. Medics weren't assigned to details like KP, guard duty, and digging latrines, so we knew it had to be something else; but what that might be, we hadn't an inkling—not until the truck arrived and we caught sight of what was in the back, four litters and a pile of mattress covers, and then saw that the officer up front, sitting next to the driver, was "a fucking chaplain, for Christ's sake," muttered one of the men.

When we set out it was already brutally hot and still, except for the distant sound of artillery. For maybe an hour we drove over a rough, hilly terrain before pulling to the side of the road, and it was only then, after we dismounted, that our detail was explained to us. "Let's get to it, men," concluded the pale, frightened-looking chaplain. We hung back, having assumed he was coming with us—why else would he be in charge? But he shouted, "Go on! You have your orders," and remained with the driver while the rest of us paired off and, with litters and mattress covers, fanned out over the area where, two days earlier, one of the companies in our regiment had seen action for the first time and had suffered unusually high casualties. Because the bodies would quickly decompose in the intense heat of mid-July, the evacuation had to be done without delay. So, off we went in search of corpses that lay scattered about, over low, rolling hills, in ravines and rifts. But as I tried to describe to

Dr. Abel what it was like—how I felt, what the men did, said, how they re-acted—my memory became clouded. I couldn't remember feeling anything but a strange numbness. "What was happening didn't seem to be happen-ing," I said. "Does that make sense?" Dr. Abel nodded for me to continue. I vaguely remembered laughter—but over what? The absurdity of the situa-tion? Then, clearly, I remembered my partner shouting to the others before we went our separate ways, "Let's not let the rear echelon bastards get any-thing." And that, I seemed to remember, was what happened, though several of us had no part of it: bodies—torn, bloody, rotting, exuding the stench of decomposed flesh, with flies and bees buzzing around them—would be stripped of watches and money before they were slipped into mattress cov-ers and placed on litters that with great effort were lugged down to the road, where the chaplain stood waiting beside the truck. He would mumble a prayer, clutching his Bible, his eyes averted, and we'd toss the bodies onto the truck as though they were sacks of flour or meal. We'd take a ten-minute break, then get fresh mattress covers and go off to collect more bodies strewn over the Umbrian hills; and after a while, the pale, frightened-looking chap-lain didn't bother to say a prayer over the dead men but kept his distance, moved away when we approached, urged us to hurry and not waste time. "The son of a bitch," said my partner. I remembered all that; I could see the scene clearly as I spoke to Dr. Abel. "Yes, yes," she would say. Now it was late afternoon, the sun still blazed mercilessly, the bodies were four deep in the truck and our work was done. Before long, a truck with a kitchen unit ar-rived—this I remembered more clearly than anything else, no doubt be-cause it was a reprieve, a welcome end to the day's grisly activities: a line of steaming vessels was quickly assembled and we knew we weren't getting C or K rations, which was what we expected, but a hot meal that we set to like ravenous dogs, our appetites keen from our arduous labor. "Vut else?" said Dr. Abel when I was finished. "Nothing," I said, "that's it." She sat quietly across from me, waiting. "You told me you received a medal," she said. "Tell me about that. Vut did you do?" I said I couldn't remember exactly, but I knew it was nothing; it was just something that happened. "And I wasn't scared," I told her, "not like in my dreams when I stand up in my foxhole and

scream, and then the others know I'm a coward." She asked if I had my cita-
tion; that would tell us what happened. "I lost it in Italy," I told her. "You have
no record of it?" she said, clearly surprised. "There was a story about it in my
hometown paper," I said. "I'm sure my mother kept it; she was very proud of
my medal." Dr. Abel had me write home for the newspaper clipping, and a
couple of weeks later I brought it to one of our sessions. She had me read it
out loud:

SOLDIER WEARING BRONZE STAR
RETURNS TO HUNTINGTON PARK

Pfc. Joseph M. LeSueur of Huntington Park, who recently returned
with the 91st Infantry Division from Italy, is a typical example of the
heroes who form the medical corps in action.

During action near Monghidoro, Italy, Pfc. LeSueur was with his
platoon in a building taking shelter from an enemy bombardment.
He saw a vehicle receive a direct hit and one of its occupants thrown
seriously wounded on the road under heavy artillery fire. Immediately he hurried to the wounded man.

Because the man was too seriously hurt to be moved, Pfc.
LeSueur stayed in the impact area and treated him under fire. After
he had rendered sufficient medical attention to the man, he carried
him to the building and continued his treatment. For his courageous action, Pfc. LeSueur was awarded the Bronze Star medal . . .

And there you have it, the story—the cause—of my psychosomatic ailments
and their cure.)

In the weeks that followed, we continued to talk about my experiences in the
war—or I did; Dr. Abel merely prompted me on occasion. "How did you do
that?" I asked when my headaches, nosebleeds, and strange sleep paralysis
had ceased. "Dat is not important for you to know," she answered, reminding me more than ever of Ouspenskaya. In the ensuing weeks, months, and
years, we moved on to archetypes, the collective unconscious, my persona,
my anima—all by way of the wild, primordial dreams I was having and of

which I kept a record. At each session, three times a week for three years, I described my nocturnal life and free-associated while Dr. Abel sat in brooding silence, her curiously beautiful dark brown eyes burning holes through me. We rarely touched on the quotidian; whom I was seeing, what I was doing, whether I was happy or unhappy—none of this seemed to concern Dr. Abel; my soul was all that mattered. Not until my last session did I think to inquire about my homosexuality. All she said was: "You do not have to be homosexual. Follow your nature."

Perhaps what was most extraordinary about my analysis had to do with the role Humphrey played. He was no longer involved with me once we broke up, yet he paid for all of my sessions without asking to be recompensed. That I didn't pay for my own analysis was a matter Dr. Abel and I had to deal with, or rationalize, at the outset; it was resolved the first day I came to her Riverside Drive apartment, so desperately in need of help was I. Meanwhile, during the three years of my analysis, Humphrey was helping others, all without question more deserving than I—Howard Swanson, for instance (I'd gone to that Town Hall concert with him because Humphrey was suddenly indisposed); and there was another black musician, a pianist named Eugene Haynes, whose debut at Carnegie Hall was made possible thanks to Humphrey.

I don't remember ever expressing my gratitude; I imagine I didn't. But when someone saves your life, how do you thank that person? You can't; you don't.

This brings us back to New Year's Eve 1951, when Paul Goodman said, "There's a poet named Frank O'Hara I think you'll like," and led me across the room to him.

DIGRESSIONS ON SOME POEMS BY FRANK O'HARA

LINES TO A DEPRESSED FRIEND

[1 9 5 3]

Joyous you should be,
of all things sweet the most constant and most pure,
eager for what might be obtained—

Luck and life and hideous certainty preventing,
ease and certainty inclining to neglect,
so that real world, blue in the eye! this
umber sky about us drowns. And where
emptiness appears bounding along, of
unrest the most diligent athlete and keenest mate,
remember the pleasure, even there, your beauty affords.

It always struck me as appropriate that a twin bed doubling as a couch was the most imposing and virtually the only piece of furniture in the tiny apartment at 348 East Forty-eighth Street, a living area that might have passed muster as a bachelor's apartment but not when occupied by two, which was the case for a year or so in the early fifties when it was the epitome of the cloying expression "love nest," the very words pronounced by Frank when I showed him the place not long after we met. It was then that we began spending mornings together, always at his place around the corner, on East Forty-ninth Street, because it was more commodious and welcoming than the close quarters where I nested, very happily, very snugly, with my

darkly attractive boyfriend, a first-generation American who called himself
Gianni Bates. In "To Gianni Bates," written a year after "Lines to a Depressed Friend," Frank capriciously alluded to Gianni's being

> Like a piano concerto your black
> and white eyes, your white face and bright black hair.

At first, Frank wondered about my lover's name. I told him it was "Gianni," not "Johnny," and confessed that I used to think it had been appropriated from *Gianni Schicchi,* since I knew he was crazy about Puccini's operas
and not too crazy about his given first name, Carmen, which was dropped in
favor of what I learned was his actual middle name, Gianni. As for his sur-
name, which Frank found outrageously incongruous, I explained that it had
long ago supplanted the mellifluous but too Italian-sounding DiOrio, and
that was thanks to Gianni's father, the proprietor of a midtown after-hours
club who was as eager to play down his Italian heritage as his son was proud
to proclaim it, *Quattrocento* being Gianni's byword whenever he spoke of his
glorious lineage, about which I always had my doubts. But one thing for sure:
Gianni was (is) a first-rate photographer, as witness the elegant picture of
Frank that adorns the frontispiece of the Knopf edition of *Collected Poems*
and, in a cropped version, can be found on the cover of the paperback
reprint.

And what has any of this to do with "Lines to a Depressed Friend," which
had two earlier titles, "To Joe" and "Umber of the Sweetest Evocation"? Just
this: it was Gianni who, by taking a new lover, caused me to be the "depressed
friend" of Frank's title, thereby occasioning the poem itself. And the time
and place would naturally come into it, for this was when I first knew Frank
while the place so buoyantly brought to mind, that tiny single-room apartment, was where love and lust were conjoined, causing a male neighbor to
pound on our wall late one Sunday afternoon and shout, his voice that of the
frustrated queen whom we'd run into a couple of times in the hallway: "It's
the Sabbath! You must stop what you're doing in there!" I keenly remember
how selfish and wise we were not to desist because of the Sabbath or some
pathetic queen.

DIGRESSIONS ON SOME POEMS BY FRANK O'HARA

Frank's poem for me—here is what happened. My heart having been broken for the first time in my life and my vanity blown to smithereens, I went to him with my tale of woe, poured out what was left of my heart, with of course no mention made of my hurt pride. Why Frank? Why was he the one I sought out for solace? Later (it was after Frank's death, a time of summing-up) Gianni would say, "He had an old soul." I think all of his friends went to him in times of travail, sadness, rejection; it was as though he knew something we didn't know, had the understanding, depth, experience, the *soul* of an older person—"It was from a previous life," Gianni insisted.

And there at the reception desk of the Museum of Modern Art, amid the clamor and confusion of a crowded Saturday afternoon, I became the only person of any possible interest or concern to him. "What was he like?" I demanded. "Tell me the truth—I have to know, even if it hurts me." Frank knew what I wanted and needed to hear, and bolstered my self-esteem with assurances that I was more attractive than the stud Gianni brought by the museum one day. Later he called me at home. "Don't be depressed," he said. It must have been then that he wrote these lines to console me.

Lines to a Depressed Friend · 33

SECOND AVENUE

[M A R C H – A P R I L   1 9 5 3]

. . . "Nous avons eu lundi soir, le grand plaisir de rencontrer
à l'Hôtel Oloffson où elle est descendue, la charmante
Mlle. Anne R. Lang, actrice du Théâtre Dramatique de Cambridge.
Miss Lang est arrivée à Port-au-Prince le mardi 24 février
à bord d'un avion de la 'Resort Air Line.'
Cette belle artiste a visité les sites de la Capitale
et est enchantée de tout ce qu'elle a vu. Elle est fort
éprise de notre pays." . . .

he thoroughfare that gives its name to this work played an important
part in our lives over the years; whether uptown or downtown, it seemed
always to be our mainstay, where we did so much of our shopping, eating
out, and moviegoing. I even ended up there, at 26 Second Avenue, after
we broke up; it was my last place in New York. But it is Frank's "Second Avenue," his longest poem, that concerns me now and enlivens my fancy, for it
was during the period of its composition that we became close friends. If my
note on "Lines to a Depressed Friend" was the ideal place to start, this is the
logical follow-up.

Larry Rivers tells us that "his long marvelous poem 'Second Avenue' was
written in my plaster garden studio overlooking that avenue." Well, not every
last line and definitely not what Frank tossed right smack into the middle of
it on an April morning in 1953. I can't remember whether it was a feature

story or an item on the society page, I only remember that it was a clipping from a Port-au-Prince newspaper. It came in the mail that morning, enclosed in a letter from Frank's peripatetic friend Bunny Lang, who was knocking around the Caribbean, "Up to no good, no doubt," said Frank with a smile, before reading the clipping aloud, his uninflected, nasal voice an encumbrance to his French accent: "Nous avons eu lundi soir, le grand plaisir de rencontrer à l'Hôtel Oloffson où elle est descendue, la charmante Mlle. Anne R. Lang, actrice du Théâtre Dramatique de Cambridge. Miss Lang est arrivée à Port-au-Prince le mardi 24 février à bord d'un avion de la 'Resort Air Line.' Cette belle artiste a visité les sites de la Capitale et est enchantée de tout ce qu'elle a vu. Elle est fort éprise de notre pays." Then, with great deliberation, after delivering a rapturous rundown on his correspondent and assuring me I'd meet her soon, he strode to his typewriter and promptly picked up where he left off—it was as if Bunny's clipping was what he'd been waiting for.

At the time he was writing "Second Avenue," I lived around the corner from Squalid Manor, which was what Bill Weaver called Frank's apartment at 326 East Forty-ninth Street, and the name stuck, even though it was quite a nice place. I used to drop by mornings before Frank had to check in at the Museum of Modern Art front desk. My favorite day was Wednesday, because that was the day the Modern was closed and we had the entire morning to ourselves. We'd sit around and drink coffee and smoke Camels and listen to a program called *Piano Personalities* on WQXR that started at 9:05, which meant I had to race over to Frank's as soon as I saw my lover off to work at a quarter to nine. Unlike Frank, not to mention my lover who worked as assistant to the fashion photographer Francesco Scavullo, I had a lot of time on my hands, the fifty-minute, three-day-a-week sessions with my Jungian analyst being my only occupation, if it can be called that and if you don't count the master's degree in English I was desultorily working toward at Columbia University—a perfect setup for me, since attendance was never taken in any of my courses. Thus, after seeing my analyst, whose Riverside Drive apartment was near the campus, I'd occasionally look in on one of my classes, nonchalantly, in the same spirit that characterized my strolls through museums and art galleries.

DIGRESSIONS ON SOME POEMS BY FRANK O'HARA

It wasn't until I'd been living with Frank for about six months that I finally met Bunny, who by then had assumed near-mythic dimensions in my imagination. I can't remember where she'd been when she swept into town, en route to Boston or Cambridge, but I know from what Frank told me later that she didn't phone before turning up at the museum, a suitcase in each hand. And Frank didn't phone either—phone me, I mean, to let me know the situation, that he gave her the keys to the place, told her about me, said he'd be leaving the museum and heading home at six, a half-hour after I was through work at the Holliday Bookshop, and that I'd find Bunny Lang ensconced *chez nous*, very comfortably ensconced, as I discovered, the impression she gave being that of someone settling in for a week at the very least.

First, there was music from the radio—*popular* music, which Frank never played; I could hear it in the hallway, before I had my key out. Next, stepping warily inside, I spied two open suitcases and women's clothes strewn about, a bra here, panties there, hose draped over a chair. Then came her voice, warm and intimate, from the direction of the bathroom, for all the world as if we were old friends, even lovers: "Joey, is that you? It's Bunny," she went on, as I closed the front door. "I'm taking a bath, come on in." The bathroom door was wide open and I could see her leaning forward, craning her neck as though she couldn't wait to catch a glimpse of me. I moved to just outside the bathroom and told her hello, not the least self-conscious; she was so relaxed, clearly not an exhibitionist out to shock me, that I was immediately put at ease. And only later did I realize that she was neither beautiful nor especially pretty, so disarmed and dazzled was I by this striking tableau, our grimy, grayish bathtub being a perfect foil for her fresh blond good looks. Was she on the fleshy side, were her lips too full, did she seem a bit jowly? Who cared? Her compelling brown eyes bespoke such wit and intelligence that you sensed right away that this was a blonde with a difference, someone to reckon with and adore. "Frank told me all about you," she said with satisfaction, smiling up at me. "Why don't you make us a drink? And sit there," she added, lowering the lid on the toilet seat. I was never so quickly won over by anyone. And within the year she would be dead from Hodgkin's disease.

HOMOSEXUALITY

[MARCH 1954]

So we are taking off our masks, are we, and keeping
our mouths shut? as if we'd been pierced by a glance!

The sound of an old cow is not more full of judgment
than the vapors which escape one's soul when one is sick;

so I pull the shadows around me like a puff
and crinkle my eyes as if at the most exquisite moment

of a very long opera, and then we are off!
without reproach and without hope that our delicate feet

will touch the earth again, let alone "very soon."
It is the law of my own voice I shall investigate.

I start like ice, with my ear, my ear
to my heart, that proud cur at the garbage can

in the rain. It's wonderful to admire oneself
with complete candor, tallying up the merits of each

of the latrines. 14th Street is drunken and credulous,
53rd Street tries to tremble but is too at rest. The good

love a park and the inept a railway station,
and there are the divine ones who drag themselves up

and down the lengthening shadow of an Abyssinian head
in the dust, trailing their long elegant heels of hot air

crying to confuse the brave "It's a summer day,
and I want to be wanted more than anything in the world"

These trenchant, wittily observed lines that touch upon an unsavory aspect
of Manhattan gay life in the 1950s have led to a misunderstanding about
the way Frank conducted his sex life. Which is to say, the poem is not as
confessional or as autobiographical as some of his readers might assume.

It was in the fall of 1955, about a year and a half after he wrote "Homosexuality," that he underwent what I came to regard as his conversion, a secular conversion I played a part in implementing. But the greater credit must
go to Chester Kallman—actually, to his mouth. That's right, his mouth, as in
Samuel Beckett's maddeningly minimal play performed on an otherwise
dark stage with a single spot trained on a mouth (or is it two mouths?) endlessly spewing words. Yes, that is the image that springs to mind when I think
of Chester, and I am confident that anyone who knew this outrageous and engaging poet will know why that analogy occurred to me: his mouth, at any social gathering, was usually center stage, the star.

Overripe is the first word that leaps to mind in an attempt to describe his
lips. They were full, heavy, roseate, and moist from a never-ending supply of
spittle, while the orifice his lips encompassed was, one imagined, sufficiently
commodious to accommodate the most splendidly endowed piece of trade
Chester could hope to entrap within, where lurked a masterly tongue that
knew its way around a cock as well as it knew how to caress and expel words,
words, and more words. And that, not his rapacious cocksucking, is what will
mainly concern us here, his fabulous mouth and agile tongue teamed together as seasoned spinner and spewer of wonderfully formed sentences—

in this instance, sentences expostulating on a subject even closer to his heart than his beloved opera and about which he was even more obsessive.

So as not to do Chester an injustice, I want to stress that ordinarily when he held forth at the San Remo, it was in the honored tradition of high camp. This meant that a very classy homosexual wit, irony, and bitchiness informed his unsparing palaver, but not, alas, on a particular night in the fall of 1955. And those of us who caught his act—Frank, John Button, and I, plus two or three other San Remo regulars—listened in consternation as he went on and on and on about some gorgeous, extravagantly hung hustler he'd brought home just the other night to the St. Mark's Place flat he shared with W. H. Auden, and how Wystan, awakened by the goings-on, called out, "Ches-ter! Is that you?" and how Chester, unwillingly disengaging himself from the giant phallus he was devouring, answered, "Yes, Wystan," and immediately went back to doing what he called "the Lord's work," as Wystan now asked, "Ches-ter? Are you alone?" and Chester, again coming up for air, called out, "No, Wystan, go back to sleep"—all of this accompanied by the telling and obscene gestures of Chester's lascivious mouth going down and then coming up, graphically indicating the great length of the hustler's member as well as the great pleasure Chester took in servicing him.

When at long last he had finished, none of us knew where to look or what to say. I remember not having been able to take my eyes off his mouth, so dumbfounded was I by its virtuoso performance, unfortunately at the service of sex talk as sordid and raunchy as any I'd ever heard from a sex-crazed queen. Yet I must admit to having allowed a vestige of vicarious pleasure to encroach upon my response, no doubt inescapable since I knew from experience how thrilling it was to give head to a passive straight stud.

In the cab on the way home—actually, the instant the door was shut and the meter began running—I heaved a sigh of relief, sat back, composed myself, and addressed these words to Frank: "Promise me something. If you ever catch me talking the way Chester did tonight, get a gun and shoot me. Don't ask me if I want to be shot, just shoot me." I expected Frank to laugh; instead, he fell silent, and I wondered about that.

Flash forward to a year and a half later, by which time we were living downtown, at 90 University Place. For quite a while, I'd noticed that Frank no longer engaged in wild sexual exploits—like, for example, his regularly making out with a guard at the UN during its construction, right there in the small, temporary station house, always after midnight, or like the time he boarded the subway, blind drunk, missed his stop and ended up in Queens, where he blew the Negro in the change booth before catching his train back to Manhattan.

Well, naturally, being a good and concerned friend, I became curious when such activities were curtailed, so I asked him what was up: I thought something might be the matter.

"You're responsible," he said.

"How so?"

"Or partly responsible." He then reminded me what I said to him the night in the cab after we left Chester Kallman. "I thought about it a lot, about the way Chester talked, and I decided I didn't want to be like that."

I was silent a moment, then told him I wished I could follow his example. "It isn't in me," I said, almost apologetically. "I just can't help myself. I love making out with strangers."

"Don't worry about it, you're fine the way you are," said Frank, who never preached to me; and about Chester, whom he liked and respected, he had not meant to be judgmental.

The conversion had been immediate and complete: his friends—gay, straight, and nominally straight—were henceforth his sole sex partners. And to the end of his life, so far as I know, Frank never made out with a stranger again.

There was another homosexual subculture of New York that flourished around the time Frank wrote his boldly titled "Homosexuality," a subculture that had nothing to do with subway latrines, public parks, and railway stations. Indeed, it was an enclave so rarefied that it might be wondered how I, an upstart from trashy Los Angeles, found my way inside its covert perimeters. Well, it was by chance, through no effort on my part, unless one counted my sporting a specious Ivy League outfit (Brooks Brothers jacket, regimental striped tie, scuffed white bucks), venturing alone into the Oak Room of the Plaza, and then, after taking a stool at the bar, not disallowing a glib conversation with an elegant stranger of fairly advanced years.

"Dress like Joe College. You have the blond crew cut for it," I'd been advised by a gay bar acquaintance when he recommended a visit to the Oak Room, whose unique cruising opportunities awaited anyone of my youthful mien and good looks. Right away, I saw what he meant. Graciously, with no strings attached, I was invited to what would be the first of a number of parties held in an imaginatively decorated West Fifties railroad flat whose hosts, an accommodating couple named Fred (Butch) Melton and Wilbur Pippin, made their digs available for what can truly be described as a gay salon, the likes of which I'd never seen and would never see again, certainly not fifteen years hence in the wake of the populist gay liberation movement, which dealt a deathblow to gatherings as precious and sequestered as those arranged by Butch and Wilbur.

What was so special about their salon? Its distinction stemmed, in the first place, from being sponsored—*paid* for, let's be blunt about it—by no less a presence on the cultural scene than Lincoln Kirstein, who in those days was witty and fun-loving, not yet the scowling figure dressed from head to toe in funereal black, with dark, daunting eyes you dared not meet at New York City Ballet intermissions. It was, then, the approachable Kirstein whom these parties reflected. And as pardoxical as it might sound, the atmosphere was rather manly, not the least effete.

Skeptical? Then let me compare this upfront gay salon with another one that flourished around the same time, the Frenchified Sunday afternoon gatherings Leo Lerman presided over at his commodious, fussily decorated, ground-floor Lexington Avenue apartment, where (thanks to Ned Rorem) I was once a guest and where I noted that the male guests, all of them gay, were scrupulously closeted even though the female guests knew the score. In other words, the salon fronted by Butch and Wilbur made no pretense of being *comme il faut*. Those manly evenings were strictly stag affairs, but with a difference: despite the absence of the fair sex, each and every guest would be impeccably decked out, in black tie, a cummerbund, a blazer, a three-piece suit—you name it.

I have to say that at first I thought it absurdly inappropriate that all these men should be dressing up for each other. I should have remembered that just a few years earlier, when I first arrived in the city from casual, laid-back southern California, I was just as taken aback by the same dress code that prevailed at midtown gay bars, the so-called Bird Circuit, where giddy queens were clad in coats and ties as they stood around discreetly ogling each other and singing the latest show tunes blaring on the jukebox. (It was a wonder they ever made out, so refined were gay men in those days!) Now as for the impulse behind the finery that characterized the Kirstein-sponsored salon, I not long ago postulated what it was all about. Those gay gentlemen, the crème de la crème of the New York homosexual world, were functioning socially as both sexes—thus, through their fastidious attire, together with their deportment that brooked no overt cruising, groping, or untoward activity in the john, they were unconsciously contriving a scene that was a parody of a proper straight salon.

Having posited that observation, I hasten to add that the scene was played out on its own terms, faultlessly and with undoubted success, as a gathering place of accomplished gay men and their acolytes, comely, well-spoken, only occasionally la-di-da or swishy youths, the equivalent of the chic, attractive women you'd meet at a salon like Leo Lerman's. And what did I, one of those youths, feel about hobnobbing with the likes of Cecil Beaton, Philip Johnson, Glenway Wescott, Monroe Wheeler, George Platt Lynes, Donald Windham, George Tooker, Pavel Tschelitchew, Paul Cadmus, and the legendary Bill Miller (regarded as the most beautiful man in New York gay society), plus the salon's host, the towering Lincoln Kirstein—were they just so many names, names to drop if I chose to? Not at all. For me, it was a thrill, an education to be in their company.

To pick up the strands of my narrative: I wrote my thesis, passed my exams, got my M.A.—and lost my lover, who then (in the time-honored tradition of gays) became a close friend for life. In the subsequent year and a half, I lived fifty miles upstate and—well, this is an important part of my story, so I'll cover it in some detail before getting back to Frank and my digressions on his poems.

First of all, it might be wondered how I tore myself away from my beloved New York. But what might summon even greater wonder is the enterprise in which I allowed myself to become involved: I taught school—*fourth grade!*—in once-fashionable Tuxedo Park, celebrated for having given its name to the evening jacket first worn at one of its fancy balls in 1899. By the time I arrived on the premises—how disappointed I was!—few vestiges of its former glory remained. Oh, it had social pretensions all right, but the place had become dowdy and middle class: the chapel (Episcopalian low church) was ordinary, the Tuxedo Club had neither swimming pool nor golf course, and at the entrance to the scrubby grounds of the Park was an ostentatious wrought-iron gate where a guard made sure you were expected, as though it were still the modish enclave of yore. The school itself—Tuxedo Park School—occupied the premises of a once-grand estate where Edith Wharton, I was told more than once, spent weekends at the turn of the century. Coeducational, with grades one through eight, it had boarders as well as day pupils from the Park; and predictably, it was the kind of school that was big on discipline, etiquette, and conservative teaching methods.

How had I ended up in such an unlikely place? To begin with, there was not much else I could do with my sketchy liberal arts education except apply for a teaching job at a private school. But why Tuxedo Park? I had no choice. True to form, once I decided to try teaching as a profession, I dragged my feet and kept changing my mind, so that I didn't sign up with a teachers' agency until after the beginning of the school year, by which time they naturally had no openings. Then Tuxedo Park's fourth-grade teacher had a nervous breakdown over the Christmas holiday—not a good omen, but I told the agency I'd be interested in applying for the job. Dr. Abel encouraged me when I called her about it (I was no longer a patient), and Frank said, "Try it, you might like it; weekends when you're off, you can stay with me." One more thing: my recently completed analysis (all those dreams!) made me aware of what I perceived to be my collective guilt and a concomitant obligation to do some good in the world for a change—a sophomoric sentiment, I suppose, but it fired me up for my interview with Mr. Potter, the headmaster, who hired me without seeing anyone else, as I was told later by the agency.

I had no idea what I was letting myself in for: no sex, no parties, no late hours, no decent food and drink—in short, a monastic experience, and after three days I was convinced I'd made a mistake and would be living for the weekends. Then something unexpected happened. Once I'd adjusted to the routine, I found the work oddly exhilarating and fulfilling, and I was pretty good at it as well—not at maintaining discipline (mine was the only noisy classroom in the school) but at getting through to the kids, even teaching them something. And my emotional life, such as it was, found nourishment in the symbiotic relationship I had with them, particularly with three boys whose beauty pierced me to the quick. The special attention I paid them, the horseplay and the fondling, evolved more out of their needs than mine, as they were homesick boarders starved for affection that found surcease only through pleasurable physical contact. Then one of the girls, a girl of whom I was especially fond, complained not to the headmaster but to me, thank God, that I liked the boys better than the girls. That gave me pause and made me more circumspect and less abandoned in my dallying with those three boys, who at the same time, I want to stress, didn't so much arouse as enliven and beguile me, the way cuddly animals always have. Still, it was unsettling, at once stirring and frustrating. I knew I was doing no harm—to the boys, I mean—but I wondered if it was good for me, since my sex life was virtually nil, weekends being my only time to make out. Then, too, teaching those young children drained me, so that at the end of the day, stripped of my identity, I was left with no life of my own, as if my students had endowed me with whatever significance I could lay claim to—all of which explained, I thought, why just about every teacher I'd ever had seemed spent, dry, sexless.

Was that how I wanted to end up, I asked myself. The question was a variation of the one that still nagged at me: Why had I come to New York? In one of my somber, soul-searching talks with Paul Goodman, I phrased it still another way: "I don't know what I want to do with my life." This made him pull on his pipe. "That is one of the most beautiful problems you can have," he said portentously. Easy for him to say, I thought, since it was a problem he doubtless never had . . .

Nevertheless, in spite of the hard work and long hours, the frustration and loneliness, the feeling of being adrift, I would very likely have remained in the teaching profession had it not been for Frank and my weekends with him in New York, first and foremost our Saturday afternoons together. As we made the rounds of the galleries, so few you could cover in one day all the shows that had opened during the week, art was revealed to me in a new light, as a vital and ongoing human endeavor, as a part of life more down to earth and yet more inspiring than anything I could possibly have imagined, whereas in the past it had been cut and dried, remote and historical. This, then, was an epiphany for me, one that emanated from a pilgrimage—as admittedly high-flown as that sounds for an activity as literally pedestrian as gallery hopping—which would find Frank leading me from one exhibition to another, looking at works by artists who were not only still living but living in New York, artists (this was the most extraordinary part of it) I was then beginning to meet at parties and at Frank's and even on the street, which was how I met de Kooning, on Third Avenue near Tenth Street.

We'd come downtown to see a group show that turned out to be nothing special—at one of the cooperative galleries, the Tanager or the Hansa—and on that quiet, otherwise forgettable Saturday afternoon in the autumn of 1954, the artist of whom Frank spoke most highly interjected, after we'd been standing on the street for maybe ten minutes, the two of them talking animatedly while I quietly attended to the beautiful sky blue of de Kooning's eyes and the captivating, amused lilt of his Dutch-accented voice: "Hey, Frank, you and your friend wanna go to the Cedar for a beer?" Not one for hero-worship, Frank seemed to make an exception with Bill de Kooning, but without ever fawning over him or otherwise making an ass of himself. And that fall and on into winter, Frank introduced me to other artists, artists of a younger generation than de Kooning's—of *my* generation, which I found thrilling and gratifying.

DIGRESSIONS ON SOME POEMS BY FRANK O'HARA

Joan Mitchell's show at the old Stable Gallery, her third solo exhibition in New York, stands out in my memory—her paintings really bowled me over, as did Joan herself. The same goes for the gallery. Located at Seventh Avenue and Fifty-eighth Street, with a service station at the corner (right in the heart of Manhattan!), it was given its name for good reason, borne out by the faint but unmistakable odor of hay, horses, and manure that permeated its two floors. Intense, bug-eyed Eleanor Ward, assisted by Hal Fondren, ran the gallery, and it was one of the most prestigious and interesting in town. They showed all kinds of talented artists who were new on the scene, Joan being the one who made the biggest impression on me. Still in her twenties, she had already broken away from the influence of artists like Gorky; and in 1954, her canvases were restrained and subtle, with squiggly lines crisscrossing on a washed-out umber background. Far more than the work of other painters who were friends of Frank's, this highly individual gestural painting moved and impressed me. So when I met Joan at a party in the Village the same week her show opened, I impulsively emulated Frank's extravagant way of telling an artist how much he admired their work; and as I spoke, I had the terrible feeling I was making a fool of myself. But I was mistaken, apparently, for what I said went over fine with Joan, and we immediately became friends.

From then on, I came close to gushing when Frank introduced me to a number of these up-and-coming artists, who fortunately took me at my word—they knew they had no cause to be cynical or indifferent. Later, when the same artists were established, I was reluctant to say very much to them, because praise struck me as superfluous at that point in their careers, and, besides, I was afraid that anything I said would be suspect and I'd be regarded as yet another trendy, celebrity-mad sycophant. Thus, because Jasper Johns became famous so fast, I was able to tell him only once how much I liked what he was doing.

It was the first time I saw his work, when Frank took me to Bob Rauschenberg's studio just off the Bowery—on Pearl Street, I think—and Bob said, after we'd looked at some of his things, "Let's go see Jasper. He expects us." At the time, Jasper was unknown—he'd not yet had a one-man show and I guess he and Bob were still doing window displays—but I'd already seen some of Bob's collages and paintings at Charlie Egan's gallery. It would have been on a Saturday afternoon in early January 1955 that Frank, having already reviewed the show, took me to see it. "A lot of people are ridiculing his stuff," he warned me on the way there, "but I think you might like it." And I did— I'd never seen anything so unconstrained, risky, and original, or so odd, either. I remember most vividly the companion pieces that wittily delineated the male and female sex organs, which Frank cited in his review that appeared in the January 1955 issue of *Art News* (and note that in those days it was Bob, not Robert, Rauschenberg):

> Bob Rauschenberg, *enfant terrible* of the New York School, is back again to even more brilliant effect—what he did to all-white and all-black in his last show and to nature painting with his controversial moss-dirt-and-ivy picture in the last Stable Annual, he tops in this show of blistering and at the same time poignant collages. Some of them seem practically room-size, and have various illuminations within them apart from their technical luminosity: bulbs flicker on and off, lights cast shadows, and lifting up a bit of pink gauze you stare out of the picture into your own magnified eye. He provides a means by which you, as well as he, can get "in" the painting. Doors open to reveal clearer images, or you can turn a huge wheel to change the effect at will. Many of the pieces are extrovert, reminiscent of his structure in the Merce Cunningham ballet, *Minutiae,* but not all are so wildly ingenious: other pieces, including two sex organs (male and female) made from old red silk umbrellas, have a gentle and just passion for moving people. When you look back at the more ecstatic works they, too, have this quality not at all overshadowed by their brio. For all the baroque exuberance of the show, quieter pictures evidence a serious lyrical talent; simultaneously, in the big inventive pieces there is a big talent at play, creating its own occasions as a stage does.

Although it wasn't an opening—weren't they all on Tuesdays in those days?—Bob was in the gallery that afternoon, flashing his big, friendly smile at whoever happened to appear. But not many people turned up during the fifteen or twenty minutes we were there, and that gave me an opportunity to become acquainted with this oddball young artist—also, to get a good look at him; and I remember liking what I saw. With his open expression, ruddy complexion, and unassuming manner, he seemed more like a farm boy than an artist, particularly an artist as bizarre and iconoclastic as he was. I think it was while we were there that he and Frank set a date for Frank to pay him a studio visit, and Bob made a point of asking me to come.

Did we go the following Saturday? I think so—remember, I was still at Tuxedo Park, so the visit had to be on a weekend. I don't remember whether Jasper's studio was above or below Bob's—their identical lofts were in some old industrial building—and I have only the vaguest recollection of what Jasper showed us. They were small, neat works, I remember that, and I impulsively said I liked them. He gave me a cold, noncommittal look, the first of several he would give me over the years. "I don't think Jasper liked me," I told Frank later. "What he didn't like was the way Bob kept looking at you," Frank said.

It was a long time before I saw Jasper again, but Bob and I ran into each other a few weeks later at a big loft party where we were all drunk and dancing and talking loudly and excitedly. That was when I first heard Bob's laugh, which was loud, unsettling, even maniacal. I still liked him, still found him attractive—but the laugh gave me pause and no doubt partly accounted for my being sardonic and indifferent, even insulting to him. I couldn't help myself, couldn't resist trying to be witty and irreverent, because at the time I was polishing a style that I hoped would lend an interesting contrast to my appearance, a distressingly wholesome appearance that prompted Joan Mitchell to say I looked like a choirboy and Arthur Gold to comment that I could be taken for an angel until I opened my mouth and shit came out.

SONNET

[J U N E   1 4 ,   1 9 5 5]

The blueness of the hour
when the spine stretches itself
into a groan, then the golden cheek
on the dirty pillow, wrinkled by linen.
Odor of lanolin, the flower
pressed between thundering doubts of self,
cleaving fresh air through the week
and loading hearts to the millennium.
Go, sweet breath! come, sweet rain,
bewildering as a tortoise
embracing the Indian ocean,
predictable as a porpoise
    diving upon his mate in cool
    water which is not a pool.

just came for the weekend and stayed longer than I usually did, I wrote
in "Four Apartments," and that puts it very well—I got it right the first
time. I only want to underscore how casually we began living together and
to state firmly that Frank never came right out and asked me to live with
him, nor did I ask him if I could—it just happened, the way two people start
seeing each other and then before they know it, certainly without their planning it, they've fallen in love. One thing for sure, and I imagine it's obvious

by now: we didn't get together for convenience's sake, simply to share expenses and otherwise lead separate lives the way a lot of gay roommates do. But we were by no means inseparable, nor did we share all of the same friends. With the exception of Joan Mitchell, Elaine de Kooning, Mike Goldberg, and one or two others, the artists I met never became friends of mine independent of Frank. Grace Hartigan once said to me, "I know that Frank loves you, so I love you, too." Did she expect me to be won over and touched by that? I much preferred the style of the acerbic, wary Jane Freilicher; it took something like twenty years for her to warm to me, and that came about mainly because she could see that I was fond of her husband, Joe Hazan, obviously the love of her life.

Still, I felt at home with most of his friends—more than Frank ever did with anyone he met through me, Gianni Bates and J. J. Mitchell excepted. In this respect, it is perhaps significant that he tried, and usually managed, to avoid going to parties with me that were given by friends of mine, people who had only a vague idea of who he was. Why this disinclination of Frank's? It has occurred to me that it might have had something to do with a need or desire to be known wherever he went. Certainly he was in the habit of being the center of attention, of being accorded the status of a star whose credits, so to speak, were recognized. Socially, Frank was poised and sure of himself, but maybe this was the one side of him that betokened insecurity—or was it exactly what it appeared to be, a star's egocentric demand for the limelight, to be center stage?

In any event, if there was going to be a satellite, it wasn't going to be Frank. Was that my role, the part I was born to play? Frank never treated me as such, but there were those, mercifully very few, who did, particularly when I first came on the scene. What springs to mind now is the day of Frank's twenty-ninth birthday, June 27, 1955, less than a month after I moved in with him. But now, just this minute, it has dawned on me that in retrospect the day, apart from being Frank's birthday, was notable for something far more significant than pointing up any slight I may have suffered.

Jimmy Schuyler, Arthur Gold, and Bobby Fizdale decided to throw a surprise party for Frank—at our apartment. Jimmy still had his keys to the place, and the three of them, plus Hal Fondren, who had prepared some hors d'oeuvres for the occasion, let themselves in while Frank and I were at work. I should mention that just as I'd taken over Jimmy's place as Frank's roommate, I'd taken over his job at the Holliday Bookshop, and I had Jimmy to thank for that; he had recommended me as his replacement when he went off to live with Arthur Gold. Anyway, Frank was indeed surprised when he came home, and so was I. We had a few drinks and then Frank and I were suddenly alone, faced with the prospect of dining on two frozen chicken pies, frozen peas, and frozen french fries—all we had to do was light the kitchen range and turn on the oven, our idea of making dinner.

"I'm sorry I didn't know it was your birthday," I said. Frank said nothing. During the festivities he had appeared out of sorts, possibly angry about something, I thought, and now that we were alone he looked around furiously, trying to contain himself. Then he fixed his smoldering gaze on me. "It was nice, wasn't it?" I ventured, wondering what I had done. "It was a surprise to you, too, wasn't it?" he said. "Well, yes," I said. "I thought so!" he said, his eyes blazing. "How dare they not let you know what they were planning. They should have told you—even asked you if it was all right. This is your place, too," he added quietly, after a moment.

It was the first time he'd acknowledged that we were living together, that I wasn't a guest as I had been from time to time over the past year and a half. But his anger hinted at something else, feelings for me that transcended those of friendship. And now I remember something else—sitting at the kitchen table with Frank a few days later, the morning of the first day of July, to be exact; we were having coffee when I abruptly said, "Isn't the rent due today?" "I'm glad you reminded me," he said. "How much is it?" I said. "I should pay half, and split the phone and Con Ed bills with you." He smiled. "Not half of the phone bill," he said. "I use the phone ten times more than you do." I could see he was pleased, not because the money would come in handy, which it would, but because I'd made a commitment, I'd let him know I planned on staying around a while.

If I seem to be making a lot out of this, it's because I'm getting at something—how, from the beginning, we unconsciously fostered a friendship that would be different from what either of us had with anyone else. There would be strings attached, there would be a trade-off: Frank would be made to feel he was more important to me than anyone in my life—and he was, as it turned out—while I, at the same time, would continue to have my sexual freedom. Did we know what we were getting into? I certainly didn't; only in hindsight have I been able to sort this out—even now, I'm not sure I have it right. It was all unspoken; we'd not yet had sex; and in the end, the ambiguous nature of our relationship would be our undoing.

The "Sonnet," which is dated June 14, 1955 (a day or two after the school year ended at Tuxedo Park), was the first thing Frank wrote after I turned up at his place with my few belongings, my teaching days clearly behind me. The poem was originally called "To Joe," and I don't know why the change was made. Well, the same thing happened to Bill de Kooning when his name was removed from "Second Avenue," so I'm in good company and shouldn't take umbrage.

"Odor of lanolin," Frank writes in this sensuous poem, and I can assure you that he wasn't thinking of wool grease but of the little tubes of lanolin ointment he always had around the house. Convinced that it did wonders for your skin, he got me to using it, just as he put me on to sandalwood—except sandalwood, a pale yellow, intensely aromatic liquid with which he liberally doused himself before going out, proved much too heady for me. Lanolin was different. Though unscented, it had a natural but slightly medicinal aroma, and I suspect I went overboard with it, hence Frank's reference to its odor. This, however, wasn't the first or last time he mentioned lanolin in one of his poems. Five years earlier, in "V. R. Lang," he admonishes Bunny to "Be always high, / full of regard and honor and lanolin" (maybe she introduced him to the stuff?), and time and again we run across mention of it, most elaborately in the 1961–62 "Biotherm (For Bill Berkson)"—specifically, in Frank's note on the poem: "Biotherm is a marvelous sunburn preparation full of attar of roses, lanolin and plankton . . ." What was it with Frank and his thing about lanolin? I draw a blank; I wish someone would enlighten me.

AT THE OLD PLACE

[J U L Y   1 3 ,   1 9 5 5]

Joe is restless and so am I, so restless.
Button's buddy lips frame "L G T TH O P?"
across the bar. "Yes!" I cry, for dancing's
my soul delight. (Feet! feet!) "Come on!"

Through the streets we skip like swallows.
Howard malingers. (Come on, Howard.) Ashes
malingers. (Come on, J.A.) Dick malingers.
(Come on, Dick.) Alvin darts ahead. (Wait up,
Alvin.) Jack, Earl and Someone don't come.

Down the dark stairs drifts the steaming cha-
cha-cha. Through the urine and smoke we charge
to the floor. Wrapped in Ashes' arms I glide.

(It's heaven!) Button lindys with me. (It's
heaven!) Joe's two-steps, too, are incredible,
and then a fast rhumba with Alvin, like skipping
on toothpicks. And the interminable intermissions,

we have them. Jack, Earl and Someone drift
guiltily in. "I knew they were gay
the minute I laid eyes on them!" screams John.
How ashamed they are of us!   we hope.

his lighthearted poem, written about a month after I began living with Frank, catches some of the atmosphere of that summer; never again would we be so carefree and downright silly—or so resolutely gay. I am even tempted to call this Frank's Gay Period, and I mean that to encompass more than his mood and activities that summer. Consider the things he wrote: the present poem with its gay goings-on, the effetely tender "blueness of the hour" sonnet, the excessive James Dean outpourings, the lines celebrating blond-haired males, the poem about two homosexual friends bedding down for the night ("Johnny and Alvin are going home, are sleeping now")—all culminating in an extravagant, glittering poem that only a movie buff who was gay could possibly have written, "To the Film Industry in Crisis." Have I made my case? Not until Frank's love poems to Vincent Warren would his being homosexual play such a prominent role in his poetry. I am aware, at the same time, that "At the Old Place" is the only overtly gay poem of the lot. For that reason, Frank couldn't have gotten it published if he had tried, since in those days, the unenlightened fifties, there was no place to send it. Significantly, it first saw the light of day a few months after Stonewall, in the November 1969 issue of a short-lived magazine called *New York Poetry*.

According to a note in the *Collected Poems*, the Old Place was "a dance-bar in Greenwich Village." Actually, it was a *gay* dance bar, a world of difference, as one would have been hard put to find a straight person in that seedy, out-of-the-way basement bar. And when I say the place was gay, I don't mean it was anything like what came later, in the sex-crazed seventies, the pre-AIDS period when you sniffed poppers, snorted coke, and had sex on the dance floors of the more raunchy queer joints. No, the Old Place was sweet and innocent, more limp-wristed than S&M or pseudo-macho, and it was about as wild as a high school prom of years past. Frank, who in the time I knew him never cruised gay bars, liked going to the Old Place for one reason only, because he loved to dance, and he was terrific at it, the Lindy being his specialty—or at least that's what the comely, effervescent Abby Friedman told me recently, and she should know; an expert dancer herself, she was Frank's favorite partner at downtown loft parties and at parties in the Hamptons.

So what do we have in this crisp, campy poem? To begin with, it's probably as close to reportage as anything Frank ever wrote—indeed, it is fairly literal in its description of a frivolous summer evening in downtown New York, a scene brought alive with but one editorial comment, the very last line that characteristically, in true O'Hara fashion, pulls the whole thing together. Can we also regard "At the Old Place" as the first of his celebrated "I do this, I do that" poems? Maybe. But one thing's for sure, it is not "about the discovery that someone thought [to be] straight is really gay," as one professional gay writer, Stuart Byron, humorlessly asserted in a review of *Selected Poems*. Interestingly, it took a woman, the redoubtable Helen Vendler, to recognize the poem's special quality and straightforward narrative: "An evening is improvised, in 'At the Old Place,' and the gay bar-scene is sketched with no retrospective frame, noted down exactly as it happens. I'm not sure why this method succeeds, except that the mixture of frivolousness, bathos, high-pitched boredom, and self-satire is not one that men have allowed into poetry very often, if ever." She quotes the poem, then goes on: "The wish *not* to impute significance has rarely been stronger in lyric poetry. It happened, it went like this, it's over." Very astute, and she is on target in realizing that it's all "noted down exactly as it happens": Frank and I are standing around in the San Remo, nursing our fifteen-cent draft beers and feeling so restless and bored that we're thinking of leaving, as it's not a good night—for one thing, Chester Kallman's not there, camping it up; he's in Ischia for the summer with Wystan. Over at the bar, where he's trying to get another beer, or maybe he's cruising someone, John Button catches our eye and frames the unmistakable words, "Let's go to the Old Place." Frank's eyes light up. "Yes!" he says, and I agree to go along. Alvin Novak, Howard Griffin, John Ashbery, and Dick Stryker are also at the bar that night, and so are Earl McGrath, Jack Spicer, and the nameless "Someone." We all agree we'd have more fun if we went dancing—everyone except Earl, who obviously thinks that the Old Place is too gay and tacky, and of course he's right, and of course that's why we want to go there. Leaving Earl, Jack, and Someone behind, we gaily wend our way farther west, to the other side of the Village where the Old Place is; and to our delight, the joint is jumping. We're not there fifteen minutes, dancing up a storm, when Earl, Jack, and Someone appear at the edge of the dance floor, barely able to bring themselves to look at us. John Button, never at a loss, screams, "I knew they were gay the minute I laid eyes on them!" We all scream and laugh like nellie queens, and Earl, Jack, and Someone don't know where to look. That's it. "It's over," as Ms. Vendler says. With the exception of one detail, Frank was unfailingly accurate: I'm not and never was a good dancer, so to describe my two-steps as "incredible" was stretching it—though the word is admittedly ambiguous.

(Some readers might not recognize everyone in the poem. Howard Griffin was a sweet, soft-spoken professorial type who wrote poetry and did secretarial work for Wystan Auden. He died some years ago. I don't know what became of Dick Stryker, a nice-looking, good-natured composer who was, dismayingly, the lover of one of the great blowhards of American poetry, Harold Norse. Earl McGrath was—and is—a tireless wit who went from being secretary to Gian Carlo Menotti to some sort of executive at 20th Century-Fox to manager of the Rolling Stones and to art dealer in both Hollywood and New York, always managing to land on his feet. Jack Spicer was a good friend of Earl's and probably had a crush on him. A West Coast poet and great guy in spite of being quite impossible, he didn't get along with Frank and was forever taking swipes at New York, reason enough for Frank to put down San Francisco. I suspect Jack secretly liked Frank, and vice versa.)

There's an offensive faggot expression some readers might not be acquainted with: "dinge queen." Not only was this an expression Frank never used, it was in no way applicable to him. For there was nothing I perceived as fetishistic or obsessive about the "thing" he had for black men, which is another way of saying that he was drawn to all kinds of racial, ethnic, and physical types. Still, his passion for blacks was exceptional, since it encompassed affection, compassion, and a genuine interest in them along with sexual desire, all of which I imagine became apparent to anyone who knew him well. My own awareness came about shortly after I moved in with him.

It would have been a Saturday morning—in mid-July, I believe. Frank was off somewhere, possibly covering a show for *Art News,* and I was still in bed, sleeping off the night before, when I was awakened by a loud banging on the door, immediately followed by a deep, resonant voice announcing, "Mailman!" Frank had told me all about his black mailman, so I was not the least surprised to see that the letter he'd trudged up five flights to deliver bore an ordinary three-cent stamp. Only his initial trip, a couple of months before I moved in, had been on the level. On that occasion, he had a registered letter that required Frank's signature.

Here, roughly, is what I remember Frank telling me about that first visit: "I had such a terrible hangover that morning that I could barely hold my head up, much less answer the door. But somehow I managed to drag myself out of bed and slip on those skimpy old gym shorts of mine. To give you an idea of the daze I was in, it wasn't until after I'd signed for the letter that I noticed the mailman was a Negro. Then when I saw that the poor guy was sweating profusely from the climb, I offered him a glass of water. He said he'd be much obliged and came right in, closing the door after him. I didn't think much about that, I just got him his glass of water and handed it to him. Well, you can imagine my surprise when he patted me on the ass as I turned to sit down. 'It's pretty nice down there,' he said. I wheeled around and found him smiling in the friendliest way. I asked him how much time he could spare, and he said he had enough time. Since then, he's been back twice, both times on Saturday when he knows I'm not at work." Frank also told me his name— it was Ed, I seem to remember—and in a burst of generosity, he said I should feel free to ask Ed in if by chance he popped up when I was home alone.

And how did Frank describe Ed? I remember him saying, "He's enormous, Joe," and I was given the impression that he was attractive. Well, just plain "fat" would have been more like it, though it was true he was well over six feet tall, and I found him to be about as prepossessing as Howard Swanson. Not that it mattered what I thought, since Ed's look of disappointment and the abruptness with which he handed over Frank's letter made it abundantly clear who it was he wanted to spend time with. It must be added— this, after all, is essential to the point I want to make—that what Frank stressed in his description of Ed was not his appearance but how warm and sweet and considerate he was. Well, so was Howard Swanson, who died a number of years ago.

POEM

[A U G U S T   1 9 5 5 (?)]

All of a sudden all the world
is blonde. The Negro on my left
is blonde, his eyes are brimming
like a chalice, he is melting
the gold.
         Beside me, passed out
on the floor, a novelist burns a hole
in my pants and he is blonde,
even the cigarette is. Some kind
of Russian cigarette.
             Jean Cocteau
must be blonde too. And the music
of William Boyce.
            Yes, and what
comes out of me is blonde.

I think of this as Frank's "blonde" poem, and I'm taking it out of the order in which it appears in *The Collected Poems*, because I remember its having been written earlier than Don Allen indicates—sometime in August, I would imagine. Like "At the Old Place," it magically encapsulates some of the goings-on that made my first summer with Frank memorable.

As elsewhere in Frank's poems, "blond" is feminized, which is odd inasmuch as he's almost invariably referring to blond males. I asked him about this once but I don't remember what he said, probably because he offered no sound reason for his aberrant spelling. Here's my own admittedly oddball explanation: in Frank's scheme of things, there is something so special about being blond-haired—mythic, glamorous, sexy, anomalous—that the word is given that piquant *e* in order to draw attention to it, and to enshrine and elevate it. But he can also be acerbic even as he pays homage to blonds, as in one of his "Lines for the Fortune Cookies" (1961 or '62): "You will meet a tall beautiful blonde stranger, but you will not say hello." To complicate matters, Frank's idea of what constitutes being a blond is as arbitrary as his spelling of the word. Thus, when he describes someone as having blond hair, that person is not necessarily what most of us think of as a real blond; he can be light-, golden-, or flaxen-haired—or even sandy-haired, like James Dean. Of course there had to be something special about each and every one of these honorary blonds; and in his "blonde" poem, he goes so far as to confer the distinction upon someone who is black, not the wonderful, truly phenomenal Joe Ford, with whom he will soon become involved and about whom I'll write later, but—who? Sorry, I can't remember anything about "the Negro on [his] left." But I do remember—how could I forget?—the passed-out novelist responsible for burning a hole in Frank's pants, and indeed he's the only reason I can so easily call to mind the drunken Upper West Side sex party where everything and everyone suddenly seemed blond to Frank.

Lanky, languorous, and brooding, with a sexy Adam's apple, generous mouth, and full, crimson lips, always drunk yet always in an accommodating state of at least semi-tumescence, he was exactly what he seemed, a much-sought-after type of crypto-, quasi-, or semi-gay trade who, if you went about it the right way, let you have your way with him—I mean, you could do about anything to or with him, just so long as he didn't have to exert himself too much. Frank and I fought over him that night until Frank realized that the Negro on his left was up for grabs, having been abandoned by some dumb queen who'd gone off to get another drink.

Charles Ingle was the novelist's name—everyone called him Chuck—and he'd just had a novel published, *Waters of the End,* one of those sensitive autobiographical first novels with a lot of fine writing in it. Dawn Powell gave him a rave review, met him, and then made the mistake of inviting him to dinner. "I think I barfed," Chuck said vaguely, in describing his drunken behavior that ruined the party. And I remember that e. e. cummings was this fledgling author's mentor, or so Chuck claimed. I also remember that he was given to using parentheses in his writing, which Bill Weaver said was a sign of faulty technique. That didn't bother me, I was still mad for him—so mad for him that, upon learning he was homeless, I talked Frank into letting him come and stay with us until he got a place of his own.

Apart from his languorous sexiness, what we all remembered about him later was the fact that he had a fatal illness. I never learned exactly what it was, but I naturally found the whole thing romantic, as though I were Rudolfo to his Mimi, while Frank soon became bored seeing him lying around the apartment. "If Chuck's going to die," he said after less than a week, "why doesn't he? What's he waiting for?" But so far as I know, he never bit the dust; he simply disappeared from my life, as so many other sexy boys I took up with did. His hair, by the way, was a light chestnut brown—about the same color as Vincent Warren's hair, come to think of it. In "Personism: A Manifesto," Frank wrote: "It [meaning Personism] was founded by me after lunch with LeRoi Jones on August 27, 1959, a day in which I was in love with someone (not Roi, by the way, a blond)." And that blond who was not a blond was, of course, Vincent Warren; given the date of composition on the manuscript, it could not have been anyone else—in fact, their affair had just begun. (I'm sure Frank thought of light-haired Bill Berkson as a blond, but they'd not yet met.)

Wait a minute. Why did Frank suddenly drop the *e*? It's true that "blond" is used as a noun in "Personism," but what difference could that have made to him? The *e*, you'll note, isn't dropped when, in the very first line of "Meditations in an Emergency," he poses the tantalizing question, "Am I to become profligate as if I were a blonde?"—which, incidentally, is further evidence of the special regard Frank had for blonds, for he seems to be saying that they are entitled to be licentious and extravagant. But my point here is, he doesn't drop the *e* as he does in his manifesto. So what's up? Since it was the only time he ever spelled the word correctly, he must have been aware of what he was doing and he must have had a reason for it. Here's what I think: the *e* was dropped in honor of Vincent, as a mark of respect and affection, and to make clear to readers that he was in love with a male, not a female. Besides, it would have been hypocritical to give the impression he was involved with a woman—Frank had never been in a closet and he wasn't about to step into one now. That's my explanation, and after all these years I'm content with it, I can live with it. For there was a time when I was puzzled by this reference to Frank's being in love with a blond—puzzled and somehow outraged, defensive. "Were you the blond Frank O'Hara was referring to?" said Robert Phelps, a gentle, gracious man who was the highly respected editor, translator, and Colette authority who died some years ago of Parkinson's disease. We were at Ned Rorem's, shortly after Frank's death. "Well, yes, it had to be me," I said. Ned rightly pointed out that Frank wasn't in love with me—not at the time he wrote "Personism," anyway. "What are you talking about?" I said. "I just don't see how he could have meant you," said Ned, very gently. "Because I'm the only blond!" I cried. "I'm the only blond!" But now, as I write this, I realize, as I have for some time, that that was never the case.

One day around 1960 the teenage idol Tab Hunter was in the Modern doing publicity shots, and Frank was commandeered (if that's the word I want) to show him around. As he was leaving his desk to go downstairs, the phone rang and it was Grace Hartigan calling to say she was in the lobby and could she see him. Explaining what was going on, Frank asked if she'd like to join him and Tab Hunter. "Tab Hunter!" she cried, incredulously. "If it was Picasso, I'd jump at the chance, but a movie star like Tab Hunter—no, I'd be too excited, I couldn't stand it." Though the tour took under forty-five minutes, I was led to believe that Tab showed great interest in the paintings and made some intelligent comments. But most of all, Frank went on about how great he looked. "A blond Adonis," he pronounced. "Blond with an 'e'?" I said. "Absolutely," Frank answered.

THE JAMES DEAN POEMS

[O C T O B E R   1 9 5 5]

Welcome me, if you will,
as the ambassador of a hatred
who knows its cause
and does not envy you your whim
of ending him. . . .

s "To an Actor Who Died" the first in the series of poems occasioned by the
death of the now-legendary movie star who was killed in a car crash in the
fall of 1955? In his note on this poem, Don Allen tells us that it was "probably written in late summer or early autumn of 1955 on Great Spruce Island." But Frank, I happen to know, was back in New York by September 30,
the date of the accident, so that rules out James Dean. Don Allen doesn't give
us a clue as to which other actor it could have been, and neither does Frank
in the poem itself—at least so far as I can discern from a close reading. In any
event, "For James Dean" is the first in the series I remember his writing.

Its publication in *Poetry* created a small stir. In *The New Republic,* a
writer named Sam Astrachan criticized the poem for implying that Hollywood or society at large was responsible for the untimely death of the
twenty-four-year-old actor, who was killed driving his Porsche racing car.
And the final stanza—

Men cry from the grave while they still live
and now I am this dead man's voice,

> stammering, a little in the earth.
> I take up
> the nourishment of his pale green eyes,
> out of which I shall prevent
> flowers from growing, your flowers.

—sounded morbid to one Turner Cassity, who wrote in a letter to the editor of *Life* magazine: "The James Dean necrophilia has penetrated even the upper levels of culture," a view shared by the ever-critical Paul Goodman. "What does Frank think he's doing, writing poems about dead movie stars!" he said to me one night at the San Remo. Earlier, before the poem appeared in *Poetry,* Frank's good friend Bunny Lang expressed similar reservations, advising against publication and suggesting that the poem was "too out" and that "you'll be sorry." And was he? In his answer to her letter, he made the point that "if one is going to start being embarrassed about one's work I don't know where it would stop, or rather it would stop."

In his O'Hara bibliography, the usually unerring Alexander Smith, Jr., mistakenly identified "For James Dean" as the poem read by Vittorio Gassman on Italian radio, when it was actually the next one Frank wrote, "Obit Dean, September 30, 1955." In somewhat the same spirit as "For James Dean," though minus that poem's astringency, it centers on an even more outrageous conceit, that of Frank's introducing James Dean to Carole Lombard in heaven:

> Miss Lombard, this is a young
> movie actor who just died
> in his Porsche Spyder sportscar
> near Paso Robles on his way
> to Salinas for a race. This is
> James Dean, Carole Lombard. I hope
> you will be good to him up there

And how did this come about, Gassman's reading "Obit Dean" on Italian radio? Simple. Our friend Bill Weaver, who by that time was living in Rome, had been helping out on the translation of some of Frank's poems for a small book to be published in Italy. When Bill wrote and asked Frank for another poem, Frank obliged him by sending something he'd just written, his second James Dean poem; a translation into Italian was promptly made and shown to a radio producer who was planning a program in memory of the actor, a program on which the handsome and smoldering Gassman had agreed to appear. Thus, some fifteen years before it was published in its original language, the poem was read by this renowned star of the Italian stage and screen. Since the sensational *Bitter Rice* was still astir in Frank's memory, as was Gassman's appearance in the more recent *Rhapsody,* he was understandably titillated when Bill wrote to tell him what had happened. In the same letter, he wrote that a number of grief-stricken Italian queens, avid fans of James Dean, had thrown themselves into Venice's Grand Canal. Did that really happen? Well, the story was no more fanciful than many such stories that circulated in the wake of the young actor's death.

Whatever possessed Frank to write these poems in memory of James Dean, what was that about? I suppose the answer is obvious: he was crazy about the kid, liked his looks, moody personality, overwrought style of acting—plus, of course, the pathos he elicited. And I egged Frank on, I was part of the whole thing. (Come to think of it, maybe it wasn't coincidental that camp and gay overtones entered Frank's poetry at about the time I began living with him.) I don't mean to suggest that I felt as intensely about Dean as Frank did: *East of Eden* I saw only three times, twice with Frank, while he saw it more like a half-dozen times, always dragging with him a friend who had not seen it, just as he'd dragged friends to see *Island of Desire* three years earlier.

Now I think all of us know what made James Dean so appealing in Elia Kazan's frenzied melodrama: he was the embodiment and idealization of youth at bay—difficult, sensitive, and gorgeous, of course. And if you happened to be queer and had not had an easy relationship with one of your parents, or with both of them, it was somehow thrilling to identify with James Dean's Cal, whose confusion seemed more that of an incipient gay adolescent than a straight kid with growing-up problems. My reason for arriving at this conclusion is simple: if a youth as bright, good-looking, and personable as the James Dean character were straight, he would have nothing to rebel against; he'd be popular at school, he'd have a girlfriend, he and not the goody-two-shoes Aaron would be the favorite son. How could he possibly be a miserable loner if he were straight? The same goes for the character he plays in *Rebel Without a Cause*.

Evoking an androgyny that brings to mind the famous photograph of Nijinsky in *Jeux* (Dean actually resembles the dancer) and possessing an ambiguous sex appeal no less unsettling than Garbo's in *Queen Christina* and Brando's in *A Streetcar Named Desire*, James Dean was blessed with a face as expressive as it was beautiful; and while not the possessor of a beautiful body, he moved beautifully and boasted at least one beautiful anatomical feature, a great derrière, which was displayed to maximum advantage in *East of Eden* thanks to snugly tailored pants and artfully revealing camera angles— oh, without question, *beautiful* and not "handsome" or "good-looking" was the word to describe James Dean!

Frank was at the Cedar when I heard the news of Dean's death on the radio, and I immediately phoned him there, as though the troubled actor had been a close friend of ours. Meanwhile, in a small town in Arkansas, the future film director James Bridges, whom Jack Larson would soon bring into our lives, was as distressed as I was and as Frank proved to be, and like Frank, he would compose an elegy to James Dean (though not until 1978), in his case a cinematic requiem in memory of the young movie star who touched his life so indelibly. In a sense the tender and beautiful *September 30, 1955* was twenty-three years in the making, in Jim's heart and soul all that time— how unashamedly Frank would have wept at the final scene: in the gathering dusk, there is a ravishing long shot of an old-fashioned, small-town movie theater marquee and a workman on a ladder removing the letters that spell out EAST OF EDEN and replacing them with MARILYN MONROE IN SEVEN YEAR ITCH. It is an extraordinarily privileged moment in the American cinema. (And how unfortunate that this underrated movie of Jim's isn't better known. It missed, it seems to me, because Richard Thomas, in the lead, lacked the necessary sex appeal, beauty, and temperament.)

DIGRESSIONS ON SOME POEMS BY FRANK O'HARA

There is another link between Frank and Jim, between Frank's poetry and Jim's movie: at the opening of the scene, it is still light out when the marquee is turned on, and I cannot conceive of a more convincing demonstration of the truth of these lines in "A Step Away from Them":

> Neon in daylight is a
> great pleasure, as Edwin Denby would
> write, as are light bulbs in daylight.

Still another connection: when I phoned Jim in Los Angeles to check on details of that final scene, he mentioned something he'd never told me—how, as a student at Arkansas State Teachers College, he idly picked up a copy of *Poetry* in the school library and leafing through it ran across "For James Dean."

Two final notes on *East of Eden* to demonstrate how the movie continued to reverberate through Frank's abundant imagination during the coming years.

As he's writing "Causerie de A.F." (July 21, 1961), a favorite line of his from the movie apparently occurs to him. Maybe you remember the context: James Dean's Cal has tracked down his mother, now running a bordello; she makes a crude witticism, gets no immediate reaction from him, and then speaks the line that becomes the poem's epigraph (note that the actress is credited with the line, as though it originated with her and not with the screenwriter): *"If you don't think that's funny, you better not go to college."—Jo Van Fleet*

And this from "Lines for the Fortune Cookies" (1961): "Who do you think you are, anyway? Jo Van Fleet?"

Well, it was no more than a day or two after the actor's death that Frank began writing "For James Dean," and as soon as it was finished he wrote "Obit Dean." I said, "Write another one, Frank," and he did, he wrote it in the sand one weekend at Morris Golde's place in the secluded section of Fire Island called Water Island, where on a similar weekend eleven years later he would have a freak accident that would result in his death. Did he really write in the sand what would become the first of his "Four Little Elegies," the third one being "Obit Dean"? Yes, I seem to remember seeing him trace the words, letter by letter:

> *James Dean*
> *made in USA*
> *eager to be everything*
> *stopped short*
>
> *Do we know what*
> *excellence is? it's*
> *all in this world*
> *not to be executed*

When I say "seem to remember," I do so for the simple reason that I may have imagined it so intensely, seeing Frank on his knees in front of Morris's beach house, more like a child playing in the sand than a man of twenty-nine, that in time it became a reality, something I actually witnessed.

By now, some readers are going to start wondering about us: What kind of lives were we living, anyway? Pretty outrageous ones, I'd say; we indulged ourselves, abided by our every whim, did pretty much what we pleased. And why not? There had to be some advantages in being queer, and we made sure that there were. For one thing, we didn't feel compelled to project those hardhearted qualities of masculinity so often expected of straight males our age—how dispiriting and tiring that must be! Like so many gays, we were young for our age, thus slightly giddy and sometimes heedless; we had no responsibilities beyond making enough money to pay the rent, buy food and booze, and go to the movies and the ballet as often as possible. "Be glad you're gay"—that was how Jack Larson put it once, trying to talk some sense into a confused, self-pitying youth who didn't understand that turning queer was his escape hatch from the dreary middle-class existence fate had assigned him, as indeed had been the case with both Jack and me—less so with Frank, whose exceptional gifts were enough to dislodge him from the rut of ordinary bourgeois life. "There are other reasons for being homosexual"—

that was Frank's way of expressing how relieved and content he was to be queer. What he meant was, going to bed with our own sex was just part of it, the great freedom we enjoyed assuming such importance that in his view it was more than sufficient compensation for being thought of as sexual pariahs and, in some quarters, as detested perverts. So we lived our lives the way we saw fit, and if it was our fancy to go gaga over a movie star, that was our business. The James Dean poems may not be among Frank's greatest achievements, but no excuses should be made for them. They are sincere and felt, and they show us a side of him revealed nowhere else in his poems. As Frank himself acknowledged to Bunny Lang, in reference to his first James Dean poem, "I've had more embarrassing sentiments than that one."

TO THE FILM INDUSTRY IN CRISIS

[N O V E M B E R   1 5 ,   1 9 5 5]

Not you, lean quarterlies and swarthy periodicals
with your studious incursions toward the pomposity of ants,
nor you, experimental theatre in which Emotive Fruition
is wedding Poetic Insight perpetually, nor you,
promenading Grand Opera, obvious as an ear (though you
are close to my heart), but you, Motion Picture Industry,
it's you I love!

In times of crisis, we must all decide again and again whom we love.
And give credit where it's due: not to my starched nurse, who taught me
how to be bad and not bad rather than good (and has lately availed
herself of this information), not to the Catholic Church
which is at best an oversolemn introduction to cosmic entertainment,
not to the American Legion, which hates everybody, but to you,
glorious Silver Screen, tragic Technicolor, amorous Cinemascope,
stretching Vistavision and startling Stereophonic Sound, with all
your heavenly dimensions and reverberations and iconoclasms! To
Richard Barthelmess as the "tol'able" boy barefoot and in pants,
Jeanette MacDonald of the flaming hair and lips and long, long neck,
Sue Carroll as she sits for eternity on the damaged fender of a car
and smiles, Ginger Rogers with her pageboy bob like a sausage
on her shuffling shoulders, peach-melba-voiced Fred Astaire of the feet,

Eric von Stroheim, the seducer of mountain-climbers' gasping spouses,
the Tarzans, each and every one of you (I cannot bring myself to prefer
Johnny Weissmuller to Lex Barker, I cannot!), Mae West in a furry sled,
her bordello radiance and bland remarks, Rudolph Valentino of the
    moon,
its crushing passions, and moonlike, too, the gentle Norma Shearer,
Miriam Hopkins dropping her champagne glass off Joel McCrea's yacht
and crying into the dappled sea, Clark Gable rescuing Gene Tierney
from Russia and Allan Jones rescuing Kitty Carlisle from Harpo Marx,
Cornel Wilde coughing blood on the piano keys while Merle Oberon
    berates,
Marilyn Monroe in her little spike heels reeling through Niagara Falls,
Joseph Cotten puzzling and Orson Welles puzzled and Dolores del Rio
eating orchids for lunch and breaking mirrors, Gloria Swanson
    reclining,
and Jean Harlow reclining and wiggling, and Alice Faye reclining
and wiggling and singing, Myrna Loy being calm and wise, William
    Powell
in his stunning urbanity, Elizabeth Taylor blossoming, yes, to you

and to all you others, the great, the near-great, the featured, the extras
who pass quickly and return in dreams saying your one or two lines,
    my love!
Long may you illumine space with your marvellous appearances, delays
and enunciations, and may the money of the world glitteringly cover you
as you rest after a long day under the kleig lights with your faces
in packs for our edification, the way the clouds come often at night
but the heavens operate on the star system. It is a divine precedent
you perpetuate! Roll on, reels of celluloid, as the great earth rolls on!

DIGRESSIONS ON SOME POEMS BY FRANK O'HARA

What can I say that might illuminate this heavenly poem? Not much; it speaks for itself, and speaks with great eloquence, wit, and precision because of its authentic and evocative details and its deft description of the idiosyncrasies and physical attributes of quintessential movie stars who for Frank exemplified Hollywood, particularly as manifested during what has come to be known as its Golden Age—roughly, the period from 1930 to 1945, which corresponds with the childhood, adolescence, and early youth of Frank's (and my) generation, thereby entangling our formative years with Hollywood's golden years. Note, by the way, that his passion for movies is reflected not only by this poem but also by the astonishing number of poems that have references to movies and movie stars. In one poem he goes so far as to pay tongue-in-cheek tribute to a hack composer of Warner Bros. background music ("How do you like the music of Adolph / Deutsch? I like / it better than Max Steiner's"—from "Fantasy"), and in another he drops the names of two character actresses most readers would not recognize (Googie Withers and Blanche Yurka in "Biotherm"). By my rough count, something like fifty-five poems are movie related—"rough," I should explain, because I found Frank's cinematic citations so drenched with nostalgia that my mind kept wandering so that I lost count.

I would imagine that anyone around our age who went to the movies regularly is bound to be touched and amused by this poem, and overcome with nostalgia. On the other hand, readers who grew up with TV would be too young to have ever cared about what was happening to the film industry during the early fifties, the period when TV was coming into its own while causing, with reckless disregard, the decline of the studio system, dwindling box-office receipts, and the razing of the nation's great movie palaces. Yet, ironically, it was the detested tube that made it possible for us to see some of our favorite movies when, beginning in the mid-fifties, they were made available on those great *Late Late Shows*. Not that Frank and I had a set that early; we had to wait until 1962, which was when Norman Bluhm gave us a hand-me-down black-and-white job. But John Button had a set and it was at his place on East Second Street that we met regularly to see some of our favorite movies from childhood.

72 · *To the Film Industry in Crisis*

Is "To the Film Industry in Crisis" an example of camp, as one critic has suggested? If so, it was high camp, even serious camp, as Frank shamelessly meant every word—*felt* every word, which is why the poem is so touching. But not everyone found it so. Paul Goodman, who humorlessly hated everything about Hollywood, was its most vocal critic. "What is happening to Frank?" he asked when I ran into him after he'd read the poem in *Meditations in an Emergency* (1957). And then there was the letter from a Father Francis O'Hara, who lived in Baltimore, Frank's birthplace. Writing under the safe assumption that Frank was born into the Catholic faith and that his baptism name was Francis, which meant that they shared the same name and religious background, he wanted to know how Frank, in good conscience, could have committed to print the blasphemous reference to the Roman Catholic Church as being "at best an oversolemn introduction to cosmic entertainment"? He concluded his letter by advising Frank to make amends, get back into the Church, and go to confession.

Herewith my notes on the movies that turn up in "To the Film Industry in Crisis":

Richard Barthelmess as the "tol'able" boy barefoot and in pants is the 1921 *Tol'able David* directed by Henry King. Perhaps Frank's favorite silent film, it is an infinitely sweet and beautiful movie largely photographed in natural daylight that is unlike anything you see in films today. We wept together over this tale of rural innocence at the Modern, where we saw other great works from the silent era like Murnau's *Sunrise,* von Stroheim's *Greed,* and Seastrom's *The Wind* with the incomparable Lillian Gish.

Jeanette MacDonald of the flaming hair and lips and long, long neck could be in reference to any of her movies co-starring the wooden Nelson Eddy— or possibly, on the other hand, Frank was thinking of the earlier, more sophisticated movies she made with Ernst Lubitsch, one of his favorite directors. "If only M-G-M had never teamed her with Nelson Eddy," opined Frank, "think how divine she could have been!"

Sue Carroll as she sits for eternity on the damaged fender of a car / and smiles is—well, I wish I remembered the title of the charming, simple-hearted romantic comedy (another silent film) Frank is thinking of; but it was, as I recall, a damaged running board the adorable Sue Carroll sat on. An innocent ingenue version of Clara Bow, she is not to be confused with Nancy Carroll, who was far better known and had a bigger career.

Ginger Rogers with her pageboy bob like a sausage / on her shuffling shoulders, peach-melba-voiced Fred Astaire of the feet can refer to any number of their great musicals, as Ginger Rogers often wore her hair in a pageboy; but I imagine the Astaire-Rogers vehicle he had in mind was the 1936 *Swing Time*, which he will recall once again in a later work, the fabulous love poem called "Steps" whose opening lines are "How funny you are today New York / like Ginger Rogers in *Swingtime*." And how irresistibly Frank wraps up the poem (this quote is a digression on a digression on a digression):

> oh god it's wonderful
> to get out of bed
> and drink too much coffee
> and smoke too many cigarettes
> and love you so much

Eric von Stroheim, the seducer of mountain-climbers' gasping spouses vividly evokes *Foolish Wives* (1921) in which "the man you love to hate" plays an officer cad and swindler who has a mysterious way with women.

With *the Tarzans, each and every one of you (I cannot bring myself to prefer / Johnny Weissmuller to Lex Barker, I cannot!)*, is Frank being just a tad disingenuous? Because there is no question in my mind that like me he preferred the most famous of the Tarzans, the great Olympic champion swimmer Johnny Weismuller; and his favorite Tarzan movie was surely *Tarzan the Ape Man* (1932), in which Weismuller sported a precensored, incredibly flimsy loincloth that barely covered his gorgeous, hairless buns. Memorably, we saw it on TV at Aaron Copland's place in Ossining, where Bob Cornell had taken us for the weekend, and Aaron, always so proper, had to be a little shocked by the way we squealed over the Weismuller physique and ass.

Mae West in a furry sled, / her bordello radiance and bland remarks describes a scene from *Klondike Annie* (1936), the least of her comedies, so obviously it was the image of her smothered in white fur that caught Frank's fancy and remained locked in his memory bank through the years.

Rudolph Valentino of the moon, / its crushing passions can only be the great Latin lover in *The Son of the Sheik* (1926), as it was about the only movie of his I remember Frank's ever seeing—again, at the Modern.

and moonlike, too, the gentle Norma Shearer best describes the Norma Shearer of the 1936 *Romeo and Juliet;* but Frank's favorite Shearer vehicle was probably *Riptide* (1934), which we saw at one of John Button's TV evenings.

Miriam Hopkins dropping her champagne glass off Joel McCrea's yacht / and crying into the dappled sea makes me wonder if the movie wasn't *The Richest Girl in the World* (1934), in which case it would have been Hopkins's yacht, as she played the title role to McCrea's indigent suitor.

Clark Gable rescuing Gene Tierney / from Russia is the 1953 *Never Let Me Go*, and I don't know what made Frank think of this clinker, filmed near the end of the great Gable's career.

and Allan Jones rescuing Kitty Carlisle from Harpo Marx is easy—it's *A Night at the Opera* (1935), the first of the Marx Brothers M-G-M comedies and the beginning of both their decline (their movies hereafter were leaden and overproduced) and their resurgence as big box office.

Cornel Wilde [as Chopin] *coughing blood on the piano keys while Merle Oberon* [as George Sand] *berates* is the 1945 piece of kitsch, *A Song to Remember.*

Marilyn Monroe in her little spike heels reeling through Niagara Falls is obviously *Niagara* (1953), actually quite a decent thriller.

Joseph Cotten puzzling and Orson Welles puzzled and Dolores del Rio / eating orchids for lunch and breaking mirrors is a composite, a very neat conflation: the three actors appeared together in the ill-fated 1943 *Journey into Fear*, which Welles (as director) was not allowed to complete and for which he did not have final cut, while the reference to del Rio "eating orchids for lunch and breaking mirrors" sounds like *Bird of Paradise* (1932), though I'm only guessing.

Gloria Swanson reclining, / and Jean Harlow reclining and wiggling, and

*Alice Faye reclining / and wiggling and singing, Myrna Loy being calm and
wise, William Powell / in his stunning urbanity, Elizabeth Taylor blossoming*
could have been inspired by any number of their movies.

So, if this wonderful, witty tour de force isn't an example of camp, does it
follow that its author could just as well have been straight? Or to put it another way: Could a straight poet have written it? No way: read John Hollander's poem on the movies and you'll see what I mean. His poem isn't at all
bad, Hollander being an accomplished poet, but it's a little square—the
product, I'm afraid, of a sensibility too determinedly heterosexual.

Writing about all these movies has naturally brought to mind many movie-
related experiences I shared with Frank. Here are just two, coupled here because they are curiously analogous.

1) In 1954, just a year before we began living together, we saw an unlikely
double feature at the Loew's Lexington: *On the Waterfront,* which was the
main draw, and *The Member of the Wedding,* the B movie on the bill despite
its Carson McCullers source and its having been directed by Fred Zinne-
mann. Seeing those two movies, one after the other, was an emotionally
draining experience, but it wasn't until we were leaving the theater that I
saw how badly shaken Frank was. Assuming he'd been as bowled over by
Brando's performance as I was, I made a reference to the terrible ordeal endured by Terry.

"Who? What?" Frank cried. He sounded put out, almost outraged.

"The character played by Brando," I explained.

"Who's thinking about him? The scene where Frankie is dragged from the
car was more violent and horrible than anything in all of *On the Waterfront.*"

2) A number of years later, when we were living at 441 East Ninth Street,
we saw a revival of *Modern Times.* It was a new print and for that reason it
was an especially rewarding experience—marred, however, by a transparent
curtain that appeared prematurely, lessening the beauty and impact of the
final scene in which Chaplin waddles off into the sunrise with Paulette Goddard. "They ruined the movie!" I shouted.

Indignant, I sought out the manager and bitterly complained. But the insensitive lout didn't seem to know what I was talking about, and Frank said, "Come on, Joe," practically dragging me away. "And what was that all about?" he asked when we were out on the street.

"I wanted everything to be just right when I finally got to see *Modern Times*."

"You never saw it before?" Frank said, surprised.

"No, I hadn't." I spoke as though it were a confession.

"So that was why you wanted so badly to see it . . ."

"I knew it was a new print and . . ." Then I explained why I had never seen it as a child. It was being shown in a special road-show presentation at a theater in the southern California town where my family lived during the Depression, and I was all set to attend the Saturday matinee with my two brothers when my mother took me aside. I knew immediately what was coming. My older brother had just taken on a magazine route selling *Liberty* and *Photoplay,* and my mother decided that my younger brother and I should be his assistants. We could keep half of what we made and the other half would be used for buying groceries. But all I did was pore over *Photoplay* while my brothers went boldly from door to door, by the end of the day selling every magazine except the one I had confiscated. "As punishment for not doing your part," my mother said, "I can't let you go to the movie." But she relented a little and let me drive with them to the Fox California where, in front of the theater, a man dressed up like Charlie Chaplin was directing traffic. Seeing the Little Tramp was what got me crying, and I bawled all the way home.

"Oh, Joe," Frank said when I was finished. "That's the saddest story I ever heard."

And in the untitled poem whose first line is "I don't know what D. H. Lawrence is driving at," written on August 24, 1959, which would have been around the time we saw *Modern Times* together, there's an homage of sorts to the movie: "and when someone looks sort of raggedy and dirty like Paulette Goddard / in *Modern Times* it's exciting, it isn't usual or attractive . . ."

To the Film Industry in Crisis · 77

RADIO

[D E C E M B E R   3 ,   1 9 5 5]

Why do you play such dreary music
on Saturday afternoon, when tired
mortally tired I long for a little
reminder of immortal energy?
                                        All
week long while I trudge fatiguingly
from desk to desk in the museum
you spill your miracles of Grieg
and Honegger on shut-ins.
                                        Am I not
shut in too; and after a week
of work don't I deserve Prokofieff?

Well, I have my beautiful de Kooning
to aspire to. I think it has an orange
bed in it, more than the ear can hold.

The picture is before me as I write—actually, it's a photograph of the painting, a 1943 oil on composition board entitled *Summer Couch*. "Private
collection, courtesy Alan Stone Gallery, New York, 36" x 51"," reads the
caption in the catalogue where the reproduction appears. Semi-abstract
and influenced by Gorky, it has brilliantly contrasting colors, predominantly

bright orange and bright green, along with blue, pink, yellow, light purple, and umber. The central figure, which is surrounded by biomorphic and triangular shapes, always seemed to me to be a chaise longue, while Frank, as we know from "Radio," thought it was a bed.

I wasn't with him when he saw the painting in the living room or parlor or one of the many other rooms in the labyrinthine sprawl of a house in Southampton where Anne and Fairfield Porter and their large family lived. That would have been in the early fifties. "It was out of the blue, completely unexpected," Frank said in describing how Fairfield came to give him the painting. I had a pretty good idea what he meant. Though not someone I knew well, I'd seen Fairfield around enough to spot him as a noncomformist who did things his own way. No question about it, he was the most abrupt person I'd ever seen in a social situation. Never one to waste words, he'd suddenly rise in the middle of a conversation, head for the door, and be out of the place before anyone realized he was leaving.

It seems he was just as abrupt when Frank began going on about how great the painting was. "It's yours," Fairfield said. "I never really liked it." Frank said it was as if someone had admired Fairfield's tie and he was now whipping it off and handing it over. "You mean he started taking down the painting?" I asked. "Just about," Frank said. And when Frank told him he couldn't possibly accept it, Fairfield became impatient—it was Frank's painting, and that was that. Finally, Frank said he'd accept it on the condition that Fairfield could have it back anytime he wanted it. That raised Fairfield's dander, and he insisted that it was an outright gift and Frank was never to mention it again—if he did, their friendship would be in jeopardy.

Thus, from the moment he took possession of the painting, Frank thought of it as his de Kooning, which of course was how he referred to it in "Radio," as "my beautiful de Kooning"—made a public announcement of it, as it were—and after a while, I thought of it as mine, too, the way you feel a place you live in is yours, no matter that it is rented.

And now in my small study in Springs, less than a mile from where Frank is buried in Green River Cemetery, I gaze wistfully at the reproduction, savoring the many associations the painting has for me: the shabby apartments where this elegant work incongruously hung (it never made it to our sleek Broadway loft) and our day-to-day lives of which it was no small part, simply getting up in the morning and having the painting there—in Frank's phrase, "a little reminder of immortal energy"—and the times we entertained and the friends who shared our pleasure in this fabulous painting whose title and date remained unknown to us all the years we had it.

"That's Bill's, isn't it? Terrific! You can always tell a de Kooning," Frank reports Franz Kline as saying when he entered our University Place apartment, already unleashing the rush of words from which Frank would fashion his tour de force, "Franz Kline Talking." But most of all—need I say it?—I associate *Summer Couch* with Frank. He lived with the painting, thought of it as his, for something like eight years. Then in 1961 or '62, Fairfield phoned him at work one morning, barely said hello, naturally got right to the point. As abruptly as he'd given away the painting, he now took it back: he needed to raise some quick cash, he said. And that was that.

Frank didn't tell me how he reacted, what he said to Fairfield; but I know that things were never the same between them after that. But what could Frank say? The painting he'd enjoyed all those years was thanks to Fairfield's beneficence. Would you like to know how much it went for? So would I—but it wasn't much; Elaine de Kooning, who knew what it fetched, laid into Fairfield for selling it for so little.

And where, I can't help wondering, is the painting now, what became of it? Does its owner love it as much as we did and does he know its history, that a poet had it for several years and wrote a terrific poem about it? Is that not part of its provenance? And I remember a casual friend telling me, not too many years ago, that he saw *Summer Couch* in a rich collector's house in Beverly Hills, I think, and now I had to hear how beautiful it looked in its present surroundings, "so much better than it did when you and Frank had it." I never spoke to that person again: that was how much the painting meant to me—not as a possession, but as a integral part of my life with Frank.

I was in Los Angeles, on one of my periodic visits to see my parents, when Frank had to return the painting to Fairfield, and it was not until I was back in New York, back in our terrible East Ninth Street apartment, that I learned what happened. "I didn't have the heart to write or phone you," he said, as I stared in disbelief at the tragic empty space between the two sooty windows that looked out on the street. "You could have prepared me!" I protested angrily. "I'm sorry," he said. "How do you think I feel?" he added, as if he had to ask. I apologized for losing my temper, and we never spoke of the painting again.

This is part two of my note on "Radio." It concerns the real subject of the poem, as indicated by its title. "Why do you play such dreary music?" Frank asks his little radio. What set him off—and me, too—was that both classical music stations, WQXR and WNYC, persisted in playing overly familiar works like the Brahms First, the Schumann Piano Concerto, and the Mozart *Jupiter*. Even worse, we had to gag down heavy doses of Beethoven that they were forever prescribing—not infrequently played Beethoven (the string trios or a late piano sonata, for example) but the *Emperor*, the *Moonlight*, the *Eroica*, the *Pastorale*, the *Pathétique*, etc., etc. In other words, Frank underplayed the seriousness of the situation, since it wasn't only on Saturday afternoon that "dreary music" held dominion but on virtually any afternoon of the week. I'm referring to the time before I moved in, when Frank was jobless and I'd drop by for a visit, sometimes for lunch (which I usually made, unwittingly priming myself for the culinary duties I'd assume when we became roommates). I have a very distinct memory of one tired warhorse after another galumphing through the airways. Not that it greatly mattered what was on the radio, so long as it was off the beaten path, for it mainly served as background music for a *gemütlich* domestic scene—indeed, it was as if we were already living together, for soon after my arrival, Frank would return to his writing or reading or whatever else he was doing, and then he'd be on the phone half of the time I was there, with Jane or Grace or someone else, while I lay around reading and daydreaming and listening to music, as cozy and content as I'd ever been in my life, a feeling I never had growing up in a family of six children. So what was true of my mornings with Frank could be said of those languid afternoons: nothing momentous happened. Yet a day in which I spent an hour or so with him would become transformed and hold some special promise. What he did to bring this about, what alchemy he practiced so effortlessly, I still find difficult to fathom and impossible to describe. But whatever power or gift he possessed, however you describe it, I'm sure had a lot to do with his inexhaustible energy, whose source must have been a fearless love of life.

But what drew him to me? Out of the blue, he'd sometimes pay me a compliment on my looks, a boon to someone as vain as I was. He did the same thing with his women friends, so I was not alone, the difference in gender notwithstanding. More important, Frank was not close to his brother, anymore than I was close to either of mine—that, quite possibly, had something to do with what drew him to me. I know it was true of me, because early on I realized that my feelings for him were at least partly fraternal.

"If you're writing, I'll leave," I said the first time I found him in the middle of a poem. "No, don't go," he said, not looking up from his typewriter. "I won't be long." And he wasn't. From then on, I realized that my presence didn't inhibit him, and I'm sure the same was true of all of his friends; our presence, on the contrary, must have inspired and galvanized him. This had less to do with his ability to concentrate than it did with the *way* he concentrated, for whatever happened around him often became part of the creative act in progress. The radio could be blaring, the phone could be jangling, people could be dropping by, someone could be in the same room with him (*talking* to him); and when we lived on East Ninth Street, in a second-floor apartment so close to the street that it seemed an extension of it, a cacophonous symphony of ugly urban sounds played fortissimo outside our window, punctuated regularly by the sound of the Ninth Street crosstown bus making its stop next to the downstairs doorway—incredibly, these distractions not only failed to impede but seemed to spur the steady stream of words rushing from his teeming brain to his two nimble index fingers that decisively, at full tilt, struck the keys of his trusty, overburdened Royal portable, of which he ran through three over the fifteen years I knew him. It would, then, be wide of the mark to say that he was tuning out, doing what I tried in vain to do under the same trying circumstances—"I can't hear myself think!" I'd shout, and

DIGRESSIONS ON SOME POEMS BY FRANK O'HARA

toss aside the book I was endeavoring to read, while Frank appeared unwilling or unable to shut out the world that engulfed us.

"Is everything grist for your mill?" I remember asking him, impatiently, on one of those frustrating occasions.

"What?" he asked, as he continued typing.

"The city! The noise outside!"

He smiled, and that was his answer: nothing deterred him, for the world was his oyster, especially the city of New York, whose sights and sounds, character and ambience, and above all its people, he never allowed his heart and mind to renounce. He wrote, "I can't even enjoy a blade of grass unless I know there's a subway handy, or a record store or some other sign that people do not totally *regret* life," words from "Meditations in an Emergency" that, sans the italicizing of "regret," can now be found in bold brass letters on the plaza fence of renovated Battery Park, appropriately beside the words of another poet who celebrated New York, a poet close to Frank's heart, a poet whose spirit and sensibility and long line had a salutary and felicitous influence on Frank's poetry—Walt Whitman, of course: "City of the sea! Proud and passionate city—mettlesome, mad, extravagant city!"

JOSEPH CORNELL

[1 9 5 5]

Into a sweeping meticulously-
detailed disaster the violet
light pours. It's not a sky
it's a room. And in the open
field a glass of absinthe is
fluttering its song of India.
Prairie winds circle mosques.

You are always a little too
young to understand. He is
bored with his sense of the
past, the artist. Out of the
prescient rock in his heart
he has spread a land without
flowers of near distances.

s it possible that the reclusive, otherworldly Joseph Cornell saw the manuscript of this poem, which has directions, in Frank's hand, "print like
boxes"? Could someone have shown it to him—for example, Rudy Burckhardt, who had recently made a movie with Cornell? As generous as he was
eccentric, this great American surrealist was known to give away his artworks
impulsively, so isn't it possible (to pursue my point) that he wanted to give

DIGRESSIONS ON SOME POEMS BY FRANK O'HARA

Frank a box because of the poem, not because of Frank's perceptive review in *Art News*? And the poem, with its references to sky, violet light, and a glass of absinthe that bring to mind Cornell's haunting work—is it not an example of concrete poetry and therefore about the only poem of its kind in the O'Hara canon? Finally, isn't it appropriate that a note about the enigmatic Joseph Cornell, whom I never knew and therefore am unqualified to write about, should be embellished with so many question marks?

My passing reference to the box Cornell offered Frank needs to be amplified—by way of another of my digressions, which will lead to other digressions, one of which will reveal what happened to that promised box.

... *you could hardly notice the walls for the paintings*, I observed in "Four Apartments," alluding to the many artworks Frank acquired through the years. That puts it rather ineptly. How about: ". . . you could hardly *see* the walls for the paintings"? Which was what I meant, and it was true, I wasn't exaggerating; and after a while, as we moved from place to place, so many works accrued that we soon ran out of wall space. And how, you might be wondering, did Frank come by these wonderful works? Virtually all were gifts from his artist friends, while there would usually be several on extended loan. "It's like a group show," said Elaine de Kooning when she visited us for the first time, at 90 University Place. Under the circumstances, you'd think someone would have suspected that a form of payola was involved; but as far as I know, nobody questioned the propriety of Frank accepting works of art as gifts—this, in spite of his being a sometime critic and a member of the Museum of Modern Art staff. I guess it helped that he didn't throw his weight around. More important, he was known as a poet, first and foremost; certainly, his artist friends thought of him that way—to them, he wasn't a museum person or a critic. "He was our Apollinaire," Philip Guston intoned into my ear as he bear-hugged me at Frank's funeral.

Not all of his colleagues at the museum understood that, at least judging from what one of them said to me at a party we gave at our 791 Broadway loft a few months before I moved out—our last joint party, come to think of it, the one graced by the attendance of Huntington Hartford, who took one

Joseph Cornell · 85

look at the paintings on the walls and beat a hasty retreat. "I can't help being jealous," confessed the colleague of Frank's, miserably, having just told me about the big-time artists who made a habit of dropping by Frank's office when they came to the museum. "I don't know how you stand it," he added—meaning, of course, how I could stand living with Frank and not die of jealousy.

"It's very simple," I told him. "Just remember he's a poet and those artists think of him as one of them. You have no right to be jealous," I concluded.

He looked at me for a moment, unhappily, and then glanced around at the paintings—covetously, I thought, and for a moment I considered explaining to him that Frank was the least acquisitive person I'd ever known. While I was about it, I could have told him of the time Frank didn't feel up to taking a subway to Queens to keep a Saturday morning date with Joseph Cornell, thereby missing out on a box Cornell wanted to give him. I think he felt uncomfortable about it, since his laudatory review of a show of Cornell's had just appeared in the September 1955 issue of *Art News*. The exhibition, at the Stable Gallery, Cornell shared with Landes Lewitin, a now largely forgotten artist who practically lived at the Cedar. Here is what Frank wrote about Cornell:

> Cornell's genius is apparently as unfailing as it is unique, for his work has no ups and downs; the total and well recognized excellence of his *oeuvre* is complete and distinct in each individual piece one sees. The pieces shown on this occasion can be described in detail, one with little liqueur glasses filled with a marble or a piece of wood, one posing a dark Renaissance man in a zodiac, others to be handled so the layers of white, pink and blue sand, held separate by glass, will shift across the plane to reveal the objects at the bottom obscurely and with a variety of films between it and the eye. But the effect of their beauty was so singular as to defy description; they are moving, too, as evidences of so pure and so uncompromising a spirit in our midst.

To drive home the point I was trying to make to Frank's colleague, I could have compared Frank's attitude toward collecting art with my own. For at

DIGRESSIONS ON SOME POEMS BY FRANK O'HARA

that time, several artists had begun giving me things, but whereas I found myself eagerly, if not to say greedily, looking forward to getting another painting or drawing, Frank clearly had what I'd describe as an unaspiring, almost indifferent attitude toward the whole thing, as for example when he forgot to take up Philip Guston's offer to give us each a gouache for our new place on Broadway. At the same time, he obviously loved his paintings and took great pains to see that they were properly hung.

Including those who collaborated with Frank as well as those who lent him works for long periods of time, these are the artists who contributed to his collection, often with as many as three or four works, and it's significant to note that it's a motley crew of the famous and the unknown, the talented and the not-so-talented: Alex Katz, Joe Brainard, Felix Pacilis, Al Held, Grace Hartigan, Marc Berlet, Lee Krasner, Jean Dubuffet, Norman Bluhm, Robert Motherwell, Basil King, Michael Goldberg, Cy Twombly, Matsumi Kanemitsu, Nell Blaine, Jasper Johns, Jane Wilson, Mario Garcia, Golda Lewis, Larry Rivers, Jane Freilicher, Jean-Paul Riopelle, Willem de Kooning, Elaine de Kooning, Fairfield Porter, John Button, Mario Schifano, Giorgio Cavallon, Allan d'Arcangelo, Franz Kline, George Spaventa, Joan Mitchell, Wolf Kahn, Paul Jenkins, and Helen Frankenthaler. Have I missed anyone? Probably.

And several of these painters, when I was first living with Frank, used to come around for a couple of hours in the afternoon—on Saturdays, I seem to remember, or when Frank had a day off—and they would come singly, never two or more at the same time: Frank's was a *salon à deux*, if you will, for it was clear to me that these artists, being self-absorbed and having a lot to say, didn't want to talk to Frank *and* each other, they wanted to talk to Frank alone—about art and poetry, mostly, but in a manner different from what I would have expected. Casual and freewheeling, yet serious and intense, the talks they had were never academic or highfalutin but of a more practical nature, nitty-gritty and from the inside out. And they didn't sit quietly, exchanging ideas: they moved around a lot, I remember—they'd pace as they spoke or one of them would get up excitedly, as he made a point, and the other would get up, too, or Frank would go to the kitchen to make coffee

Joseph Cornell · 87

and his guest would follow him, or they'd wander into the other room where I was reading and maybe half listening to what they were saying and then I'd end up joining them.

Wisely, I did a lot of listening in those days, and looking, too—for example, at what seemed to me to be a very odd painting by Cy Twombly. He brought it by and left it with Frank for several months, maybe for as long as a year. It was black and white, with a lot of scratchy lines and doodles, not like one of the later and more elegant blackboard pictures but a modest-sized painting that looked unfinished, seemed careless and impromptu, as though it just happened without the artist giving it much thought. That's what I felt at first. But I kept looking at it—it's one of the advantages of living with a painting, you can really get to know it—and after a while, I saw how beautiful and interesting it was. Later, I read what Edwin Denby said about his first experience looking at de Kooning's paintings, and that made me feel smart, because I'd instinctively gone about it the way he had: "Seeing the pictures more or less every day, they slowly became beautiful, and then they stayed beautiful."

But I already knew I was on the right track for the simple reason that I began to feel about painting the way I did about music, as something that would always be there for me. (Poetry meant as much to me later, partly by being around Frank.) Some of the paintings gave me no problems at all. The heavy impasto still life Felix Pacilis brought by was easy to get at—it was like a van Gogh, I thought—and the luminous landscape Wolf Kahn lent Frank was just as accessible. Same thing with a painting by Larry Rivers from his Bonnard period. (Whatever happened to Felix Pacilis, anyway? And what happened to that painting of Larry's? How beautiful it was!)

I liked all of the painters who came by, and Mike Goldberg I found the most expansive and approachable. And physically attractive—sexy, that is: he exuded an extremely masculine yet by no means macho sexuality with which he was so comfortable, and about which he was so secure, that he wasn't the least bothered by the unmistakable admiration of two very up-front queers. But Frank didn't simply like Mike's rough good looks, burly presence, and warm, forthright manner, he was also infatuated with him and remained so over the years, through Mike's affair with Joan Mitchell and his marriage to Patsy Southgate, and of course through Frank's own various liaisons or affairs or whatever you want to call them (friendly couplings might be closer to the mark).

Did Frank have an affair with any of the straight and nominally straight painters who used to come by? Hard to say; he was awfully discreet and I never asked questions, just as he never asked questions about my sex life. (His affair with Larry was over by then, incidentally, so I never saw what they were like together.) Cy Twombly—gangly, dark-haired, curiously good-looking Cy, with his irresistible Southern drawl and quiet, easygoing manner—I remember as coming around not just afternoons but at night as well, and then I'd make myself scarce. Soon thereafter, this great charmer and wonderful artist was off to Italy, where he took up residence and married a contessa—or maybe it was years later, I'm not sure. Anyway, it was a long time before I saw him again, and he was as unassuming and as attractive as ever, no more affected by his growing fame than Guston, Kline, and de Kooning were by all the attention they got.

EDWIN'S HAND

[1 9 5 5]

Easy to love, but
difficult to please, he
walks densely as a child
in the midst of spectacular
needs to understand.

Desire makes our
enchanter gracious, and
naturally he's surprised to
be. And so are you to be
you, when he smiles . . .

On the heels of "Joseph Cornell" comes this acrostic poem in the *Collected Poems*. Its subject is another unexampled American original of the same generation as Cornell: the equally retiring, the gentle and fragile, yet strong and resilient Edwin Denby, modest possessor of a prose style of singular luminosity, simplicity, and elegance, and a ballet critic, poet, and flaneur about whom Frank wrote in his introduction to *Dancers, Buildings and People in the Streets:* "He sees and hears more clearly than anyone else I have ever known."

He was not what he seemed. Far more prodigious, and certainly more complex, than his soft voice, mild manner, and timorous pale blue eyes suggested, he was held in such high esteem and his considerable virtues were so magnified, mainly by each new crop of young admirers who seemed to turn up annually, straining to catch every word he whispered, that a backlash was inevitable. Thus it was said that Edwin had a mean streak, that he was severe and judgmental, and not as generous as he seemed. I remember a waggish friend of Frank's and mine, tired of hearing Frank go on about Edwin's endless virtues, insisting that it was all a pose, that "Edwina" was too good to be true and a disingenuous goody two-shoes. Then there was someone, a disgruntled poet in whom Edwin doubtless showed little interest, who went so far as to hint that Edwin, sweet Edwin, was a misogynist and troublemaker, more monster than saint. Both judgments—Edwin as saint and Edwin as monster—were wide of the mark and canceled each other out. Yet there were two sides to the man, which Frank, if he were alive today, would deny, because when he loved someone as much he did Edwin, he was oblivious to any flaw in that person and stubbornly refused to acknowledge that any existed even in the face of compelling evidence. But if, on his own, he detected a flaw in someone, all hell broke loose and his feelings about that person would change overnight. I saw it happen on several occasions. I saw it happen with me.

This poem of Frank's first appeared in print on an invitation to an enormous buffet in celebration of Edwin's sixtieth birthday on March 15, 1963, which happened to be shortly before Frank and I moved into the loft on the third floor of the building at 791 Broadway, where the party took place. The festivities spread out over two floors, the second floor where Donald Droll and Roy Leaf lived, and the fourth where George Montgomery and Dan Waggoner lived. Edwin's great friend Bob Cornell was the principal organizer of the event, but it was Frank Lima, our poet-chef, who presided over the making of great vats of boeuf bourguignon; I remember rending an unbelievable amount of prime beef into two-inch cubes under his exacting instructions. With the exception of the rigorous Lincoln Kirstein, who let it be known that he didn't believe in such celebrations, everyone who was invited showed up; but I have no idea how many of us there were—at least fifty or sixty, I should imagine. Virgil Thomson proposed the main toast to Edwin, and after dinner, Red Grooms provided the entertainment (a puppet show?). And that's about all I can remember; my memory isn't very good when it comes to formal occasions, I suppose because they're too cut and dried to be memorable.

How did Edwin like the evening? Unlike his friend Virgil, who basked in the slightest attention paid him, he was clearly not the sort who liked a fuss to be made over him. On the other hand, if he was not what he seemed . . . Now that I think about it, his eyes were more attentive and alive than ever, and an especially benign smile played on his lips. He was all graciousness, an exemplary guest of honor—and to me, he seemed remarkably unchanged from when I first knew him eleven years earlier. Not that he looked young for his age: it's that when I met him, he had already settled into the look he'd have for the rest of his life, so that at the relatively early age of forty-nine he was well on his way to becoming the ethereal, silver-haired aesthete whose unearthly radiance so often caught people's eye at New York City Ballet intermissions. (Aschenbach of *Death in Venice* come to life? Not quite; Edwin's countenance lacked the necessary hint of decadence.) I believe it was during one such ballet intermission that we met, and Frank may very well have introduced us. I do know that my sharing Edwin's passion for cats was partly what made him feel friendly toward me; and when, as part of the Francesco Scavullo entourage, I went off with Gianni for a week's winter vacation in Palm Beach—such was the frivolity of my life on the fringes of the high-fashion world—Edwin cared for our exceptional Siamese, which was named Junior, as though it were the offspring of our gay marriage. Another thing Edwin undoubtedly liked about me was that I was with Gianni, whom he seemed to regard as a stereotypically sexy southern Italian. I guess I'm suggesting that Edwin's interest in sex was vicarious and voyeuristic; or, to put it another way, he seemed not to have had much actual sexual experience—he was ascetic, no question about that.

And naïve about romantic love, whose fickle nature and inconstancy he failed to perceive or understand. Years after I broke up with Gianni, he reproached me for allowing our affair to come to an end. How he got around to this I don't remember, but I do know we were at home, in our East Ninth Street apartment, when he asked me, almost angrily, while Frank was in the other room on the phone, "Why didn't you stay with Gianni? He was what you wanted—you were right for each other!" And Frank and I weren't? Or, putting it another way, I wasn't right for Frank—I wasn't good enough for him? He stopped himself; those words seemed to hang in the air, unspoken but implicit, a judgment passed on me that I wasn't in the same league as Frank—yes, that was how he made me feel, what he said to me being all the more devastating because of his gentle manner and soft voice that could only belong to someone in the right.

About the same time, John Button did something quite shocking: he phoned Edwin and took him to task for speculating about, and making a smutty reference to, what John and his new lover, Scott Burton, did in bed— why, imagine talking in such a disrespectful way to this older, kindly man we all looked up to! Well, that was John for you. Frank was more compassionate, and what comes to mind now is one of our nights with Edwin. The three of us—Frank, Edwin, and I—would sometimes adjourn to Edwin's loft on West Twenty-ninth Street after the ballet at City Center. We'd drink bourbon, nibble on whatever tidbits Edwin could rustle up, reflect on the ballets we'd seen that night, and then go on to related aesthetic matters. The loft was like Edwin, immaculate and spartan; relatively few possessions were in evidence, but there always seemed to be at least one kitten for me to hold and fondle. Also, before he decided he could no longer afford to keep it, he had a wonderful early de Kooning—on an otherwise bare wall all to itself, the work assumed the force and significance of an icon.

The night I'm thinking of went on a bit longer than usual: we drank more than usual, talked more than usual, became more emotional than usual—not just about a new Balanchine ballet (was it *Agon*?) but also, on this occasion, about life's bitter disappointments and other lachrymose matters. After we'd finally torn ourselves away from Edwin and were almost all the way downstairs, Frank came to an abrupt halt and took hold of me, as though something was wrong. "What is it?" I said. "It's Edwin," he said. "What about him?" I said. "He's lonely," Frank said. "We can't leave him up there by himself. One of us should go back and spend the night with him." "Oh, Frank," I said, "we can't do that." Reluctantly, Frank gave up the idea, but I don't remember how I talked him out of it.

Edwin's Hand · 93

And here is what Edwin said to me when we were alone for the first time after Frank's death—a paraphrase, needless to say, yet close to his exact words, since what he said meant so much to me: "I know this is hard for you. I'm older and I've gone through more things. For me, it means—" He paused to find the right words, then said quietly, "I always took comfort in the idea that I'd have Frank around as long as I lived." Then after he read "Four Apartments," in *The World,* having told Bill Berkson and me that he couldn't write a memoir himself, he said: "If I wrote a piece about Frank, I'd want it to be like yours." Later, after it appeared in the *Homage* volume, the other side of Edwin appeared: "You didn't say what Frank had done for you, that he helped make a man of you."

So Edwin could give and he could take away.

> Easy to love, but
> difficult to please

is how Frank begins his poem—and there, in a nutshell, is Edwin, his affability and kindness tempered by his high standards and expectations of excellence. Thus Frank seems to be acknowledging that Edwin could be demanding, even severe. When I complained mildly about someone, Edwin took up my cudgel and coldly pronounced words I repeated to Frank, whose response was a knowing smile: "You have to draw the line somewhere and you might as well start at the bottom." To bear the brunt of Edwin's disapproval—now there was an experience not easily forgotten. On one memorable occasion, it was nothing more than a glance and gesture, a withering look Edwin shot me, accompanied by an almost imperceptible shake of his head, simply because I made the mistake of waxing enthusiastic over a flashy Ravel piece from *Gaspard de la nuit* played by a pianist named, I think, David Porter—anyway, a friend of Bob Cornell's, at a musicale Bob threw one night in 1958. Frank was so busy coming on to young David, who, unusual for pianists, was straight, that he didn't notice a thing; then later, when I mentioned to him how Edwin looked at me, he had the nerve to say it was all in my imagination, adding that it would be unlike Edwin to make me feel small.

Then there was Edwin's handwriting (surely Frank had it in mind when

he hit on the title "Edwin's Hand"): minuscule, spidery, indecipherable—
what does that tell us? I saw a sample of it on a postcard Frank once received,
possibly the only time Edwin ever wrote him. Frank pored over that card as
though it were in code, then passed it on to me; I took one look and gave it
back. Frank, however, didn't give up that easily; so curious was he to know
what Edwin had written him that he kept the card out and sometimes over
drinks would puzzle over it. But after a couple of weeks, having pieced together no more than two or three phrases, he admitted defeat. Consistent
with Edwin's handwriting was the diffident way he spoke in public—yes, I actually witnessed one such rare occasion. Was it in the late seventies at a reception in Lincoln Center when he received the Capezio Award for dance
criticism? Anyway, he was expected to say something, and he did—except he
couldn't be heard, he wouldn't *let* himself be heard.

So what can we deduce from handwriting that can't be read and a voice
that can't be heard—what do they tell us about Edwin? That he was secretive, disinclined to communicate, determined to frustrate and confound? I
don't know, I really don't know. And now I'm beginning to wonder how some
of Edwin's admirers might feel about what I've written here. Have I been
gratuitously bitchy and negative? Have I inappropriately allowed captious
comments and snide observations into a note purportedly about a poem
whose subject, let's face it, Frank certainly didn't hold up for disapprobation?
To such charges, I would plead "not guilty"—but Frank, I'm sure, would rule
against me. I can hear him now, the voice not of our pre–Bill Berkson/
Vincent Warren days when he doted on me, seemed to like everything about
me, but that of 791 Broadway, the end of the line, when at long last he discovered I had a fault and it was that "You're petty, Joe!" (Sorry—I'm getting
ahead of myself; I'll go into all of this later, at the appropriate time.) All right,
I'm a Virgo; I seize on small things, I dwell on them, I'm too critical. But
when it comes to what I've just written—no, it isn't what it might seem. In
fact, it's the exact opposite, a testament to Edwin Denby's splendor. Or so it
seems to me. For what I'm saying is, his flaws were so few and insignificant
that they merely serve to remind us how exceptional he was and why I, like
so many others, revere his memory: I think of his stubborn refusal to seek

Edwin's Hand · 95

fame and of his willingness to let fame come posthumously, should it come at all; I think of the encouragement he offered writers, poets, painters, dancers—all of us; I think of his sharing with us, his younger friends who loved the Balanchine ballets, what he saw and heard, always interested in what we saw and heard, drawing us out without patronizing us; I think of what appeared to be his social unease, his charming inability to remember anyone's name, particularly when forced to make an introduction; and I think of his suicide, I think of that, too, his courageous, clandestine decision to leave us because he felt it was time to check out—what a way to go, what a lesson for us all! And his writing. Let others extol the virtues of his poems; I'm content to concentrate on his prose for a moment, his criticism and his occasional pieces—sharp, simple, direct, on target, the words falling on the page as right as rain, shaping supple sentences and creating subtle rhythms, as here from the opening paragraph of his piece on the thirties and how he came to know Willem de Kooning:

> Pat Pasloff asked me to write something for the show about New York painting in the thirties, how it seemed at the time. The part I knew, I saw as a neighbor. I met Willem de Kooning on the fire escape, because a black kitten lost in the rain cried at my fire door, and after the rain it turned out to be his kitten. He was painting on a dark eight-foot-high picture that had sweeps of black across it and a big look. That was early in '36. Soon Rudy Burckhardt and I kept meeting Bill at midnight at the local Stewart's, and having a coffee together. Friends of his often showed up, and when the cafeteria closed we would go to Bill's loft in the next street and talk some more and make coffee. I remember people talking intently and listening intently and then everybody burst out laughing and started off intent on another tack.

After Frank's death—or perhaps a year and a half earlier, at the time of our breakup—whatever friendship existed between Edwin and me began to falter, to lose its intimacy and warmth, until finally we merely greeted each other perfunctorily when we met, rarely engaging in conversation. It was not what I wanted, but there was nothing I could do. It was Edwin—seemingly shy, diffident, passive—who called the shots; but of course, I knew that all along.

CAMBRIDGE

[J A N U A R Y   1 2 ,   1 9 5 6]

It is still raining and the yellow-green cotton fruit
looks silly round a window giving out on winter trees
with only three drab leaves left. The hot plate works,
it is the sole heat on earth, and instant coffee. I
put on my warm corduroy pants, a heavy maroon sweater,
and wrap myself in my old maroon bathrobe. Just like Pasternak
in Marburg (they say Italy and France are colder, but
I'm sure that Germany's at least as cold as this) and,
lacking the Master's inspiration, I may freeze to death
before I can get out into the white rain. I could have left
the window closed last night? But that's where health
comes from! His breath from the Urals, drawing me into flame
like a forgotten cigarette. Burn! this is not negligible,
being poetic, and not feeble, since it's sponsored by
the greatest living Russian poet at incalculable cost.
Across the street there is a house under construction,
abandoned to the rain. Secretly, I shall go to work on it.

What could he have been thinking? Why didn't I stop him? What was wrong with me—with *us*? To let myself off the hook, I can say in all honesty that Frank hadn't yet begun turning to me for advice on practical matters. In fact, he barely broached the subject and instead blithely presented the whole thing as a fait accompli. "Joe, there's something I have to tell you," he announced one day in the fall of 1955. "I've accepted a fellowship at the Poets' Theatre in Cambridge—you remember my telling you about it, don't you?"

I was taken aback. "Does that mean you have to go there?"

"It's only for six months," he said—a little sheepishly, I thought. "It begins the first of the year."

But why, why go—whatever possessed him? I still to this day don't know. Had Bunny talked him into it, or George Montgomery, whom I had not yet met? Bunny more than likely, as she'd also been granted a fellowship. Then there was the possibility that he felt the fellowship would give him time to write. After all, wasn't that the main reason for his resignation from *Art News,* because he was forced to write reviews he didn't want to write, which in turn took him away from the writing he wanted to do? But by the fall of 1955, he must have realized that he thrived on life in New York, that the city had become the lifeblood of his poetry. I also liked to think he was happy living with me.

No, it made no sense for him to return to the scene of his college days. You can't go home again, and you can't, by the same token, go back to college either—which he must have realized the minute he stepped inside the creepy one-room apartment he'd sublet from Lyon Phelps, a Harvard classmate. Why creepy? Because, in the first place, the room was dominated by a large, unbelievably ugly mahogany coffee table whose concave top was covered with a bed of sand two inches deep. It was that kind of apartment, one with a plethora of appalling personal touches and nothing in sight to alleviate the horror—even Lyon's many books failed to warm the room or give respite. "You must miss your de Kooning," I said after taking one look at the place when I paid him a visit one weekend in late spring.

DIGRESSIONS ON SOME POEMS BY FRANK O'HARA

And how, you might wonder, was I doing in New York, with Frank away serving time, which was how he characterized his fellowship? For one thing, I found it necessary to get a temporary roommate to help with the rent and utility bills—an unavoidable recourse Frank hadn't taken into account, just as I imagine Jimmy hadn't when he went off to Europe with Arthur Gold. A friend of mine named Jules Cohn moved in with me, poor guy. A Rutgers graduate who was as unworldly as he was intellectual, he had become acquainted with me at what must have been his first place of employment, a dumb research firm from the Stone Age called Facts, Inc., where from nine to five we sat next to each other at a long conference table, clipping news items from the *Times* and putting them in folders. That would have been in 1951.

We were uneasy friends from the beginning. While I was out of the closet, he seemed to be straddling the fence, to mix tired metaphors. I said everything I could think of to shock and entertain him, and I had plenty to say. A great audience, he hung on my every lascivious word, thus becoming more committed than ever to a life of safe, vicarious, homoerotic thrills. To a large extent, that formed the basis of our friendship—that and our shared passion for the theater, which at the time was still alive and kicking on Broadway. I don't remember why Jules needed a place to stay for the six months Frank would be away; perhaps he merely wanted to observe a wild and unrepentant faggot in his habitat. Anyway, he moved in and lived to regret it—but not because of me.

Wary of Frank from the moment he met him, Jules fully expected him to be safely out of the way, in Cambridge; instead, he came storming back to New York every chance he got. At the time, I didn't realize anymore than Frank did how hard those periodic weekend visits were on Jules, who regarded Frank as wanton (his very word), while Frank, as far as I know, never bothered to form an opinion of Jules. I imagine he wondered why I had him for a friend—but would that be any reason to treat him so abominably? Not that I was blameless: I was Frank's craven accomplice, for I did nothing to stop him. He didn't just keep poor Jules up half the night with his drunken revelry (I'd be drinking along with him, of course), he also rode roughshod

Cambridge · 99

over him, teasing and goading him, and taking over the place as if he and not Jules were paying half of the rent.

For a long time after, I wondered what lay behind the ferocity of Frank's ill will. Then several years after his death, I ran into Jules and we began reminiscing about the old days. "I'd never known anyone like you and Frank," he said at one point, his tone one of disapprobation. I waited, knew he had something unpleasant to say. "You lived as though life was to be enjoyed," he said, "as though nothing mattered more than that." Exactly. And what, I might have asked, did he think mattered? Why, what else but the opposite—living as if life were drudgery, something to be endured, not something to find joy in. And Frank, I'm pretty sure, sensed that Jules had this crippling attitude toward life and he must have disliked him for it. At the same time, the mere presence of anyone in the apartment with me while he was stuck in Cambridge would have been enough to frustrate and provoke him. If you have any doubt that Frank was not in his element during his months away from New York, note the small number of first-rate poems he wrote, maybe three at the most.

So what happens upon his return to New York? Before a month is out, he's written one of his signature works, "In Memory of My Feelings." Yet, that fine poem notwithstanding, it would appear that his dry spell dogged him from Cambridge to New York, because that summer and on into the fall and winter, he was anything but prolific. Could he not get his bearings and put the Cambridge experience behind him on account of its dire repercussions? Yes, that was partly true, I guess. But that fall, something else began to go awry in his life, and in mine. But I am getting ahead of myself . . .

And the poem "Cambridge"? All it brings to mind is the prevalent feeling I had of incompleteness—I don't know how else to express it. I wanted Frank back in my life.

IN MEMORY OF MY FEELINGS

[J U N E   2 7 – J U L Y   1 ,   1 9 5 6]

> . . . Grace
> to be born and live as variously as possible . . .

From "In Memory of My Feelings," a poem as terrific as its title, comes the epitaph on Frank's simple slate headstone. But the way Frank broke the line wasn't observed, and it came out:

> Grace to be born and live
> as variously as possible.

Which is probably preferable—for a headstone, I mean. As is perfectly obvious, the poem is Frank at his most Whitmanesque, and I guess it's about as confessional as he ever got. I like reading it from time to time, like certain other of his poems, and just now I read it over to see if a personal response might be triggered, a comment or observation that could probably come only from me. Nothing. But I do have a few things to say about the poem's dedicatee, Grace Hartigan, a pivotal figure in Frank's life, a frequent source of inspiration to him in his work, and surely the most controversial of all of his women, which is saying a great deal, considering who some of them were. Going out on a limb, I've drawn up a list of them in safe alphabetical order (he was closer to four of these women than any of the others, while several made the list simply because he had a special affection for them): Elaine de Kooning, Helen Frankenthaler, Jane Freilicher, Maxine Groffsky, Barbara Guest, Grace Hartigan, Irma Hurley, Lee Krasner, Bunny Lang, Camilla

McGrath, Joan Mitchell, Renée Neu, Maureen O'Hara, Gaby Rodgers, Jane Romano, and Patsy Southgate. Have I left anyone out or put someone on the list who doesn't belong there? Maybe. I will eventually have something to say about all of them, but right now, I want to concentrate on the woman whose name ended up—appropriately, she no doubt contends—on the modest slab at the head of Frank's grave, a vigorous stone's throw from the imposing boulder where Jackson Pollock is buried, with a puny rock nearby that discreetly marks the spot where his wife, the indomitable but now vanquished Lee Krasner, is interred. But how, it might be wondered, can I state unequivocably that Grace Hartigan was the most controversial of Frank's women when Joan Mitchell's name is on the list? Simple. Anyone who knew Joan in the old days would surely agree that no woman Frank spent time with was more headstrong, stubborn, contentious, intractable, self-indulgent, irrepressible, and just plain downright difficult. Or more talented, I'd add. So where's the controversy?

Grace was different, and still is; she had (has) her detractors and she had (has) her champions. (I belong to both camps.) Take her appearance at the tribute to Elaine de Kooning a year after that fabulous woman's death. This "marathon memorial," as Rose Slivka described it, took place at New York City's Cooper Union on March 12, 1990, which would have been Elaine's seventieth birthday, and it went on so long (close to three hours) that an intermission was required. No fewer than twenty-five people delivered eulogies, which, besides failing to do justice to her, were dull, conventional, and fairly predictable—except for Grace's speech. She took it upon herself to tell how hard it was on Elaine when Joan Ward had Bill's baby and how, with characteristic verve, Elaine turned up at the hospital and said to Joan, with apparent good humor, "Bill and I always wanted a baby," as though Joan were a pioneer in surrogate motherhood. Some people liked the story, others felt it was at best in questionable taste—and that sums up the effect Grace had on many of us back in the fifties and early sixties, when I used to see her.

She was never dull, but gauche she could occasionally be, as when she made that remark about loving me because Frank loved me. I could have responded, "Grace, I feel the same way about you and for the same reason."

And it was the truth. Thus, it was Frank neither of us could resist, not each other: we were swept along by his feelings, found that we had no choice but to have a warm regard for each other—he wouldn't have it any other way. With Jane Freilicher, it was different, for no such tactic would have worked, and he knew it. So it was Grace, the more outgoing and generous of the two, who consistently extended herself to me, never concentrating solely on Frank when the three of us had drinks or dinner together.

Frank was crazy about her, somewhat to the dismay of several of his friends. He delighted in her gutsy style, especially as manifested by her bold, unbeautiful, but striking paintings, and he was always eager to learn more about her touching New Jersey adolescence as limned in the five-and-dime-store diary she read from, no coaxing necessary. In time, it became clear to me that his love for her was so great that he was physically drawn to her, as a mass of steel is drawn to a magnet. "Heterosexuality! you are inexorably approaching. (How discourage her?)"—that from "Meditations in an Emergency." But heterosexuality, or the opposite sex, was not so much in pursuit of him as the other way around, as witness the number of women he sought out and of whom he became enamored. And the point should be made that his appreciation of the comeliness of women was quite different from that of gay hairdressers, couturiers, fashion photographers, and the like, whose interest is strictly aesthetic and professional. I am not suggesting that Frank was bisexual, at least not in any active physical sense. But really, "bisexuality" has not so much to do with sexual preferences as with making accommodations, adjusting to a situation—for example, if a straight man in prison has sex with another man that doesn't mean he's gone queer or become bisexual. I guess I'm saying there's no such thing as bisexuality if it means being equally attracted to both sexes; we all have a preference, and if we didn't, we'd go crazy. As for Frank, I'd say that he was pansexual, a term that better suits him inasmuch as it implies a Whitmanesque grandeur, generosity of spirit, and inclusiveness.

And now I think I've stumbled onto something, the key to understanding his sexuality. Like Walt Whitman before him ("my great predecessor"), he wasn't a ticking sex bomb—his libido resided more in his feelings than in his groin. But unlike the avuncular and vicarious Whitman, also unlike Edwin Denby, Frank had at various times both the desire and the determination to make out with a great majority of the people to whom he was attracted, their diversity being truly mind-boggling: big guys, little guys, macho straight men, flagrantly gay men, rough trade, gay trade, friends, friends of friends, offspring of his friends, blonds, blacks, Jews, and—women: Grace Hartigan, for example.

Hefty, big-boned, nicely proportioned, with expressive eyes and skin all aglow, she seemed to me to be in the Ann Sheridan mold, a compliment I didn't hesitate paying her. Yes, I really thought she was something. To begin with, I never knew anyone, male or female, who appeared to have more self-confidence and determination. And though she had as many feminine wiles as any woman you were likely to run across at the Cedar Street Tavern, she could hold her own with the most rough-and-tumble Abstract Expressionists. Also, she was not above creating a scene or using physical force if she felt it was called for.

One such occasion stands out in my memory. Grace, Frank, and I had left a party that was going nowhere and were walking across Eighth Street, heading for the Cedar, when Grace suddenly decided she'd had enough of the wimpy little guy who was tagging along. If I thought long enough, I'd remember his name, but maybe it's better that he remain anonymous. To give you an idea of what he was like, though: he was an abstract painter with a pathetically small red mustache and dim little eyes, and like a number of downtown artists and would-be artists, he never had a one-man show—in short, he was a loser. And now, trailing slightly behind us as we headed for the Cedar, he was unsteady on his feet, slobbering slightly, and slurring his speech from having drunk more than he could hold. Do you think Grace felt sorry for him? No way. Without warning, she hauled off and hit him so hard on the side of the head that he landed in the gutter. Frank stopped to help him to his feet as Grace, eyes straight ahead, continued walking briskly, with me keeping apace, eager to know what had gotten into her. "Hey, Grace," I said, "why'd you do that?" "I can't stand a man who doesn't act like a man!" she said furiously. Later, when Frank and I were home, I complained about

Grace's behavior, though I was more amused than appalled. No surprise to me, Frank had by then spent his feelings of compassion for the wimp and now firmly took Grace's side. "What are you talking about?" he said. "The guy was asking for it." When it came to Grace, Frank's loyalty knew no bounds.

Was he ever in love with her? In no uncertain terms, Frank answers that question himself in "For Grace, After a Party," which he wrote a couple of years before "In Memory of My Feelings":

> You do not always know what I am feeling.
> Last night in the warm spring air while I was
> blazing my tirade against someone who doesn't
> interest
>   me, it was love for you that set me
> afire,
>   and isn't it odd? for in rooms full of
> strangers my most tender feelings
>   writhe and
> bear the fruit of screaming. Put out your hand,
> isn't there
>   an ashtray, suddenly, there? beside
> the bed? And someone you love enters the room
> and says wouldn't
>   you like the eggs a little
> different today?
>   And when they arrive they are
> just plain scrambled eggs and the warm weather
> is holding.

If that isn't a love poem, I don't know what is. But if you need more evidence, let me tell you about a Hamptons summer evening when Grace had the guest house on Alfonso Ossorio's estate, The Creeks, in Wainscott. It was sometime in the late fifties, a brief period when Grace wasn't involved with anyone romantically, and she had us out for the weekend. Our first night, we had dinner in, just the three of us, and all evening Frank had eyes only for Grace, making me feel like a fifth wheel—a new situation for me, Bill Berkson having yet to enter Frank's life. But Grace, as usual, didn't ignore me or try to keep me out of the conversation, and that night, I remember, she was particularly attentive to me. Perhaps for that reason she noticed nothing out of the ordinary about Frank—not until it came time to turn in, which was when he made known his intentions, and he did so within easy earshot of me, when he stood at Grace's bedroom door and entreated her to let him join her for the night. Well, my impression of Grace was that she took sex far too seriously to consider a proposition that promised nothing more than a friendly romp in the sack. Besides, she expected a man to be a man, right? Right. So as gracefully as she could manage, and not without a show of affection, she turned Frank down, resorting to the usual line about being friends and the likelihood that sex might complicate matters—a far cry from the way the more fun-loving Patsy Southgate handled a similar situation: see her piece, "My Night with Frank O'Hara," in *Homage*.

Later, when we were back in New York, I made a lighthearted reference to the pass Frank had made at Grace, said something about its being "far-out" or "really too much." His response surprised me, though it shouldn't have. Having taken Grace's rebuff in stride, he now turned the situation around and made me bear the brunt of whatever embarrassment or hurt he had experienced. "I'm sorry I brought it up," I said when he berated me for my insensitivity. "Just promise that you'll never mention it to anyone," he said. "Of course," I said, and kept my word until I blurted it out several years later, by which time he was no longer seeing Grace and couldn't have cared less.

A STEP AWAY FROM THEM

[A U G U S T   1 6 ,   1 9 5 6]

It's my lunch hour, so I go
for a walk among the hum-colored
cabs. First, down the sidewalk
where laborers feed their dirty
glistening torsos sandwiches
and Coca-Cola, with yellow helmets
on. They protect them from falling
bricks, I guess. Then onto the
avenue where skirts are flipping
above heels and blow up over
grates. The sun is hot, but the
cabs stir up the air. I look
at bargains in wristwatches. There
are cats playing in sawdust.
                              On
to Times Square, where the sign
blows smoke over my head, and higher
the waterfall pours lightly. A
Negro stands in a doorway agitating.
A blonde chorus girl clicks: he
smiles and rubs his chin. Everything

suddenly honks: it is 12:40 of
a Thursday.
         Neon in daylight is a
great pleasure, as Edwin Denby would
write, as are light bulbs in daylight.
I stop for a cheeseburger at JULIET'S
CORNER. Giulietta Masina, wife of
Federico Fellini, *è bell'attrice*.
And chocolate malted. A lady in
foxes on such a day puts her poodle
in a cab.
         There are several Puerto
Ricans on the avenue today, which
makes it beautiful and warm. First
Bunny died, then John Latouche,
then Jackson Pollock. But is the
earth as full as life was full, of them?
And one has eaten and one walks,
past the magazine with nudes
and the posters for BULLFIGHT and
the Manhattan Storage Warehouse,
which they'll soon tear down. I
used to think they had the Armory
Show there.
         A glass of papaya juice
and back to work. My heart is in my
pocket. It is poems by Pierre Reverdy.

Jackson Pollock's funeral took place on Wednesday, August 15, 1956, and the next day Frank wrote "A Step Away from Them." It is—can there be any doubt?—his first great "I do this, I do that" poem. It is also, quite obviously, a lunch poem: "It's my lunch hour," Frank states at the outset. Then in what might be called quasi-telegraphese, which is amazingly converted into poetry, he describes what he sees, thinks, and feels as he walks west from the museum and heads downtown toward Times Square. Aside from walking, his only activity has to do with eating and later having a papaya drink, and verbs are eschewed—yet the poem is anything but static. And then it's "back to work," he tells us, adding offhandedly that "My heart is in my / pocket. It is poems by Pierre Reverdy."

Nothing is made up in this perfect poem, right down to that little volume of Reverdy—yes, I'm sure it was in one of the pockets of his Brooks Brothers seersucker jacket. And how do I know what he was wearing? Because it was a hot summer day and because I remember his jacket, which was, incidentally, identical to the one he would borrow from me and name a poem after three years later, almost to the day. So like everything else in "A Step Away from Them," the detail about the Reverdy poems wasn't dreamed up to make the poem work, though work it does with uncontrived finesse.

Giulietta Masina he had a passion for after seeing *La Strada* the previous year, and though the connection is far-fetched, he associates her name with Juliet's Corner, where he stops for a cheeseburger and chocolate malted. It is also prescient, this unwonted mention of Masina's name. Eight or nine years later, Frank would meet the great Chaplinesque actress over drinks at Earl and Camilla McGrath's. Masina spoke no English, Frank no Italian, so Camilla acted as interpreter—Camilla, the former Contessa Pecci-Blunt, a more splendid and heavenly Italian woman one could not hope to meet, a favorite of Frank's who will appear again in these pages when we get to his last night on the town, some forty-eight hours before the accident that took his life. Without gushing, though perilously close to it, he let Masina know in no uncertain terms how great he thought she was; and when Frank met an artist he admired, he was neither stingy in his praise nor willing to check his penchant for the dramatic gesture. So down on his knees in front of this tiny, cherubic woman he went, with Camilla standing next to the chair where Masina sat, acting as interpreter: "You are not simply a great artist, you are a fact of our lives"—that was how his little speech began, and it sounded terrific when translated into Italian.

The next names to appear are those of Bunny Lang, John Latouche, and Jackson Pollock; all three had recently died, Pollock's fatal automobile accident having occurred five days earlier. "It is 12:40 of / a Thursday," Frank meticulously notes. Did he write the poem immediately after he was back at his desk? No doubt; and since the Thursday he refers to corresponds to the date on the manuscript, it's clear the poem was completed then and there— he must have got it right in one draft, as was so often the case in short poems like this. Of course, it's not surprising that Frank should be thinking of Bunny and of Latouche and Pollock, whose untimely deaths are undoubtedly all the more poignant to him because of the warm, beautiful day he brings alive so vibrantly in these few lines. It's clear that he's glad to be among the living on such a day, but he also feels close to the departed—"a step away from them." Of the three, Bunny was the only one he knew really well, and because of a falling out they had shortly before her death—it was apparently precipitated by her getting married—his grief must have been all the more difficult to bear.

I just got out Frank's *Collected Poems* and looked up "Words to Frank O'Hara's Angel." How touching and somehow appropriate that this poem of Bunny's should have found its way into the book! The manuscript was found among his papers, right where he'd put it, apparently in 1950, and as his poems piled up through the years, it remained nestled next to bona fide O'Hara poems, just as the grief over her death remained with him to the end of his life. (The poem, sad to say, was excised from the paperback edition.)

I am not exaggerating about his grief. In 1963 or '64, Kenneth Pitchford and his then-wife Robin Morgan were visiting us at 791 Broadway—I don't recall the occasion—and Kenneth, curious about Bunny, asked Frank what she was like. The mention of her name caught him off-guard; cut to the quick, he burst into tears and fled to his bedroom, as though he'd just received word of her death.

John Latouche was the second to go among the three, from a heart attack—Touche, as he was called, the kind of cosmopolitan New Yorker whom one who is new to the city dreams of meeting. A superior lyricist who was friend and mentor to the young Kenward Elmslie, he came to Frank's rescue with some quick cash Frank needed shortly after settling in New York. Not a handout, though: he hired Frank to arrange the words of one of his musicals—*The Golden Apple*?—so they would look like poetry on the printed page.

Frank hardly knew the kind and thoughtful Touche, and Jackson Pollock he knew even less well. Did Pollock call Frank and Larry faggots one night at the Cedar, either to their faces or behind their backs? It would have been at the time of their brief and unlikely affair, when Larry was experimenting with homosexuality the way he did with heroin—it was no more than a flirtation. I must remember to ask him about the Pollock incident the next time I see him; if true, it might help explain why Frank had not seemed to like Pollock and why, in later years, he appeared reluctant to say anything of a personal nature about the man, particularly in Lee Krasner's company. That is, it was my impression that if he didn't have something good to say about this controversial artist whose work he admired so extravagantly, he would rather not say anything. It is, then, Jackson Pollock the artist who is elegized along with Frank's great and cherished friend Bunny Lang and his new friend John Latouche.

A RASPBERRY SWEATER

It is next to my flesh,
that's why. I do what I want.
And in the pale New Hampshire
twilight a black bug sits in the blue,
strumming its legs together. Mournful
glass, and daisies closing. Hay
swells in the nostrils. We shall go
to the motorcycle races in Laconia
and come back all calm and warm.

to George Montgomery

The dedicatee of "A Raspberry Sweater," George Montgomery is also the person to whom Frank dedicated his first book of poems, *A City Winter*, which was really a pamphlet of thirteen pages that John Myers brought out under the Tibor de Nagy imprint in 1952. I can't remember whether it was George or Jane Freilicher who warned me, only half jokingly, that my friendship with Frank might be in jeopardy now that he'd dedicated a book of poems to me, the book being the long-deferred *Lunch Poems*, published in 1965. It was probably Jane, to whom *Meditations in an Emergency* was dedicated, because I don't think she ever got over the rupture in their friendship, whereas George and Frank, so far as I could tell, merely drifted apart, painlessly and without regret. But the warning I was given would have come a little late, for at the time I had only recently moved out of 791 Broadway. Which means that what I was told must have been more along the lines of, "You see what happens when Frank dedicates a book of poems to you? Your friendship ends."

Actually, Frank didn't have all that many fallings-out with friends, and certainly he kept more friends from his college days than most people do: John Ashbery, Hal Fondren, Freddie English, Bunny Lang, and Larry Osgood immediately come to mind. And George Montgomery. The raspberry-red sweater was his, a Shetland wool of unusually beautiful color. Frank admired it so much that George said, "I feel selfish keeping it," and promptly handed it over—in 1956, when Frank was in Cambridge on his fellowship at the Poets' Theatre.

That was where I met George, in Cambridge, on a weekend I spent there with Frank. Later, when George came to New York to live, I saw him occasionally and then quite often after we moved downstairs from him at 791 Broadway. Yet I never got close to him, nor did I ever learn what, exactly, was the basis for the friendship he and Frank formed at Harvard—he took great pictures of Frank, that's all I ever knew for sure. But I suspect that George, who entered Harvard at fifteen, was an early influence on Frank, and helped him find his way to becoming a poet. The last time I saw him, he let me know he didn't like all the commotion about Frank since his death. Frank's poetry was what mattered, he said, not his character or personality or all the people whose lives he touched.

Soft-spoken and reticent, not out to impress anyone, he was unlike any of Frank's other artist friends, with the exception of Edwin Denby, who was even more remote and retiring. What I mean to say is, he struck me as being utterly indifferent to, and definitely not part of, the frantic, trendy, mercurial New York you have to come to terms with if you're going to have a career— either you make it or, if you know what's good for you, you get out of town. George did neither; and he never changed, he remained exactly the way he was in Cambridge, as if he'd never moved to New York—he was that provincial, that out of it, such was the obstinate nature of his New England modus vivendi, integrity, and sense of himself. He wrote his poems, he took his photographs, he collaborated with Dan Wagoner on some quirky, interesting evenings of dance. And he had a nervous breakdown.

It was inevitable, perhaps, that what awaited this slight, fine-featured adherent of Zen was the fork in the road that would take him away from the hurly-burly of New York to a place where through meditation he might find peace—specifically, to his simple New Hampshire farm, whose atmosphere is evoked so tenuously, so minimally, in "A Raspberry Sweater."

Near the end of my "Cambridge" note, I stated that in the fall of 1956, something began to go awry in Frank's life, and in mine. This means that what I asserted in "Four Apartments"—*This was a fair-sized loft apartment, and we moved here in February 1957, mainly because we wanted to live downtown*—amounted to a whitewash and a cover-up, because our decision to move had nothing to do with wanting to live downtown. Frank was so happy to be back in New York that moving was the furthest thing from his mind, as it was from mine. For one thing, the apartment on East Forty-ninth Street, besides being conveniently located, was a bargain at something like fifty bucks a month. And we were getting along better than ever, because by that time we'd worked out things between us—which is to say, we'd every so often make love; it would happen casually and unexpectedly, and afterward, like adolescents on a camping trip or buddies in the service, we didn't acknowledge what had happened. Yet as offhanded as those intimacies were, they served a purpose, I believe—that of renewing and strengthening our ties while at the same time keeping Frank's boyfriends and mine from coming between us. Perhaps it wasn't an ideal situation, but we were reasonably comfortable with it, so much so that we began wearing each other's clothes— that was how close we'd become.

And happy. Years later, when we were finally, at long last, comfortably ensconced in a decent apartment, Frank said over coffee one morning, things having recently gone badly between us, "Joe, there is only one reason two people should live together: because they make each other happy." I agreed with him; and before the month was out, we were no longer living together. But the summer of 1956, we were happy and had no real problems.

114 · *A Raspberry Sweater*

Then Jimmy came back. I hate having to put it that way—it was what I preferred not to deal with in "Four Apartments"—but that was what happened: it is the truth, a painful truth for me, because from the beginning, when I first got to know James Schuyler through Frank, he was special to me and remained so over the years, as special as his poetry, which I embrace as wholeheartedly as I do Frank's. I suppose he had no place else to go after he broke up with Arthur Gold, and perhaps, too, he felt he was still Frank's roommate, at least as much as I was. So one day, without my being forewarned, he moved back in and took my room, and Frank then shared his bed with me.

A delicate matter now: Jimmy was suffering from a serious mental disorder, about which I cannot be—nor would I choose to be—more specific. Not from fear of being indiscreet, since we have Jimmy's own acknowledgment of his problems in "The Payne Whitney Poems." I will say this, though: he was not the warm, witty, immensely attractive person he was when I first knew him in 1952. The transformation in those four years, from 1952 to 1956, was astonishing; he was now more dead than alive. Twenty-five years later, when I was reading "The Morning of the Poem" and ran across "I would rather sleep than do anything," I immediately thought of those days on East Forty-ninth Street when Jimmy was in bed more than out of it—what a dispiriting atmosphere his sickly sopor created!

But it was something else that unnerved me to the point of distraction—two things, in fact. And when I tell you what they were, you might think I was the one who was crazy. "Jimmy gave me another black look today," I'd say to Frank when we were alone, perhaps as we were turning in for the night. "I got one, too," Frank might say. But he seemed to take in stride the demonic way Jimmy looked at us—it would be out of the blue, for no good reason—and I was advised not to take such looks seriously. But they were chilling, they made me think he wanted to kill me. And perhaps he did.

That was the first thing. The other had to do with Jimmy's passion for buttermilk—I think he must have drunk a quart a day. Which was all right by me. What wasn't all right, what drove me up the wall, were the empty, buttermilk-encrusted glasses he left around the apartment, as if the coffee mugs I found in the oddest places weren't bad enough. I'd been assigned, or simply took, the role of Cinderella, so naturally I was the one who every few days gathered up and washed the crockery and glasses strewn through Squalid Manor, which now more than ever lived up to its name.

I must have taken two or three months of this, and then one day, a Sunday afternoon while Jimmy was napping, I said to Frank, mildly, keeping my voice down, "I don't think three people can live together." He acknowledged that it wasn't easy, and I told him it was virtually impossible. Then I added, as though it were an afterthought and not what had been on my mind all that week, "I think I'd better get a place of my own." Frank said, "Don't leave without me."

We took the first place we heard about, from a drinking companion of Frank's at the Cedar. Jimmy stayed on at the apartment—there was no reason for him to leave—but within a couple of months, during which time his mental condition worsened, he'd also moved out. "It was a long time before I forgave you for what you did," he told me many years later at a party, the clear implication being that I'd stolen Frank away from him. I saw no point in trying to explain what happened, that Frank wanted to leave with me— that it was his idea, not mine. No question, what Jimmy said angered me, considering what he'd put me through, not to mention our loss of such a great apartment. But when I recollected what he said to me when we saw each other for the first time after Frank's death, in the fall of 1966 (Jimmy wasn't at the funeral; that summer, he was staying at, and didn't stir from, Anne and Fairfield Porter's place on Great Spruce Head Island off the coast of Maine), I completely disregarded his unjust inference of my actions. "I immediately thought of you when I got the news"—that was all he said and all he needed to say.

One more thing. Frank was capable of great compassion, he was very good in an emergency, you couldn't find a better friend. But if someone went off the deep end, his gift of empathy went out the window—that, in any event, was what I felt to be the case, which I may have been especially alert to because the same coldness, horror, and impatience engulfed me in the presence of madness. Frank couldn't get away from Jimmy fast enough—

thus (I should have made this point earlier), his "Don't leave without me" related only partly to his desire to be with me. Fortunately, Jimmy had other friends who were more indulgent and self-sacrificing than Frank, and it was their unstinting support that made it possible for him to have a productive life. He was only two years shy of seventy when he gave up the ghost, an attainment that must have surprised many people.

By the time we moved downtown, someone else ceased to be part of our lives: Paul Goodman. Of course, he'd been far more important to me, just as Jimmy was really Frank's friend; and while Frank and Jimmy would have a rapprochement within a year, I would never again feel at home in Paul's company—nor would Frank. But at best theirs had been a tenuous friendship, one that never got off the ground. "I liked him better when I didn't know him," said Frank, whose admiration for Paul's work did not pave the way for what Paul may have wanted and expected, a relationship not too dissimilar from the one he had with his foremost fan and disciple, a handsome, sexy, straight writer named George Dennison, about whom Frank said, "That I might see more of George Dennison is the only possible inducement for me to become part of Paul's entourage."

I'm not sure how Frank made it clear that he wasn't interested in playing a subservient role in their relationship. I know that he balked at baby-sitting Matthew, Paul and Sally's three-year-old, and that may have sent a message to Paul. But it wasn't until later, when I was teaching at Tuxedo Park and seeing Frank on weekends, that a definitive rift occurred between them—over a piece of music, if you will, during intermission at a Town Hall concert. We'd just heard Ned Rorem's *Poet's Requiem,* a realization of the requiem Paul dreamed up for *The Dead of Spring,* the third volume of his epic novel, *The Empire City.* It was a secular text, of course, and highly unorthodox, with quotations from Gide, Cocteau, Kafka, and Freud. Frank was very high on Ned's setting; as I recall, he was especially struck by how Ned set the passage from Freud. ("Our own death is unimaginable; and when we try to imagine it we perceive that we really survive as spectators. At bottom no one believes in his own death; in the unconscious every one of us is convinced of his own immortality.") It was then that he took out his fountain pen and, for my benefit, wrote across his program, "Great"—an exaggeration, perhaps, but that was Frank's style, decidedly hyperbolic; and I nodded in agreement.

His enthusiasm carried over into the intermission, and for some reason Paul, who joined us, was put off by the way Frank was carrying on. Or perhaps it was because his own opinion wasn't being solicited; after all, he had put together the requiem's text. Finally, when there was a lull in our discussion, Paul pronounced his own judgment on the work: "It was very un-Ned," said he, coolly. This rubbed Frank the wrong way, so that as we got into a discussion of a piece by Prokofiev—was it on the program?—he went out of his way to disagree with Paul, who naturally wrote off the flashy Russian as a lightweight. "Again, to Ludwig van Beethoven," reads the dedicatory inscription I remember seeing on the manuscript of one of Paul's plays—that barely hinted at how fanatic he was about the great Beethoven, so it can be easily imagined what he thought of a composer like Sergey Prokofiev.

Frank and Paul had other run-ins, the most memorable one occurring at a party Gianni and I threw when we lived briefly in a large apartment on First Avenue near Fifty-fifth Street. From across the room, I noticed Paul in deep conversation with Frank, who was feeling vulnerable at that time because of his recent breakup with Larry Rivers. Apparently reacting to something Paul said, Frank burst into tears and fled to another part of the apartment. Before going to him, I stopped and asked Paul what was the matter. Though clearly flustered by what had happened, Paul could not stave off what struck me as an expression of smug satisfaction. "I'm afraid I was too honest with Frank about his recent poetry," he explained. "I didn't mean to hurt his feelings," he added, "but it was for his own good." That didn't sound like something Frank would cry over; and sure enough, when I sought him out and told him what Paul said, he was incensed. "That fool!" he cried. "I was thinking of Larry, not of anything *he* said!"

Eventually, the subject of Paul Goodman was closed so far as Frank was concerned. Paul, on the other hand, never ceased assailing Frank whenever I ran into him. As the recipient of his rancor, I was a courier of sorts. I think he expected me to pass on his remarks to Frank, who assiduously kept his distance from Paul. "What did he have to say about me this time?" Frank would ask later. "Nothing worth repeating," I'd say, and then I'd repeat it, since Frank really wanted to hear. Censoriously, Paul would cite the camp element in Frank's poetry or he would complain about his taste in music, or he might deplore Frank's veneration of movie stars. On one occasion he decried Frank's looks—this from Paul, one of the most physically challenging people around! "The people's choice," he fumed when Larry Rivers entered a party celebrating the publication of May Rosenberg's novel about the art world, *But Not for Love.* "Are you blaming Frank for Larry's success?" I found myself saying, as much to my surprise as his; but I really felt Frank was behind Paul's gratuitous swipe at Larry.

Was what Paul perceived as my defection to Frank the last straw and the reason for his peevishness? It had something to do with it all right, but I always thought that if he only had wider recognition as writer, he would have been a different man. And, to some extent, I was right. For with the 1960 publication of *Growing Up Absurd* his flow of vitriol was finally stemmed, just as Harold Rosenberg's appointment as art critic of *The New Yorker* stopped Harold's infernal grousing about the magazine's shortcomings. Those two great intellectuals had a lot in common, come to think of it. Both were great talkers, deep thinkers, and committed socialist types who never compromised—except each man, in his own way, seemed to have an eye for the main chance. Or am I being uncharitable? At a Gotham Book Mart party where Paul had a cute guy in tow, I waited until the kid was out of earshot and then cheekily asked Paul if, as champion of America's alienated youth, he didn't make out like a bandit when he lectured at college campuses across the land. "I would never use my position that way," he answered, pompously, not to mention disingenuously. I stifled my laugh; I'd gone far enough, as it was. Then he brought over his trick, showed him off, explained to the wide-eyed stripling that "Joe's an *old* friend of mine—isn't he beautiful, Joe?" It was payback time: what immediately came to mind—Paul's mind as well as mine, I'm sure—was an episode whose climax, featuring the word "old," led to the beginning of the end of our on-again, off-again relationship . . .

It was the time when I was rooming with the window dresser—you remember him; Bill was his name, I think—and Paul came by one afternoon, met the guy, drew him out while at the same time reminding him that he was a therapist and maybe he could help him, all of which led to Bill's confessing that he had a sex problem, the nature of which he did not disclose to Paul. "Would you like to talk about it?" Paul asked, sounding very professional. "There's something I have to do," I said. "Why don't I leave you two alone?" And off I went on an errand that kept me away for forty-five minutes or so. When I returned, Paul was virtually chasing Bill around the room, so I knew immediately that Bill had explained his problem: he had an unusually large penis that even in repose was such a shocker that, just recently, the attendant at the St. George Hotel swimming pool in Brooklyn Heights accused him of lewdness and ran him out of the place. Paul was all sympathy but still felt he couldn't evaluate Bill's problem unless he learned the extent of it. "I'm sensitive about it, can't you understand that?" Bill cried. To his credit, Paul came around and suggested they meet at another time. "Fine," Bill said, and went into the other room. I suddenly felt sorry for Paul. How he wanted to see Bill's gigantic cock! Of course he surmised I'd seen it, and that only made it worse. "Good old Paul," I said as I put my arms around him and patted him on the back. Without looking at me, he stiffened and drew away, then departed without a word.

At that time he was about forty, slender and youthful in appearance, yet my endearment stung, as he acknowledged later when I asked why he had lately become so curt with me. It really surprised me, the way he carried on. Time and again, hadn't he given the opposite impression, that he was anything but touchy and insecure? Only a couple of weeks earlier, just before the brouhaha over Bill's cock, I had sat next to him at a Living Theatre performance of *Faustina*; like all of Paul's plays, it had the audience squirming. So wretched was this work that the leading actor, the estimable Julie Bovasso, stopped suddenly in the middle of her final speech. "I have some lines to say that are so ghastly, I don't think I can continue," said Bovasso, looking straight at the audience. "Paul, this is terrible," I whispered. "No, it's wonderful," said Paul, "it makes the play even more powerful. Julie's so moved by the words she can hardly speak them," he added, as Bovasso courageously continued,

"I'm supposed to break through the invisible wall separating me from the audience and say . . ."

Paul died of a heart attack in 1972, a month before his sixty-first birthday. There was a well-attended memorial service for him; distinguished intellectuals spoke, Eugene Istomin played the slow movement of a Schubert sonata (a last-minute substitution for Beethoven's *Waldstein*), and Ned Rorem's settings of poems by Paul were sung by Betti McDonald, with Ned at the piano. David Sachs, the Goodman disciple I met at Maxwell's that fateful night, sat next to me. When the service was over, he turned to me and solemnly predicted that Paul would have a brilliant posthumous career.

For a while it looked like that might happen. Within a year, his *Collected Poems* was published by Random House, and not one but two biographers, Raymond Rosenthal and Taylor Stoehr, were set to write his life story. And then what? The biographies have long since been canceled. Memoirs by his colleagues barely mention him. (Was he really so disliked, even hated, by his peers? It would appear so.) In articles about the Jewish intellectuals of New York his name is skirted, as though he never wrote for *Partisan Review, Commentary, New Republic,* and *Dissent.* Thus he is being dismissed as cavalierly as he was back in 1949 when Edmund Wilson, in a letter to the editor of an obscure literary magazine, made this cruel assertion in his complaint about Paul's review of Mary McCarthy's *The Oasis,* whose most damning phrase, "a toothless satire," I somehow remember: "Paul Goodman is a hoax—he doesn't exist."

POEM READ AT JOAN MITCHELL'S

[F E B R U A R Y   1 5 ,   1 9 5 7]

. . . I hope there will be more
more drives to Bear Mountain and searches for hamburgers, more
    evenings
        avoiding the latest Japanese movie and watching Helen Vinson
        and Warner Baxter in *Vogues of 1938* instead, more discussions
        in lobbies of the respective greatnesses of Diana Adams and
        Allegra Kent,
more sunburns and more half-mile swims in which Joe beats me as Jane
        watches, lotion-covered and sleepy, more arguments over
        Faulkner's inferiority to Tolstoy while sand gets into my
        bathing trunks
let's advance and change everything, but leave these little oases in
        case the heart gets thirsty en route . . .

Just now, I realized that if, among our friends, there hadn't been wed-
dings and birthdays, no poems would have emerged from Frank's typewriter during our first couple of months at University Place. And that
strikes me as significant. For the confluence of these two occasions,
along with their respective poems, offers strong evidence of his having taken
to heart a point Paul Goodman made in a 1951 *Kenyon Review* piece entitled "Advance-Guard Writing, 1900–1950," namely that the future of such
writing, its supreme expression, is in the occasional mode—an oversimplifi-

cation of mine, I confess. Anyway, this densely written essay seems to have had an influence on Frank's writing, possibly playing a part in the development of his "I do this, I do that" strategy. But now I'm moving into an area of criticism I ordinarily, and rightly, leave to others . . .

"Poem Read at Joan Mitchell's" was what Frank ended up calling the first thing he wrote after our move downtown, its original title being the more cumbersome "Poem Read at Joan Mitchell's in 1957." But to me, both sounded more like labels than titles for a poem, and I mistakenly assumed he hadn't yet decided what to call his epithalamium, that being the last thing this forthright, informally inclined poet would settle on. While the poem credits Joan with "surprising [Jane Freilicher and Joe Hazan] with a [wedding] party for which [Frank] was the decoy"—the ceremony itself, a small family affair, took place the next day in Queens, on a Sunday, February 17, 1957—Mike Goldberg, in all likelihood, dreamed up the idea of marking the occasion. I say that because later, when he was married to Patsy Southgate, he liked playing host so much, not infrequently deciding on his own to throw a dinner party, that Patsy sometimes called him, with a mixture of exasperation and affection, "Sociable Mike." But Joan and not Mike was the one who had a decent, good-sized place, not to mention the money to foot the bill, so the party, an after-dinner affair, was given at her studio apartment on St. Mark's Place.

"I'm serving cognac and nothing else," I remember her announcing, "and I don't want to hear any bitching." No reason why she should have, since she served excellent cognac, Rémy Martin at the very least. John Myers said he wanted to bring Tennessee Williams. "Oh no, the party's for friends of Jane and Joe's," said Joan or Mike, and they were calling the shots. I told Frank it was a case of reverse snobbism, that it was Tennessee Williams's fame that made him persona non grata. "Tennessee's welcome as far as I'm concerned," Frank said with a shrug as he continued working on his poem. Only later did we learn that Joe knew Tennessee in Provincetown during the late forties, and I'm sure John made a point of this when he asked if he could bring him along. But as I said, Joan and Mike were calling the shots. Was it also their idea for Frank to write a wedding poem and read it that night? No, it was something he did on his own, mainly because it was practical: painters gave artworks as gifts, Frank gave poems. And at that time, his being a poet really came in handy, since we were so broke from having recently moved that what we ended up giving Jane and Joe was an art book, Kenneth Clark's *The Nude,* which as an employee of Holliday Bookshop I got at a 40 percent discount. I think it was the discount that made Frank decide to write a poem for them.

It was completed just in time for the party. Packed with nostalgic references to experiences he shared with the couple, the poem also looks to the future, anticipates more good times—or so he claimed. More than likely, he suspected that the intimate friendship he had with Jane was now terminated, something similar having happened a year earlier when Bunny married Bradley Phillips. But Bunny's marriage led to a quick curtain rather than the long, drawn-out denouement that characterized Frank and Jane's relationship after her marriage. As if that weren't enough for Frank to contend with, it would not be long before yet another of his great loves, Grace Hartigan, took a new husband after years of being single. But in that instance, as we'll see, there would be no unhappy-making consequences, since Grace's third marriage would prove to be a minor episode in her life, a subplot that discreetly unraveled offstage, thus enabling Frank to continue playing his usual stellar role until—I'd better stop there, as I don't want to get started on Grace again, not right now. It's Jane I mean to concentrate on, even if the present poem, the nominal subject of this note, was written for both Jane and Joe. And observe how gracious Frank is in addressing them as a couple, never hinting that his close friendship has been with the bride. By then, of course, it was clear to everyone that Jane had found in Joe Hazan the man with whom she wanted to spend the rest of her life. But two or three years earlier, it must have occurred to Frank how serious her commitment was; and now that I think about it, by the time I began living with him, in the summer of 1955, their close rapport, their comradeship, was already becoming a thing of the past.

The evidence, as always, is in his poetry, so let's take a look at it. In February 1951, this original, attractive, highly intelligent woman makes her debut in "Interior (With Jane)," after which she's the subject, inspiration, or dedicatee of poem after poem right through the mid-fifties. By 1956, not only has her relationship with Joe become of ever-increasing importance to her—anyone could see that—but also, by then, another woman who paints, a woman in every way her opposite, beginning with the sort of painting she does, is making serious inroads into Frank's life and poetry, so that it is to this other painter, not to Jane, that he dedicates what is by far his most important poem of that year, "In Memory of My Feelings." I'm tempted to refer to Grace Hartigan as Jane's nemesis, but that might give the impression Jane was competing with her, and she wasn't—she had (has) too much dignity, reserve, and sangfroid for that sort of thing.

In any event, the marriage poem for Jane and Joe can be regarded as a grand and poignant gesture on Frank's part, a farewell to Jane as well as an acknowledgment of Joe's signal importance in her life. For she will now virtually disappear from Frank's poetry; subsequently, we'll find her name merely mentioned, en passant, and just twice at that, over the nine years that remain to him. The first is a glancing reference in a poem called "Two Dreams of Waking," while the second reference, which is sardonic and far more interesting, reflects the ambivalent feelings he has in relation to her marriage. A glib, offhand reference it is, too, nestled in "Adieu to Norman, Bon Jour to Joan and Jean-Paul" between a line about a mere acquaintance of Frank's and a line about an art critic who was not an intimate friend:

> Shirley Goldfarb continues to be Shirley Goldfarb
> and Jane Hazan continues to be Jane Freilicher (I think!)
> and Irving Sandler continues to be the balayeur des artistes

One would assume that Jane's exit was hard on him—and maybe it was, for all I know; Frank complained so little and knew how to cope so well that I frequently had no inkling what he felt when something in his life went awry. I do know this: whenever he stopped seeing someone who was an intimate friend, there would always be someone else around to take up the slack— one of several people, in fact. At the time of Jane's marriage, he had Mike and Larry and Grace and, well, me. (Kenneth Koch? No, his friendship with Kenneth was different, not of an intimate nature but based, it always seemed to me, on their shared passion for poetry.) Others would soon move into Frank's crowded life, turning up more or less in this order: Kynaston Mc-Shine, Norman Bluhm, LeRoi Jones, Patsy Southgate, Vincent Warren, Bill Berkson, Jim Brodey, Tony Towle, and on and on and on, right to the end—to J. J. Mitchell, dissolute, decadent J.J., whom I unwittingly brought into his life. I'm not referring to casual friends and acquaintances—they comprise another category—but to friends who saw him all the time, who confided in him, and who in some instances went to bed with him. I guess he never ran out of people. At any given time during the years I lived with him, he was involved intimately, very intimately, with at least three people besides me. Did he have a best friend? No, he never did, not while I knew him; but as Larry Rivers pointed out in his graveside speech, many people thought he was *their* best friend.

Having unburdened myself of these observations and insights, I don't want to give the impression that he and Jane stopped being friends after her marriage. Yet things were never the same again—I could tell, because when they saw each other, at a party or at an opening, they didn't *sound* the way they used to, the way they had in the early fifties, those times when I first heard them confabulating, just the two of them, one-on-one, never at a loss, always with something to say, their timing as smooth and on target as Lunt and Fontanne's. I remember, in the beginning, being bemused and taken aback by the tone and style of their talk, by the way words and phrases were spoken as if italicized, and most of all by their relentless banter, so private and arcane you were discouraged from joining in. I know I felt uncomfortable at first, as though I were not in on the joke. Later, I heard others in their circle use the same tone of voice and employ the same kind of campy, dry, superior wit, and then I knew what was going on. They reminded me of nothing so much as a high school clique, and its charter members—Frank and Jane plus John Ashbery, Kenneth Koch, and Jimmy Schuyler—were like the smartest kids in school, which I'm sure they all once were.

Tone and style were set by Jane, it seemed to me; and her subdued, astringent personality kept the others from getting out of hand—no mean accomplishment, since they were all high-spirited, far-out gays with the exception of Kenneth, who could easily have passed for gay, God knows. What I mean is, camp could well have taken over, and the badinage could have become insufferably precious as well. But it never happened that I know of, and eventually I got used to their act, got over feeling intimidated, even looked forward to hearing them hold forth. John Button picked up on their style, and so did Alvin Novak, Harry Matthews, and Kenward Elmslie. Significantly, no woman besides Jane was part of the clique, not even Barbara Guest and certainly not Grace Hartigan.

And me? I couldn't simulate their style or copy their speech pattern if my life depended on it—which was too bad, because theirs was the dominant "in" way of talking at just about every party I remember from those days. This is not to say I was snubbed or felt left out; I was simply aware that there was a distance between us, but not an uncomfortable one—and one, I might add, for which I was grateful, since it afforded me a perspective on them I wouldn't otherwise have had. I especially wanted to figure out Jane.

Fat chance of that. What it was that made her so alluring—appealing would not be the right word—I am still in the dark about, still find difficult to pinpoint. Indeed, the Freilicher Mystique, or whatever you choose to call it, defies logical analysis. She did not put herself out; she was cool and standoffish; she had a wry and subtle sense of humor but was not prone to smile; and usually, now that I think about it, she wore a look of disappointment, as though nothing in the world had ever pleased her. Yet, curiously, what all of this added up to was someone you wanted to sit next to at dinner, someone you hoped to amuse as much as she amused you.

Just as Grace Hartigan reminded me of the "oomph girl," Ann Sheridan, Jane put me in mind of Jeanne Moreau, that divine and troubling Gallic sphinx, whose sensuous, beautiful mouth also curved downward, not unattractively, not in a frown of disapproval but in grief, it seemed, over some long-ago loss or injury. After I saw the incomparable Moreau for the first time, in Louis Malle's *Les Amants* (1958), I urged Frank to see the movie because its star, I told him, was an interesting new actress who reminded me of

Jane. This got him to talking about Jane's physical attributes, and he did so wistfully, their intimate friendship by that time kaput; all I remember is his commenting on the "beautiful line of her shoulders."

And how was it left between them, following her marriage? Let me think . . . Around 1960, before the Pop Art craze, Jane had us to her studio to look at several paintings that were unlike anything she'd ever done—they weren't still lifes or landscapes, as usual, but large, rather cartoonlike portraits of Elizabeth Taylor and Mike Todd, and of Marilyn Monroe, maybe of a couple of other celebrities. I found them delightful, funny, and original, as did Frank; and we laughed, but not unkindly. The visit did not go well, or so it seemed to me; I had the feeling that she and Frank were no longer on the same wavelength, and it must have been the last time he was invited to her studio. It's possible, too, that his allegiance to Abstract Expressionism was by then so complete that he'd lost interest in the kind of painting she was doing— that would certainly have contributed to the growing rift between them. And at about this time, he angrily lamented one night, "Jane cares more about her new refrigerator than she does about her painting"—this, after spending a perfectly decent evening at the Hazans' new place, an apartment he apparently found alarmingly comfortable and middle class. Odd that he was never put off by the fancy digs of Helen Frankenthaler—but then Helen, who had the prettiest studio I ever saw, was never a buddy from the old days; moreover, she'd always had money and so could not be accused of being nouveau riche, despite the airs she gave herself. "Blue Territory," written about a month after "Poem Read at Joan Mitchell's," ushers that handsome, talented, fiercely ambitious woman into Frank's poetry—in a cameo part, it turns out, nothing like Jane's starring role. But Helen, mainly because of her marriage to Robert Motherwell in 1958, will turn up again in these pages when we reach the last two or three years of Frank's life, a period marked by his involvement with this prominent couple in the heady uptown art world.

And Jane? While what's been recorded here has hardly done her justice— she's far more interesting and complicated, not to mention more talented, than my skimpy reflections have intimated—it's unlikely that she'll be turning up again.

128 · Poem Read at Joan Mitchell's

JOHN BUTTON BIRTHDAY

[M A R C H   1 ,   1 9 5 7]

Sentiments are nice, "The Lonely Crowd,"
a rift in the clouds appears above the purple,
you find a birthday greeting card with violets
which says "a perfect friend" and means
"I love you" but the customer is forced to be
shy. It says less, as all things must.

                                        But
grease sticks to the red ribs shaped like a
sea shell, grease, light and rosy that smells of
sandalwood: it's memory! I remember JA
staggering over to me in the San Remo and murmuring
"I've met someone MARVELLOUS!" That's friendship
for you, and the sentiment of introduction.

And now that I have finished dinner I can continue.

What is it that attracts one to one? Mystery?
I think of you in Paris with a red beard, a
theological student; in London talking to a friend
who lunched with Dowager Queen Mary and offered
her his last cigarette; in Los Angeles shopping

at the Supermarket; on Mount Shasta, looking . . .
above all on Mount Shasta in your unknown youth
and photograph.

    And then the way you straighten
people out. How ambitious you are! And that you're
a painter is a great satisfaction, too. You know how
I feel about painters. I sometimes think poetry
only describes.

    Now I have taken down the underwear
I washed last night from the various light fixtures
and can proceed.

    And the lift of our experiences
together, which seem to me legendary. The long subways
to our old neighborhood the near East 49th and 53rd,
and before them the laughing in bars till we cried,
and the crying in movies till we laughed, the tenting
tonight on the old camp grounds! How beautiful it is
to visit someone for instant coffee! and you visiting
Cambridge, Massachusetts, talking for two weeks worth
in hours, and watching Maria Tallchief in the Public
Gardens while the swan-boats slumbered. And now,
not that I'm interrupting again, I mean your now,
you are 82 and I am 03. And in 1984 I trust we'll still
be high together. I'll say "Let's go to a bar"
and you'll say "Let's go to a movie" and we'll go to both;
like two old Chinese drunkards arguing about their
favorite mountain and the million reasons for them both.

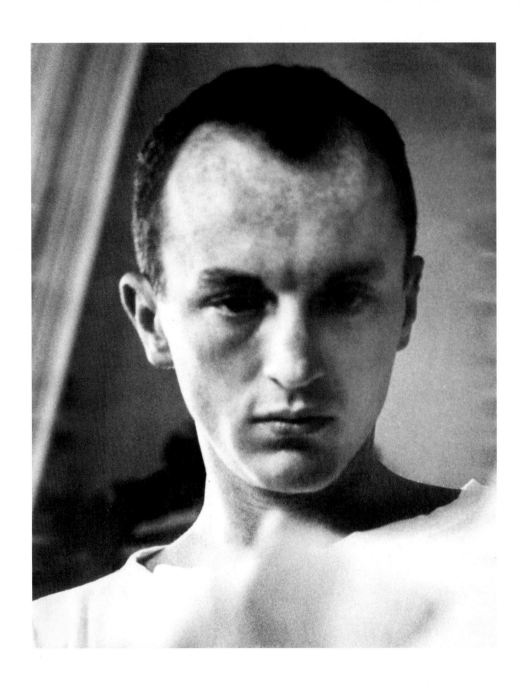

Previous page Joe LeSueur in the Colosseum, 1943 or '44

Above Frank O'Hara at the typewriter, c. 1950

[PHOTOGRAPH BY GEORGE MONTGOMERY]

Paul Goodman and Kenneth Koch at the Cedar Tavern, 1959

[PHOTOGRAPH BY FRED W. MCDARRAH]

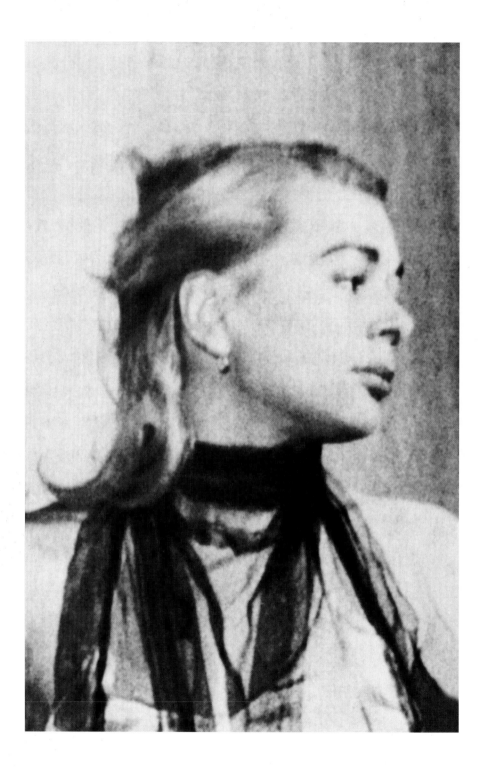

Facing Bunny Lang, c. 1953

Above Frank and Grace Hartigan, 1954

[PHOTOGRAPH BY WALTER SILVER]

Top Frank, John Button, James Schuyler, and Joe watching TV
at John Button's house, 1955 [PHOTOGRAPH BY JOHN BUTTON USING A TIMER]

Bottom Joan Mitchell, c. 1957

Facing Edwin Denby, c. 1965 [PHOTOGRAPH BY JEROME ROBBINS]

Left William Weaver, Grace Hartigan, James Schuyler
(seated in front), Frank, John Ashbery,
and Kenneth Koch in Grace Hartigan's loft, 1952

[PHOTOGRAPH BY WALTER SILVER]

Above Patsy Southgate and Mike Goldberg
at an East Village poetry reading, 1959

[PHOTOGRAPH BY FRED W. MCDARRAH]

Bill Berkson on Washington Square, 1959

[PHOTOGRAPH BY FRED W. MCDARRAH]

Vincent Warren, c. 1960

Facing Joe at 441 East Ninth Street, 1959
[PHOTOGRAPH BY FRED W. MCDARRAH]

Above James Schuyler, Joan Mitchell, Joe, and Bertha Schaefer
(back turned) attending an Adolph Gottlieb opening at R. T. French
and Company, 1960 [PHOTOGRAPH BY FRED W. MCDARRAH]

Top John Ashbery and Jane Freilicher in Water Mill, N.Y., 1962

Bottom left Joe in Water Mill, 1961

Bottom right Morton Feldman in Water Mill, 1963

[PHOTOGRAPHS BY JOHN JONAS GRUEN]

Top Clarice Rivers, Larry Rivers, Joe, and
Elaine de Kooning at the Latin Quarter, c. 1965

Following page Frank, 1963
[PHOTOGRAPH BY MARIO SCHIFANO]

Two weeks after Jane and Joe's wedding it was John Button's twenty-eighth birthday, and that elicited "John Button Birthday"—another label, I thought at the time, but now I see it differently. Like the title for the previous poem, it reminds me how assiduously Frank avoided the conventional, the overblown, the sentimental. "John Button Birthday" and "Poem Read at Joan Mitchell's"—what could be more blunt and to the point?

If there was a party for John, I don't recall it. More than likely, all we did was have dinner together, in Chinatown or at some inexpensive Italian restaurant like the Grand Ticino on Thompson Street. There would have been four of us, I imagine—John, Frank, and me, plus John's boyfriend, Alvin Novak, who had previously visited John in the summer of 1955 and had now forsaken sunny, laid-back Los Angeles for a way of life more rigorous and demanding, and with fewer creature comforts, just so he could be with John. And who could blame him—not I, smitten the moment I laid eyes on John, or Frank, also instantly enamored of him, or John Ashbery, no less enthusiastic, as we might surmise from "John Button Birthday." And above all, certainly not Jimmy Schuyler, who would have followed John to the ends of the earth. Then maybe Jimmy joined us for dinner that night. I don't know why I didn't think of it before—of course he would have. Nothing could have kept him away, unless he happened to be in Southampton, where he was living most of the time, with Fairfield and Anne Porter, who, over the years, would prove to be the most steadfast and generous of his many benefactors. But Jimmy didn't simply have a crush on John, nor was he, as the rest of us were, the recipient of an occasional letch, because what the poor guy felt—or endured—was the exquisite pain of a Proustian passion, obsessive, unrequited, utterly hopeless. And, worst of all, it was a lingering passion, spun out over several years.

I witnessed, at fairly close proximity, the onslaught of the passion that seized Jimmy in the early fall of 1956, when he was planning his return to Squalid Manor. Or perhaps he'd fallen secretly in love with John earlier—secretly, I should explain, because only John, apart from Jimmy, knew about it at the time, John being the uneasy recipient of a cascade of love letters that would come to light after his death in 1982.

John Button Birthday · 131

Here, from what sounds like Jimmy's first letter to John (there's no date, but it was obviously written in the fall of 1956, from Sneeden's Landing): "When Arthur and I had our talk, finally, last evening, and I told him that I'm going back to New York, I had no reason to think I was going away from him to any greater satisfaction. You didn't come into it, nor should you have; there's been a real estrangement between us for a long time. If Arthur's upset, he's also relieved. We haven't said we're breaking up, though that in effect is what it is."

In what appears to be his next letter (most of them are undated), he's no longer so reticent about expressing his feelings toward John, even exults in acknowledging that "I love being in love with you, it makes even unhappiness seem no bigger than a pin." He then goes on to allow, rather grandly: "I can't quite decide what day to re-enter 49th Street"—as though Frank and I, now apprised of his plans, have rolled out a red carpet, are eagerly awaiting his arrival! Poor Jimmy. His precarious emotional and mental state could only have been exacerbated by the masochism he'd latched on to, for surely he was aware that he didn't stand a chance with John, if only because John and Alvin were back together, Alvin having by then returned to New York.

"And in 1984 I trust we'll still / be high together"—how poignant those words are now, since by then, by 1984, John would be dead from a heart attack and Frank would have long since had his life snuffed out. Nor does the poignancy end there. For a litany is evoked and sent pounding through my head, a pitiless, spiraling roll call of John's and Frank's deceased friends, lovers, and associates, their names summoned, and listed herewith, not according to when they shuffled off this mortal coil—I can no longer remember when anyone died—but through free association, one name leading to another, several of them having been brooded upon when Jane phoned with news of Jimmy's death on the morning of April 12, 1991 ("Our ranks are thinning," said Jane): Edwin Denby, Virgil Thomson, Bill Flanagan, Sam Barber, Wystan Auden, Chester Kallman, Donald Droll, Fairfield Porter, Elaine de Kooning, Aladar Marberger, Harold Rosenberg, Philip Guston, Musa Guston, Jane Romano, Bunny Lang, Ted Berrigan, Tom Hess, Franz Kline, Ma-

DIGRESSIONS ON SOME POEMS BY FRANK O'HARA

tsumi Kanemitsu, David Smith, Lee Krasner, John Myers, Herbert Machiz, the majority launched into eternity by 1984, the others soon thereafter. But because they were so close to John and Frank, and died miserably at an early age, both of AIDS in their forties, perhaps Scott Burton and J. J. Mitchell belong at the head of this lachrymose list—pouty, pint-sized, urchinlike, boyishly attractive Scott, who, to his delight, caused much gnashing of teeth among the many people he drove up the wall with his snotty arrogance when, unexpectedly, he became famous as the creator of "pragmatic structures" (furniture art) after years of fruitless forays into various realms of conceptual art and experimental theater, also after his decade-long affair with John Button had come to such an ugly end that they became the bitterest of enemies; and J.J., charming, fun-loving, fabulous-looking J.J., another story altogether, as shiftless as Scott was ambitious, a spoiled rotten golden boy, an army brat (actually, son of an admiral), to no avail a Choate/Harvard graduate, an unlikely lover of mine for about five minutes, and, intriguingly, the last person with whom Frank fell in love.

Not surprisingly, given my vagueness about recent deaths and also because so many friends and acquaintances have died of AIDS, I'm uncertain when Scott and J.J. departed this life, whether it was before, during, or after 1984, a year whose Orwellian significance isn't reflected in Frank's poem—could his settling on that year have had no special meaning, been coincidental? (And exactly ten years later the heavenly Joe Brainard would be dead from AIDS, on May 15, 1994.)

Enough about those two dozen or so deaths, all more or less untimely except for Edwin's, and Virgil's, his release granted only after he lived long enough to grumble, knowing whereof he spoke, "Living past ninety is for the birds"—it's time to focus on the subject of this note, the eponymous John Button ("He's as cute as a button," I told Frank after being introduced to him), the John Button so many of us esteemed, doted on, couldn't get enough of, the John Button of a heartbreakingly brief period of splendor, its apex around the time of the birthday poem before everything began to go wrong in his life and he became a different person, someone cruelly trans-

John Button Birthday · 133

formed by bad health (cancer, heart trouble), someone who thereafter was bitter, difficult, and angry, someone who, henceforth, will be completely disregarded in this note, for it is the earlier, the real John Button I wish to celebrate here.

"The long subways / to our old neighborhood the near East 49th and 53rd"—that's in reference to our uptown digs when Frank and I first knew John, not long after he moved from San Francisco to New York. John's was a cramped, low-ceilinged, ground-floor apartment, an inadequate space for someone who painted: his single closet, I recall, was so crammed with paintings that there was no room for his clothes. And precious little light was admitted into his flat. For a while, Alvin stayed with him there—came for an extended visit, had no plans to settle in New York, then changed his mind when he was back in L.A.; I imagine he missed New York as much, or almost as much, as he did John. Possibly, you'll recall having met Alvin earlier in these pages, when we went dancing at the Old Place and his rumba with Frank was "like skipping on toothpicks." Tall, dark hair, flashing white teeth, handsome features—a pianist. And outgoing, ebullient, aquiver over art, music, ballet, and New York.

That summer, the summer of 1955, Frank wrote another poem—untitled—in which Alvin figures, as does John, and I like it so much that I'm going to include it here:

> Johnny and Alvin are going home, are sleeping now
> are fanning the air with breaths from the same bed
>
> The moon is covered with gauze and the laughs
> are not in them. The boats honk and the barges heave
>
> a little, so the river is moved by a faint breeze.
> Where are the buses that would take them to another state?
>
> standing on corners; a nurse waits with a purse
> and a murderer escapes the detectives by taking a public
>
> conveyance through the summer's green reflections.
> There's too much lime in the world and not enough gin,

they gasp. The gentle are curious, but the curious
are not gentle. So the breaths come home and sleep.

At about the time that poem was written, Frank passionately and incisively extolled the merits of a small still life John had just finished—I think it was John who said, "Frank knew what it felt like to be a painter"—and then told him, firmly, "An artist needs more space than you have, and better light, too; you've got to move, John, that's all there is to it." And didn't let it go there: in no time at all, he'd gotten John together with Mike Goldberg, who was giving up his grungy but sunny, decent-sized place in a down-and-out, nowhere part of town on the edge of the Lower East Side that would soon be known, euphemistically, as the East Village. John struck a deal with Mike—gave him key money, I think—and thus preceded our own move downtown by more than a year.

With a studio area facing the street and a living area in the rear that looked out on a small, sadly neglected section of historic Marble Cemetery, the space—I hesitate to call it an apartment—occupied the top floor of an ancient, dilapidated three-story building on Second Street near Second Avenue, and it was there, in that ruin of a once-private house, that John Button lived and worked for the next sixteen years, close to a third of his life. Unaffected by trends, ignoring the existence of any zeitgeist, and greatly admiring Willem de Kooning but not showing it, as so many of his contemporaries did, by aping the great man's style, John stubbornly went his own way, turning out—painstakingly, never in great profusion—luminous and immaculate oils, gouaches, and watercolors that were for the most part cityscapes, serene evocations of New York for which he would become known.

It was during his first five or six years at 28 East Second Street that he was most happy, I believe, and at his best as well, since it was then that his generous nature shone and he took pleasure in reaching out to people, in holding court, so to speak, with intimate dinners, musicales, late-night parties, and TV evenings, all the while finding time for the many men in his rich and varied love life: Puerto Ricans, blacks, one-night stands, fuck buddies, serious lovers, even a close friend on occasion. (Alvin? Early on—sensibly, in true homosexual tradition—his role in John's life was amended from lover to best friend.) Now, as if all these goings-on weren't enough, John had wide-ranging interests that embraced, in depth, not just art, music, literature, ballet, and film, but nature conservancy (he was an active, very involved member of the Sierra Club), photography (he took great pictures), medical matters (pathology, neurology, pharmacology, etc.), and heaven knows what else, so that it always seemed a miracle to me that he found the time to paint as many pictures as he did.

Slight, wiry, of medium height, John Button had neat, smallish features, mischievous brown eyes, not very good teeth—well, I suppose he was far from handsome—but he was the possessor of such peppery wit, insouciant charm, and sexual allure that those of us under his spell were like so much putty, stripped of all objectivity, not qualified to assess his sheer physical at-tractiveness. And now, as I think of John, of those five or six years when, pre-sumably, he was happier than at any other time in his life, I find that I don't know where to begin or know how to shape my version of the John Button story, for what flashes through my mind is a rapidly shifting profusion of scenes, images, impressions, a memory of things that were said, experiences that were shared.

His musicales—delightfully bizarre, anomalous, magical—only John could have arranged such evenings. Frank and Alvin would play duets on an upright John had picked up somewhere—Bizet's *Jeux d'enfants* I remember most vividly, perhaps because Wystan Auden was present on that occasion—and John would sing, say, a Fanny Brice number, "Secondhand Rose," or some nutty old song he'd dug up, the one beginning, "Cleopatra had a jazz band in a castle on the Nile," being my favorite. He sang brazenly, with panache—the way he did so many other things, like a trick he performed without warning, usually when there was a lull in the conversation. Seated and nonchalantly chatting with his guests, he'd suddenly throw up his legs, simultaneously striking a match which he then held to his anus just as he broke wind: *whoosh*—a great jetlike flame would shoot out of his ass.

The night Auden put in an appearance—no, John didn't light a fart for his delectation—I was ceremoniously introduced to the famous poet by Frank, who had vomited after meeting him a few years earlier, because, as he acknowledged, "I was in such awe of him." I, too, was all atwitter—but for a different reason: as I shook his hand, I saw that his tie was dangling in his drink. How humiliating for him, I thought—but there was no cause for concern, as it turned out. For when he raised his glass to his lips, he saw what had happened and casually, unfazed, flipped the tie out and finished his drink in one great gulp. "The fucking frogs," he muttered in reference to French poets and, specifically, as I recall, to Baudelaire, who would have been a great poet, W. H. Auden went on to say, if only he'd written in German. I remember seeing Auden that winter, on Second Avenue near St. Mark's Place, shuffling through the snow in his bedroom slippers—in 1960, would that have been? Yes, I think so. And I remember Fairfield Porter's turning up at John's, hanging out with us, a bunch of uninhibited gays, our sexual orientation and camping as inconsequential to him as the fact that we were considerably younger than he. It's been said that Fairfield influenced John—his paintings, I mean—but perhaps it also worked the other way around as well. And I swear that Fairfield, awkward, abrupt, upright Fairfield, was in love with John— obliquely, it might be said, the only way he could be in love with someone of his own sex, I thought at the time and said as much to Frank, who actually acknowledged that I might be right. Anyway, John was definitely the magnet, the main reason Fairfield would often put in an appearance at John's salon, which is the right word for those evenings when friends of John's came by and sat around and talked, renouncing the boob tube whenever Fairfield was present (John was the only one of us who had a television, not to mention all kinds of gadgets, appliances, stuff we never dreamed of acquiring); and from what John once said, I know that Fairfield was also given to turning up in the afternoon on those days that *Art News* business brought him to the city, at which time he'd have John all to himself.

How did I know Fairfield had a crush on John? Well, I didn't *know,* I simply intuited that was the case, because one evening, as John was relating a story with his usual flair, I happened to catch the expression on Fairfield's glowing, youthful, splendid New England face—a rapturous, transfixed expression, the unmistakable expression of someone in love, the same look I would see thirty years later on Joan Mitchell's face when, during an un-guarded moment, she had eyes for no one in the room but the young woman, a lesbian, who had become her live-in companion after Riopelle had been sent packing. Love like this, experienced by a straight person for someone of the same sex is, I feel, all the stronger and more enduring for being uncon-scious, impractical, of having no chance of developing into anything.

I could be wrong about Fairfield—about Joan, I'm on firmer ground—but that John had his hands full can't be doubted, and I'm not just thinking of the many admirers he had to discourage but also of those to whom he was attracted. A sovereign makeout artist, he impressed me so much on account of several of his conquests—sleek, sexy, dazzling men, after whom I was also, or had once been, in hot pursuit—that I couldn't help but be jealous. There was, for instance, my first black lover, the young and unbelievably beautiful Alvin Ailey, who early on lost his looks but whom I was lucky to land in his prime, just once, back in my USC days when the fledgling dancer was a stu-dent at UCLA. Well, John didn't just climb into the sack with him on one oc-casion, he had repeats; the two had, for all I know, a bona fide affair. Same thing with another modern dancer, Paul Taylor. But I was smart enough not to compete with John, who, until J. J. Mitchell appeared on the scene, had no equal when it came to scoring. And when it came to an aspect of gay life almost as important as sex—camping, being the bitch, spouting witticisms—John also reigned supreme, for he had it all, was never at a loss, more than held his own with Chester Kallman, which is saying a lot. Apropos camp, John had camp names for all of us, the best and bitchiest being those that were used behind our backs—for example, Miss Gay was what he dubbed John Gruen, the adoring but gay-acting husband of Jane Wilson; Gold and Fizdale were Girl and Fizgirl, a droll and pitiless play on The Boys, the duo-pianists' normal nickname; Kynaston McShine was Butterfly McShine; and that saturnine couple Bill Flanagan and Edward Albee were the Sisters Grimm. No, I thought of that one, and it amused John almost as much as the name I gave myself when, at a fancy fag cocktail party, he introduced me to the impeccable Cecil Beaton who said, "Sorry, I didn't catch your name," and I, drunk and sick to death of the appalling preponderance of preening queens at the party, said, "Oh, just call me Shit-face." John loved telling everyone about my triumph that night, for Beaton, he claimed, later asked John, "Who was that refreshing young man you introduced me to?"

Now, suddenly, I remember another shameful episode in my life, which also happened to be the one time in all the years I lived in New York that I had a brush with sex-related street violence. More than a brush, since I was knocked down, kicked, and pummeled by an eye-filling stripling after I made it known, in response to his come-on, that I'd be happy to oblige him with a blow job. I got away from him all right—with my nose bloodied, my lip cut, and one eye blackened. Upset and in need of sympathy, I called John from a pay phone—didn't bother to go home, as Frank was in Europe on museum business—and John said, "Come right over." Now emerged the compassionate as well as practical side of John Button, who immediately gave me a tranquilizer, then consoled, fed, and nursed me. I couldn't have been in kinder or more expert hands.

At that time—the spring of 1958—I was secretary to Gian Carlo Menotti, and the next morning, when I reported to work, he had this response to my tale of woe, to my bitter condemnation of the gorgeous gay-basher who had cruelly and gratuitously sought me out: "Oh, Joe, these are the people I want to reach with my music"—how John howled over that! And how he and the rest of us carried on when we watched old movies at his place, movies we hadn't seen since childhood—which brings to mind this pronouncement from an avid movie fan that I heard or read somewhere: "I remember my childhood but I remember the movies better." Amen—and I think Frank, Jimmy, and John felt the same way. So our seeing those old movies again meant a great deal to us—indeed, became such a habit and tradition that we met at John's even in his absence. "Frank, Joe and Vincent came over for the Late Late with *Riptide*," Jimmy informed John in a letter written in the fall of 1959, when John was in San Francisco being treated for cancer and Jimmy was staying at John's place in his absence. It might be added that *Riptide*, which starred Norma Shearer as the chic, Adrian-clad, philandering wife of decent, long-suffering Herbert Marshall, was a favorite of Frank's—and of mine, too, come to think of it. Jimmy? He had a weakness, I remember, for

Bette Davis in *Dark Victory,* while at the top of John's greatest-movies-of-all-time list were each and every one of the Busby Berkeley Warner Bros. musicals, a passion shared by Frank's twenty-one-year-old lover, Vincent Warren, who was seeing these thirties movies for the first time.

And now, abruptly, on this giddy, happy note, before I go back on my word and find myself delving into the calamitous part of the John Button story, I'll bring to a close these scattershot, lighthearted recollections and move on to the third University Place poem.

WIND

[MARCH 31 , 1957]

Who'd have thought
           that snow falls
it always circled whirling
like a thought
           in the glass ball
around me and my bear

Then it seemed beautiful
           containment
snow whirled
           nothing ever fell
nor my little bear
           bad thoughts
imprisoned in crystal

beauty has replaced itself with evil

And the snow whirls only
           in fatal winds
briefly
           then falls

DIGRESSIONS ON SOME POEMS BY FRANK O'HARA

it always loathed containment

beasts

I love evil

to Morton Feldman

he first time I caught sight of him—it was either at the Cedar or at some art opening—I remember being struck by how out of place he seemed. An immense, overweight, unprepossessing man of indeterminate age. he brought to mind the quintessential baseball umpire behind home plate. He was hardly someone you'd expect to see hanging out with artists.

All I had to do was hear him hold forth, on just a single occasion, to change my mind and realize how much he was in his element. Not only that, it soon became clear that he was the most compelling presence on the art scene of downtown New York in the fifties and early sixties. Remarkably, an alluring aura that encompassed his great girth made you forget what he looked like—he was that charismatic, so much so that he enjoyed surprising success with the opposite sex. And he loved women, truly appreciated them. It was, however, with his male companions at the Cedar and the Artists' Club that he was probably most at home; and thus, in the company of such heavyweights as Philip Guston, Willem de Kooning, and Franz Kline, he effortlessly commanded center stage with an acerbic wit and perspicacity offset by warmth, good humor, and lack of pomposity. Come to think of it, he was like Frank in that respect; and like Frank, who early on became his great friend and admirer, he sought out for companionship painters rather than practitioners of his own artistic discipline. In his case, it was music as unlike that of Ned Rorem, Frank's other composer friend, as one could imagine. Ethereal, subtle, seemingly unvaried, and very, very soft, it was experimental music that went on for hours; most listeners were either lulled or exasperated by it, and few stayed to the end of a performance. Need it be added that those performances were rare and given at less than ideal venues, like the hall at Cooper Union?

Again, like Frank, he had a cultlike following that did not extend above Fourteenth Street, while his music, in its own way as arcane as that of his famous colleague John Cage, was more written and talked about than listened to, the London music world being far more empathetic than the stodgy New York scene. But in the decade after his sudden, unexpected death in 1987— some thirty years after Frank dedicated "Wind" to him, twenty-one years after Frank's own death—something happened that surprised even his closest friends and most ardent admirers. With a frisson that recalled the posthumous fame that befell another of his downtown cronies, Jackson Pollock, he was heralded as one of the seminal figures in the history of music of the second half of the twentieth century. But Frank, I venture to say, would not have been surprised by this turn of events, which might be deduced after one reads the laudatory liner notes he wrote for a record album of this far-out avant-garde composer, who was none other than—fanfare, please—the improbable, unforgettable, magnificent Morton Feldman.

Frank's notes were written in 1959, which makes him one of Morty's earliest champions. And now, some forty-odd years later, in a volume that bears the nostalgic title *Give My Regards to Eighth Street,* they have been reprinted as an afterword to what is an irreplaceable collection of odds and ends, statements, reminiscences, and informal essays left by the composer and expertly cobbled together by B. H. Friedman. It is a lively, multifaceted introduction to the mind and heart of this legendary figure, a handsome paperback about which I have one minor complaint: nowhere in its pages is there a photograph of its extraordinary-looking author and subject. Instead, the publisher (an alternative press called Exact Change) decided to go with Philip Guston's cartoonlike portrait of Morty.

I'd like to comment on this. As is well known to many in the art world, Philip was for many years an intimate friend of Morty's; perhaps only Howard Kanovitz, who reportedly began each day with a phone call to or from the composer, was closer. But it was the great Philip Guston, the most tender and lyrical of the Abstract Expressionists, who exerted a salient influence on Morty's music; and it was, of course, the ineffably beautiful abstractions, the pre-figurative Guston, that enthralled Morty and influenced his music, while the controversial paintings that began to appear in the seventies—but let's hear directly from Morty on the subject.

"I was in Europe for a year," he stated on the occasion of a 1986 performance of *For Philip Guston* in Los Angeles, "and [Guston] was at the Academy of Rome for a year, then I came back and he had a big show . . . [at the] Marlborough Gallery . . . I was confronted with a completely new type of work . . . I was looking at a picture, he comes over and says, 'What do you think?' And I said, 'Well, let me just look at it for another minute.' And with that, our friendship was over . . . So, it's a sad story . . . we broke up because of style."

And how ironic—delightfully so, it seems to me—that an example from Guston's late period, the work Morty deplored, should find its way onto the cover of his collected writings. Then, too, doesn't the reason for their falling-out—it naturally became the talk of the art world—demonstrate how seriously New York artists once took their work? Their careers and their work were not one and the same, and it was their work that mattered more to them.

I am, by the way, cribbing from a review of *Give My Regards to Eighth Street*—written by myself, however, for the *East Hampton Star.* Which makes it all right, I suppose.

And here is a sampling of Morty's writing. In one of his many anecdotes, he tells of an evening when "I was still a newly arrived immigrant at the Cedar Bar" and of how "Elaine and Bill de Kooning casually took my arm as they passed, and said, 'Come on over to Clem Greenberg's.'

"There were just a few people when we got there," he goes on. "After a while I found myself listening to Greenberg, who was talking about Cézanne. De Kooning began to show signs of impatience and seemed to be trying to control his anger. He finally broke out with, 'One more word about Cézanne and I'll punch you in the nose! . . . Only I have the right to talk about Cézanne.'"

•

DIGRESSIONS ON SOME POEMS BY FRANK O'HARA

But have I nothing to say about the poem that triggered this note? Well, I can easily imagine Frank having dedicated it to Morty because he just saw him or thought of him or heard one of his pieces. Read the poem; make of it what you will. As for the liner notes, let me close by quoting a provocative insight that might lead you to the complete text in the hard-to-get volume called *Standing Still and Walking in New York*

> ... one of the most remarkable pieces recorded here is *Structures* for string quartet (1951). It is a classical string quartet without sonata development, without serial development, in general without benefit of clergy. Like Emily Dickinson's best poems, it does not seem to be what it is until all questions of "seeming" have disappeared in its own projection. Its form reveals itself *after* its meaning is revealed, as Dickinson's passion ignores her dazzling technique ...

POEM

[A P R I L 6 , 1 9 5 7]

I will always love you
though I never loved you

a boy smelling faintly of heather
staring up at your window

the passion that enlightens
and stills and cultivates, gone

while I sought your face
to be familiar in the blueness

or to follow your sharp whistle
around a corner into my light

that was love growing fainter
each time you failed to appear

I spent my whole self searching
love which I thought was you
it was mine so briefly
and I never knew it, or you went

DIGRESSIONS ON SOME POEMS BY FRANK O'HARA

I thought it was outside disappearing
but it is disappearing in my heart

like snow blown in a window
to be gone from the world

I will always love you

to Franz Kline

This poem has a number of associations for me, and oddly, it is Grace Hartigan who is most forcefully brought to mind—not, I might add, without
a twinge. But first of all, inevitably, I associate this lovely lyric with the person to whom it is dedicated, the person who incorporated its twenty-one
lines in an etching, an artist whose permanent fixture–like presence at the
Cedar beguiled so many of us, whether habitué of that now-legendary watering hole or occasional sojourner like myself, who took for granted that
we'd always see him there, hunched over at the bar, seldom if ever seated in
a booth, his stool midway between the entrance and the john, puffing a cigarette, quaffing a beer, coughing, chuckling, holding forth, spinning yarns,
and reminiscing about his Pennsylvania youth, but mostly telling jokes you
wouldn't remember later, so unassuming and convivial he would seem to the
casual observer, the quintessential barroom crony, a short, mustached,
blunt-featured, ordinary-looking guy who just happened to have a genius for
making black-and-white paintings of transcendent beauty—this, I probably
don't have to tell you, was Franz Kline, whom I knew through Frank from
chance encounters at the Cedar, which, apart from our University Place loft
apartment, where he came to be interviewed by Frank, was the only place I
ever saw him.

Earlier, in my ruminations on the Cedar bar scene, I may have given the
impression that I looked askance at the painters with whom Frank whiled
away so many hours. Let me offer this proviso: when it came to Franz Kline
and three of his peers, artists whose company Frank also sought, artists of the

same generation as Kline, the heroic generation—de Kooning, Guston, and David Smith—I can't remember ever feeling anything for them short of un-qualified affection and boundless admiration, exactly Frank's sentiments, I have no doubt. And was it any wonder that we felt as we did? They were forthright and approachable, they were not full of themselves, they made a distinction between their work and their careers. "If fame ever comes your way, give it the back of your hand," said Bill de Kooning to Frank, not long before Bill left New York to live in Springs, where he designed and built a rambling, fanciful, phantasmagoric studio that would have made a dandy nightclub, I remember thinking the afternoon he took us on a tour of the place shortly before its completion in 1963. "I can put up you and Edwin," he told us, as he showed us the room where we'd be staying, "but that's all; no women allowed."

Like Franz, Bill also came to our place once, to the apartment on East Ninth Street. "Yes, I know Elaine's our friend," Frank said when I started to object to his suggestion that we ask Bill to come to dinner with the woman he'd been seeing for the past year or so, the much talked-about, frequently disparaged survivor of the Pollock smashup, whom Frank had dubbed "Death Car Girl" before he decided to befriend her; and now he went on to say, "It's the right thing to do, Joe; I'm sure Bill would appreciate it." "You mean if we recognize their affair," I said facetiously, "Ruth would become socially acceptable?" "We're having them to dinner," Frank said firmly, un-smiling. "All right, all right," I said. "I just hope Elaine doesn't find out."

But find out she apparently did, for on the afternoon of the dinner, a Sat-urday in the fall of 1960, she phoned Frank to say she wanted to see him, asked if she could drop by for a drink at, say, five-thirty? She arrived at six, kept us on tenterhooks wondering when she'd leave, and was having a merry time with us when our dinner guests arrived at seven-thirty. After carrying on in her usual unflagging fashion for another hour, the adorable, improvi-dent Elaine—whom neither Frank nor I could ever fault, no matter what she did—suddenly announced, apologetically, with a glance at her watch, "Oh! I've got to run; I have a dinner date—I'm already late."

Now, I ask you: Why would this engaging, sought-after woman, who never ceased being in love with Bill, who clung to his name professionally, who never divorced him—why, in heaven's name, would she want to be found sitting with us when he arrived with the much younger, dark-haired, brazenly good-looking Ruth Kligman? What did she hope to gain or prove? You'd think she would have been afraid of losing her dignity, not to mention her composure. Well, she didn't; and the *coup d'éclat* she miraculously pulled off must have been what she had in mind when she phoned that afternoon. For if anyone was to be pitied it was poor Ruth: shorn of her customary confidence, her voice faltering, she said in an aside to me as Elaine made her leading-lady exit, with Frank slipping out with her to see that she found a cab, "I feel sorry for her." It was all I could do not to laugh.

As for the rest of the evening, I can only assume it went all right, since Elaine's dropping by for drinks is not only the only thing I remember, it's the only reason the evening sticks in my memory. Was Ruth socially acceptable thereafter? Not exactly. A month or so later, when Bill brought her to a party at Harold and May Rosenberg's, May roared, "Get that slut out of here!" "Now, May," said Frank. May then shouted, forgetting herself for a moment, "You can leave, too, faggot!" Frank gave May an indulgent smile; and Bill, who was busy getting himself a drink, seemed not to know what was going on. "Bill, what are you doing?" Ruth shrieked, outraged that he had not come to her defense. "We're leaving!" "After I've had a drink, Ruthie," Bill said quietly, his sangfroid matching Frank's. Exasperated, Ruth then helped herself to a drink, as Harold and the rest of us looked on in amusement. In the face of this, what recourse had May but to forget the whole thing? And, as I remember, the four of us—Bill, Ruth, Frank, and I—were the last to leave the party. Did we go on to the Cedar? Probably . . .

I became acquainted with Philip Guston later, through several meals Frank and I shared with him and his delicate, taciturn, deferential wife, Musa. You'd hang on every word uttered by the charming, articulate, rapturous Philip Guston, whose enthusiasm would have seemed sophomoric and inappropriate were it not for his sagacity, the marvelous things he said. But when Musa spoke—virtually whispered—you didn't simply hang on her every word, you leaned forward eagerly, hoping to encourage her to go on talking. Just to look at her broke your heart—she was that sort of woman, not protective and proprietary like, say, Rothko's wife, who in the most casual conversation referred to her husband as Rothko, or like other artists' wives, as for example, Anita Marca-Relli, whose sweet, self-effacing manner was, you sensed, a shell into which this one-time actress/model had retreated or been relegated, thus permitting the spotlight to shine solely where it belonged, on her blustering, vainglorious husband. Yes, Musa Guston was different from most of the wives of the artists we knew. For she seemed to be her own person, resilient and dégagé, with inner resources to spare, yet at the same time infinitely touching because of what you felt about her, or what *I* felt, in any event, which was that she wasn't cut out to be an artist's wife, that she'd once yearned to do something else with her life, something creative, something for herself, but had been thwarted through her modesty and beneficence, and by her love for and devotion to the man she married.

As I say, I only felt this, only intuited it. Thus, just as I was unaware that she and Philip had a child—it seemed patently clear that theirs was a childless marriage—I had no way of knowing, had never been told, that Musa had forsaken her aspirations to be an artist not long after she became Philip's wife. I vaguely remember hearing that she wrote poetry, but I never saw any of her poems, and I don't think Frank did either. In fact, not until recently, with the publication of *Night Studio: A Memoir of Philip Guston by His Daughter*, did I learn of the existence of a child, who it turns out was named for her mother (she is now Musa Mayer). At the same time, this intense and insightful book confirmed the assumption I made about the Guston ménage: it centered completely on him, on his work and career; and, too, the book revealed what would follow, that their daughter never occupied, even briefly, the Guston catbird seat. No, not once was there any mention of young Musa back in the days when the Gustons came to our place for drinks, after which we'd go on to some inexpensive Chinese restaurant—once, I remember, to Sing Wu, an ordinary eatery next to the Gem Spa on Second Avenue, where a lot of us went when we were disinclined to make the trip to Chinatown. As I recall, the night we went to Sing Wu was the night Grace Hartigan joined us—an uncommonly cold winter night, now that I think about it, because I remember her fussing with the enormous fur coat that enveloped her ample body, the coat having only just that week been acquired through one of the bartering deals artists used to make with an unctuous, vulgar furrier named Jacques Kaplan. As we were getting seated, I was struck by how self-satisfied and haughty she seemed that night. Then this: "Musa," said Grace, doing her level best, I thought, not to sound too patronizing, "you should talk to Philip about getting you a fur coat. How about it, Philip?" Before Philip could reply, Musa said sweetly, without a hint of innuendo, "I'm happy with the cloth coat Philip bought me."

Later, alone with Frank, I gently raised the possibility that Grace might have been a tad bitchy. "Not at all," said he. "It's bitchy of you to think she was." Had he meant to be unkind to me? No. Out of his usual blind loyalty to Grace, about whom he brooked no criticism, he merely felt the need to put me in my place—which of course doesn't mean I wasn't stung by his reproach. "You think Grace never says or does anything out of line," I countered, sorely tempted to let him know then and there what she'd said to me in a cab a couple of weeks earlier en route to our respective domiciles after a party: "It's nice that Frank has a sex life, but does he have to bring his boyfriends around?" These acrimonious words pronounced as soon as Frank and Vincent had gotten off at Avenue A and Eleventh Street, where Vincent had a one-room apartment (it was one of the few nights they stayed at his place, an occasion that filled me with gratitude); and I, fainthearted as usual under such homophobic-charged circumstances, did not say what I should have said before Grace took the cab farther downtown to her Essex Street studio, something along the lines of: "We put up with that boring lover of yours, don't we? Well, Vincent's infinitely more attractive"—after which I would have quickly decamped at my Avenue A and Ninth Street stop, slamming the car door behind me before she had time to respond. What a triumph that would have been! As it was, I offered no rebuttal and ended up hating myself for a long time thereafter.

I said nothing to Frank about all this—first, because it would have necessitated my confessing how lily-livered I'd been ("Why didn't you say something to her?" he would have demanded), and second, because I knew it would hurt him. And why does Grace come so forcefully to mind in connection with "I will always love you"? Actually, it's the etching that makes me think of that indomitable, frequently intimidating woman, about whom I suddenly seem to have nothing good to say. And no wonder: the etching takes me back to the period shortly before Grace, upon counsel of her cornball shrink, decided that there was no room in her brave new life for neurotic fags like Frank O'Hara and John Bernard Myers, both of whom received Dear John letters when, seemingly out of the blue, she moved to Baltimore and married a respectable member of the medical profession.

Did the etching incident occur in the fall of 1961 or '62? I don't remember. In any event, it wasn't long after she shot off her mouth in the cab and, as I said, shortly before she fled New York—an ordinary Saturday afternoon, I remember: Frank and I are reading, puttering, half listening to the Metropolitan Opera broadcast, when Grace, without calling first, turns up at our door. Frank seems as surprised to see her as I am. "I've come for the Kline etching," she explains. "Don't you remember?" "Oh, of course," Frank answers, and fetches one of the two etchings he brought home a couple of days ago. Vincent will pick up his that evening when he gets together with Frank, while the other one is going to be dropped off by me at the framers that very afternoon. Or so I thought until this minute; and I say nothing now, not a word—I just sit there, stunned, and watch as Frank hands over the etching he promised me. "I love it," Grace tells him, barely glancing at it. "How sweet of you." And kisses him, says thanks, then sweeps out of the place, for it seems she has a cab waiting downstairs and can't stay for the drink Frank offered her.

For the next couple of days, I speak to Frank only when I'm spoken to and remain silent about the etching until—I guess it was after work one evening—we were having drinks by ourselves for a change: "Why have you been so cold to me lately?" he asks. "Anything wrong?" I tell him, and he says, in the most casual way imaginable, "Oh, is that what's been bothering you," then goes on to explain that he completely forgot he'd promised the etching to me and that when he saw Grace at that party the other night and she was so unhappy, he impulsively told her he wanted her to have it. "I thought it might cheer her up," he says, "and I think it did," he adds, as though that might make me feel better. All I say is: "She sure didn't waste any time coming by to pick it up." And guess what? This proved to be about the last time Frank saw Grace before she disappeared from the New York art scene.

I was in California visiting my family when she wrote Frank his Dear John letter, and when I returned I heard about it from one of Frank's confidants, Norman Bluhm, one of two or three people he'd shown the letter, so wounded was he by it. And now he said to me, when I brought up the subject, "That's all over; I'm not going to talk about it, with you or anyone." But Grace, I'd noticed, had already ceased to be a subject of conversation, of *his* conversation, I should say, much less a part of his life. Except he did review an exhibition of her paintings six months or so after their estrangement, and significantly, he viewed her work with jaundiced eyes for the first time, no doubt because he was no longer under her spell. (No, not out of spite; if he'd liked her new paintings, he would have said so.) It was a paragraph-long comment that was part of his art chronicle for the spring 1963 issue of *Kulchur,* and as far as I know, he didn't anguish over the review or have any qualms about what he felt compelled to commit to print:

> Abstract-expressionism, which has been dying in the daily and weekly press for lo! these many months, has also been abandoned in her recent show by Grace Hartigan, a motion self-proclaimed in her catalog preface. In the largest painting, *The The,* she showed a continuance of the very ambitious figurative-abstract-expressionist expression through which she achieved considerable renown for her own "Second Generation" interpretation of the New York School style; it is a somewhat botched-up painting, but admirable in its ambitiousness and adamancy. Elsewhere, save for *The Dream,* a very interesting move towards a more subtle Matisse-ish arabesque line and more modulated palette, her defection has produced little but repetitiousness of feeling, and in at least two pictures, *Marilyn Monroe* and *Clark's Cove,* a vulgarity of spirit which is quite disheartening in that it employs illusionistic devices to further apparently unfelt ends. Strangely enough, Miss Hartigan even in her most expressionist moments of the past has never seemed more German—her Monroe here is a movie

> star as seen by Kirshner *cum* Jack Levine. But she has done remarkable and important work in the past and will, I'm sure, in the future; it may be, as Pasternak said of the early Mayakovsky, that her new pose does not yet fit her talents, that she has not yet become her pose. This is not meant in a deprecating sense, but rather in a realistic one. The techniques by which an artist keeps going are not confined to the materials of the studio.

I think the final sentence strikes a personal note: Grace, he seems to be hinting, has kept going by giving up New York for Baltimore. Well, so much for the woman who inspired so many terrific poems of Frank's . . .

I began with Franz Kline and I should wrap up this particularly rambling digression with him. A number of years ago, a book on Kline came out that questioned the authenticity of "Franz Kline Talking"; the author, Harry Gaugh, implied that the interview was largely an invention of Frank's and that Kline good-naturedly went along with it. No, Frank wouldn't pull something like that, nor was Kline as easygoing as Gaugh apparently assumed him to be. My own recollection is that Frank made notes during the interview and typed them up right after Franz left.

It was about two years after the interview that Franz made an etching which incorporated the "I will always love you" poem; the words, in Frank's handwriting, were photographically reproduced on the etching plate. I seem to remember that Franz selected the poem, which Frank then dedicated to him; but I have no idea if Frank was thinking of anyone in particular when he wrote it—possibly, like "For Poulenc," it was simply a love poem he dreamed up, or maybe Larry Rivers was on his mind? The etching was one of twenty-one published in a portfolio by the Morris Gallery; other poets included Theodore Roethke, Dylan Thomas, Harold Rosenberg, William Carlos Williams, and Richard Wilbur, while the artists ranged from the famous (de Kooning, Jacques Lipchitz, and Ben Nicholson) to the little known, artists whose names I can't recall offhand.

When Frank asked me if I'd like one of the two etchings he was getting, I naturally said I'd love to have it—then found myself pondering what he did with the set of *Stones* he'd been given in recompense for collaborating with

DIGRESSIONS ON SOME POEMS BY FRANK O'HARA

Larry Rivers on those thirteen lithographs. He gave them away, of course—
to Mike Goldberg and Patsy Southgate, as a wedding present. And now, for
God's sake, he was giving away both of his Kline etchings. "You sure you don't
want to keep one for yourself?" I said, rather halfheartedly, I have to admit.
"What difference does it make who owns it?" he reasoned. "If I give it to you,
I'll still be able to look at it." So, what happens? He ends up giving it to Grace,
because she seemed depressed when he saw her at a party. How, I now ask
myself, aghast at my avidity, could I have allowed my feelings to be hurt? I
should have seen the whole thing for what it was, yet another manifestation
of Frank's unacquisitive, generous-to-a-fault nature.

POEM

[1 9 5 7]

I live above a dyke bar and I'm happy
The police car is always near the door

                                in case they cry
or the key doesn't work in the lock. But

                he can't open it either. So we go to Joan's
and sleep over,

            Bridget and Joe and I.

I meet Mike for a beer in the Cedar as
the wind flops up the Place, pushing the leaves
against the streetlights. And Norman tells about

the geste,
        with the individual significance of a hardon
like humanity.

           We go to Irma's for Bloody Marys,

and then it's dark.
We played with her cat and it fell asleep. We
seem very mild. It's humid out. (Are they spelled "dikes"?)
People say they are Bacchantes, but if they are

we must be the survivors of Thermopylae.

DIGRESSIONS ON SOME POEMS BY FRANK O'HARA

This modest poem I find so private and enclosed that I feel proprietary about it, as though it were written for me. Perhaps for that reason, it yields a particularly rich and abundant hidden life when I decode its nineteen lines. Let me show you how it works. I start at the top, with the "dyke bar," and go on from there.

"I can't believe it's a lesbian hangout," I called to Frank, my curiosity aroused by two stout men in double-breasted suits who had just emerged from a cab and entered the—was it The Round-up? The Stirrup? The Silver Spur? Some such butch name. Our third-floor studio apartment, into which we'd just moved, was not directly above the bar but two doors up the street from it, so we had an excellent view of the action.

"I have it on good authority that it's a dyke bar," Frank said, joining me at the window.

"Whose authority?"

"Brigid told me," he said. "She's been there a couple of times."

Brigid—not Bridget, as Frank spelled her name in the poem—was (is?) Brigid Murnaghan. Long-limbed, with dirty blond hair, quite good-looking but already, in her mid-twenties, a terrible mess (though a poet of sorts), she frequented various downtown bars like the Cedar and the more literary White Horse Tavern across town, any bar where she could cause a commotion or court attention with her spectacular, wide-ranging gutter vocabulary that surpassed even Joan Mitchell's rough-and-ready way with words.

"If Brigid's right," I said, "what are those two straight men I just saw doing in there?"

At that moment another john appeared, this one sporting a homburg and exiting from the bar with a large woman in a fur coat. He hailed a cab and off they went—which was when I had my satori, if it can be called that. For suddenly I had the answer to a larger question, one I'd wondered about ever since I heard Chester Kallman run on about some straight stud he'd serviced, namely: In the heterosexual world, does there exist a counterpart to the trade queen? Or is the thrill of bedding down someone who is passive and indifferent, who isn't attracted to your sex, an anomaly only certain homo-sexuals take pleasure in? And now I had my answer. "Those men are straight trade queens!" I exclaimed, and proceeded to elaborate upon this strange psychosexual phenomenon.

"Oh, Joe, you're such a deep thinker," Frank said dryly, about as im-pressed by what I had to say on the subject as he was interested in my ideas about certain painters who hung out at the Cedar. "They come on too strong with their butch act, as if they have to prove something," I'd pronounced firmly just the other night, after we'd seen one bruiser (was it Sal Scarpita?) pick some poor guy up, turn him upside down, and deposit him in the litter basket at the corner of University and Eighth Street. "Stunts like that," I went on, "are an indication that they have something to prove, and are probably a sign of repressed homosexuality."

Frank laughed in my face when I said things like that. "You imagine the whole world's gay," he told me more than once. No, I didn't, and one artist whose staunch heterosexuality I never doubted was Willem de Kooning. My reasoning might seem paradoxical: it was because I observed that he enjoyed close, easygoing friendships with gay men like Frank, Edwin Denby, and Donald Droll, and because just about every time he met Frank, or at least every time in my presence, he greeted him with a kiss on the mouth. Funny thing was, deportment of that sort caused Lee Krasner to come to a conclu-sion opposite from mine: "He's half queer," she told me around 1980, spitting out the epithet as if she were alluding to a terrible affliction, though pre-sumably not as terrible as being all queer like the very person to whom she entrusted this spiteful canard. Although I raised no objection—you tangled with Lee at your own peril—I took offense and had to bite my tongue. Later, mulling it over, I began to wonder if her allegation might not have been a smokescreen to becloud suspicions about her late husband: maybe he, and not de Kooning, was the famous Abstract Expressionist with homosexual impulses. But I didn't get very far with my ruminations, because Frank sud-denly came to mind and all I could think about was how amused he would have been: "Bill de Kooning's half queer? I love it—if only it were true!"

The police car is always near the door . . . Briefly, I entertained the notion that the two young, not unattractive cops with whom we spoke on a couple of occasions might themselves be straight trade queens. "Why else would they be hanging around?" I wondered aloud; and this time Frank seemed to take me seriously, as possibly attested by his ambiguous assertion that their car is nearby *in case they cry.*

And then: *or the key doesn't work in the lock*—the lock of our downstairs door, which was as baffling as the presence of the police. To begin with, we had no idea who came around and locked the door at the end of the day. Also, why did our key turn some nights and other nights not at all?

But / he can't open it either—that would be the more sympathetic of the two cops who came to our aid the night we couldn't shake Brigid upon leaving the Cedar. "You guys don't have to put up with this shit," he said gruffly, handing back the key. "Speak to your super about it." But the building had no superintendent. On top of that, we were illegal tenants, since we hadn't been granted—and never would be granted—an AIR (artist in residence) status.

And what did we get for our fifty bucks a month? Nothing more than a modest-sized floor-through with a flimsy plywood partition dividing the space in two, hardly what anyone would describe as a studio, much less as an apartment. For a stove we had a hazardous hot plate, and for a refrigerator something that belonged in the galley of a small cabin cruiser. The toilet was in the hall, the kitchen sink and washbasin were one and the same, and—get this—neither a bathtub nor a shower came with the place. As to how it was furnished, about all we had were a table, three upright chairs, and a couple of beds—plus, hovering incongruously above this bleak mise-en-scène, absurdly, gloriously out of place, Frank's vibrant de Kooning from 1943. At the moment, that fabulous work crowds from my mind Frank's other paintings, by Rivers, Goldberg, Freilicher, Twombly, Bluhm, and Leslie, the earliest acquisitions in his constantly growing collection. Most were outright gifts from the artists, others would be on extended loan. With painstaking care, we hung them salon style in our humble abode sans bathing facilities, about which, by the way, we always intended to do something. In fact, during the two years of our encampment we spoke endlessly of our plans to have a shower installed while blithely continuing to use our friends' facilities. There must have been something wrong with us.

Hands down, I would rank it as the least memorable and most incommodious of our four dwellings, a place that comes to mind now only because of Frank's poem, otherwise I never think of it when, at idle moments, I dwell upon my life with Frank O'Hara—who, what's more, wasn't all that prolific there, the great emanation of his poems occurring later, after our move to the horrendous, noisy East Ninth Street apartment.

And so what happens? Directly above the door whose lock caused us so much anguish, the New York Landmark Preservation Society has seen fit to affix a plaque proclaiming a notable distinction for this very ordinary building at 90 University Place:

FRANK O'HARA (1926–1966)

WHILE LIVING HERE IN 1957–59, THE POET, CRITIC
AND CURATOR WROTE A MONOGRAPH ABOUT THE
ARTIST JACKSON POLLOCK. HIS POEMS DEALT WITH
URBAN THEMES IN AN EXPRESSIONIST STYLE
ANALOGOUS TO POLLOCK'S ACTION PAINTINGS.

An absurd assertion, the business about Frank's poems being analogous to Pollock's paintings. No matter; he would have loved his name being linked with Pollock's.

Moving right along, though it's taken me longer than I expected (the poem is opening so many doors, triggering so many memories!): *So we go to Joan's / and sleep over, / Bridget and Joe and I.* Joan Mitchell's spacious studio apartment was within easy walking distance, at 60 St. Mark's Place, on the opposite side of the street from the building that housed Wystan Auden and Chester Kallman's shabby, cockroach-ridden cold-water flat (in twenty years, the building—in its way, as ordinary as ours—would also flaunt a commemorative plaque out front). Now it wasn't just once that Joan put us up, it happened several times. Did she mind? Are you kidding? Our little sojourns gave her someone to drink with—until dawn if she had her way, and she usually did, being more determined than the two of us put together. But since Frank was a pushover once he started drinking, I was the one she took to task. "What the fuck do you think you're doing?" she'd yell when I immediately got out the blankets to make up a bed on the floor. "I'm putting you fuckers up and you can't have one fucking drink with me?" "I have to be at work tomorrow morning," I'd offer lamely. She would glare at me and resolutely put out three glasses. "Okay," I'd say, "one drink." After gagging down two or three Scotch and waters—Scotch was all she ever had and I hated the stuff—I'd stagger to our makeshift bed, leaving Frank and Joan to squabble drunkenly into the night.

Interestingly, it never occurred to any of us, even when we were older, that we drank too much, and turning to AA for help was unheard of, hardly a place where you'd find capable, socially acceptable people like ourselves. This isn't to say we had social credentials—with the exception of Joan, I hasten to add; the biggest boozer on the downtown poetry-art scene, she was still in the Social Register, Chicago edition, where her name would remain for years to come. But in 1957 I had only a vague notion of her pedigree, her irreverent references to her father as "a skin and syph man" and to her mother as someone who dabbled in poetry, barely hinting that he was the renowned president of the American Dermatological Association and she a socially prominent woman who had published several books of poetry and had helped found Harriet Monroe's *Poetry*.

I surmised, before long, that it was all a ruse, that Joan wanted everyone to disregard her background and think of her as a struggling artist, as no different from her friends and peers, Larry, Mike, Grace, Alfred, the two Janes, who hailed from the Bronx, Brooklyn, a drab New Jersey town, some godforsaken place in the Midwest. Meanwhile, she distanced herself from the one painter who had a comparable upper-class background but who, in contrast to Joan, played up her birthright: the talented and infuriatingly successful Helen Frankenthaler, who would always be a thorn in our testy friend's side. By temperament, of course, Joan was obviously more down to earth, and anything but a careerist—she simply worked hard at her painting. Still, the advantages she enjoyed since childhood made a mockery of her assertion in later years, "I've paid my dues."

Without question, though, she appeared to be the personification of the struggling female artist: no makeup, thick brown hair uncoiffed, no feminine frills in her attire, her bearing intransigently bohemian—but withal, not unattractive to me, and judging by her self-deprecating remarks, a lot better-looking than she thought she was. True, you were immediately aware of her unrefined features and protuberant eyes, but you also saw that she had a fresh, honest, scrubbed look, the look, perhaps, of a pioneer woman of the American prairie, a Willa Cather heroine, with a commanding presence that set her apart from most of the women, the camp-follower types, who hung out at the Cedar, abject, sycophantic females dubbed "art tarts" by one of us, possibly by me.

What I never understood was how Joan came to be so irrepressible and outspoken, a law unto herself—in other words, a sacred monster in the making. She said exactly what she thought with nothing, it would seem, edited out; and it mattered not at all to her if someone's feelings were hurt or if what she said gave umbrage. The only conversation she deemed worth having was one with a high anxiety potential. Here, for example, is how a friendly chat with her would begin when we hadn't seen each other for a while:

> JOAN (*sits, pours Scotch, drinks, then*): So, how are you? What's been happening?
> JOE: Nothing much. I'm fine.
> JOAN (*unconvinced*): You are?
> JOE (*hesitating*): Well, yes . . .
> JOAN: You don't sound very sure. You're not fine at all, are you? Why don't you admit it?
> JOE: I guess things could be better.
> JOAN: You're miserable—I can see! Tell me about it.

And I would. Even if I wasn't unhappy, I'd work up a story. Of course, this was when Frank and I first knew her; she'd only just gotten started and we were amused by the way she threw her weight around and dominated a conversation. Alas, that was in her youth—apropos of which, this morsel of bitter truth from André Gide is apt: "Il n'y a pas qualité si plaisante de la jeunesse qui ne puisse, à viellir, de se gâter"—roughly, "There is no quality, no matter how pleasing in youth, that does not spoil with age."

Perhaps I should move on, but my mind is still on Joan, so indulge me as I continue to stray from the stated source of my recollections . . . About a year after our move to University Place, she went to Paris for an extended stay and took up with Jean-Paul Riopelle, the French Canadian tachist who had a big reputation in Paris but not in New York, reason enough for them to remain in Paris when they decided to live together, he being a great bear of a man who was not about to defer to some woman. Virtually unknown in France during most of her thirty-five years in residence, Joan kept her St. Mark's Place studio and, usually without Riopelle, would come for long annual visits. This meant that our friendship with her was not allowed to languish, though where Frank was concerned it was a friendship fraught with constant friction. Were they in some ways too much alike? Let's just say the chemistry was all wrong between them and let it go at that.

But before Joan moved to Paris and settled down with Jean-Paul, there was a reason, a very specific reason, why she and Frank were so often at loggerheads: *I meet Mike for a beer in the Cedar.* That would be Michael Goldberg, and it seemed Frank was forever meeting Mike for a drink or going to his studio to see his latest painting or having lunch with him when Mike found himself near the Modern in the middle of the day, so that what happened was inevitable, Joan being a painter herself, an ambitious and intensely serious painter who had not quite ended her affair with the very painter Frank was lavishing so much attention on. She began to feel neglected, jealous, then suspicious. "And for good reason," I averred, "since it's obvious you're crazy about Mike." "That doesn't mean I've seduced him," said Frank, reasonably, before accusing me of taking Joan's side, this being the occasion when I was kidnapped, Frank's fanciful characterization of what transpired at the tail end of that tumultuous night in the fall of 1957.

First, a little background that touches upon something very important,

DIGRESSIONS ON SOME POEMS BY FRANK O'HARA

Frank's poetry and how it impinged on his relationship with Mike and Joan as artists. The previous year, a painting of Mike's called *Sardines* had inspired Frank to write "Why I Am Not a Painter," and it had just appeared in *Evergreen Review*. Meanwhile, in Joan's case, inspiration went the other way, from poet to painter: in manuscript, she read a poem Frank wrote in 1954, "To the Harbormaster," and was so moved by it that she began an enormous painting that from the beginning bore the title of Frank's poem. Not that any of this explains why Joan was in such high dudgeon that night . . .

As was often the case, I'd elected not to go to the Cedar with Frank, the quasi-gay San Remo being more my speed. "What happened?" I called out when I heard his key in the latch at the unbelievably early hour of eleven. "Did the place burn down?"

"Your friend," he growled, slamming the door shut. "Something got into her and we had a tiff." He strode to the other side of the partition, to his half of the loft, without so much as a glance at me.

As I returned to my reading, the fierce rat-a-tat of Frank's Royal portable— was he firing off a letter to Joan?—told me I'd better give him a wide berth. Ten, fifteen minutes passed, then came a timorous knock on the door that could not possibly be heard by Frank. As for the treacherous downstairs door, it had obviously not been locked. Fairly certain who had come calling and why, I opened the door as quietly as possible and saw that it was indeed Joan, with her finger to her lips ("shhh"). Offering no resistance, fain to do her bidding, I followed her downstairs, both of us treading gingerly so as not to alert Frank. I should point out that I wasn't taking Joan's side, I was just curious to learn what their set-to had been about.

Until well past midnight, we drank and conferred in a booth at Bradley's, a nondescript Irish bar just up the street. About our colloquy, I have only the vaguest memory of what was said; she complained about Frank and I listened. Then, after walking her to the Cedar, I managed to pry myself loose and return home where I hoped to slip into our loft as sneakily as I'd departed.

But why am I going into all of this? What am I getting at? The truth is, not until just now, in the act of writing this, did I realize what I have been so elaborately leading up to, what this account of that long-ago night is really about: Frank is its mainspring, its true subject, the why and wherefore. I opened the door and there he was, ashen, agitated, on the brink of tears. Seeing me, he was both angry and relieved, like a parent whose child, having disappeared, been lost, or thought to have been abducted, saunters into the house as though nothing has happened and asks, "What's the matter?" In fact, my very words. "Where have you been?" he cried, outraged by my question. I began to explain, but he interrupted: "You disappeared! I said something to you, from the other room, and got no reply, then I came in here—you were gone! You weren't in the john—you were nowhere! You disappeared without a trace! I thought—" "What?" I asked. "I thought you were kidnapped!" he exclaimed, and I looked at him, astonished. "By Joan," I finish for him. "The troublemaker!" Frank exploded. "I should have known she'd pull something like this." It was then that he accused me of taking her side.

But I don't want to go into that or say anything more about what led up to the evening's events: I want to think about Frank now, brood upon his extreme and moving behavior, to which I attached no significance at the time. Was that insensitive of me? Yes, I think so. At times I seemed not to have realized what was happening in my life; only later, in retrospect, have certain incidents like this one, seemingly small and insignificant, assumed their appropriate weight.

Next, a fleeting reference, one of only two in Frank's poetry, to University Place: . . . *the wind flops up the Place, pushing the leaves / against the streetlights.* Even with a nudge from Frank, nothing of interest comes to mind about this minor thoroughfare of drab commercial buildings and boring apartment houses, with equally drab and boring bars, delis, and coffee shops interspersed, from shoddy, ugly Fourteenth Street down to what was then the staid and quiet corner of Eighth and University, where one found, inexplicably, completely out of place, Frank's beloved haunt, the misnamed Cedar Street Tavern—sad to say, that was the extent of our neighborhood. "Not my idea of the Village," as I grumbled to Frank, whom I blamed for our impulsive move, a move that I, of course, initiated.

And Norman tells about / the geste, / with the individual significance of a hardon / like humanity. Clad in somber colors, with a scarf around his neck, his long black hair in artful disarray, a de rigueur Gauloise dangling from his lips, he spewed a salty American slang cum Gallic patois of his own invention, with grand words like *politesse* and *geste* tossed in for good measure—that is the Norman Bluhm I remember from the night Frank introduced us in a booth at the Cedar. Sitting beside him was Mike Goldberg, whom you've already met—except I failed to describe him. Warm, generous, voluble, upbeat even in the face of adversity (he'd never admit to you or to himself if things were going badly), he exuded a sexuality due only in small part to his good looks—no wonder Frank was drawn to him. At Joan's behest, Norman looked Mike up when he gave up Paris for New York, and they quickly became bosom buddies, soon to be joined by Frank when we moved downtown—thus the duo became a trio, a curious trio, I thought at first: Mike and Norman, earthbound and burly, and Frank, with his nasal alto voice, birdlike frame, effete way of walking on the balls of his feet, another story altogether. Years later, briefly slated to write a biography of Frank, Peter Schjeldahl would also wonder about the Goldberg-Bluhm-O'Hara triumvirate, but for a different reason. Given access to Frank's pocket-size appointment books of that period, he was taken aback and clearly disappointed to see the entry, day after day, "Drinks with Mike and Norman." Why those two, Peter wanted to know, when Frank could have been seeing—*should* have been seeing, I think he said—major artists like Johns and Rauschenberg? I shrugged, said nothing, but thought to myself: He has a Hollywood-movie concept of an artist's or poet's life.

Actually, Frank did hang out with some pretty big names: de Kooning, Kline, and Guston come to mind. All of them fairly macho, I suppose, but they accepted Frank as one of them, even invited him to become a member of The Club. So far as I know, only Jackson Pollock, probably the least secure and most conflicted of all the downtown painters, expressed hostility toward gays: "a couple of faggots" he was said to have groused when Frank and Larry Rivers, at the height of their affair in 1954, turned up at the Cedar together—which, come to think of it, was about the time John Myers carried on about their appearance one night on the staircase of City Center, at a New York City Ballet performance: "There they were," he simpered, in his usual excessive fashion, "like Rimbaud and Verlaine, covered with blood and semen!"

And now: *We go to Irma's for Bloody Marys . . .* Near the end of Strindberg's harrowing *Ghost Sonata*, the Daughter (no name given) passionately decries "the toil of holding the dirt of life at bay," which is from the translation of Michael Mayer, as is the title—it's the only English-language version of the play I've been able to lay my hands on. But when the Living Theater produced the work on a shoestring in 1955—it was performed in the vast, high-ceilinged Upper West Side apartment of Julian Beck and Judith Malina—the title was *The Spook Sonata* and the line just quoted I remember as being a lot more earthy and hard-hitting, something on the order of "washing away the dirt of life" in the translation the Becks used. (In "Meditations in an Emergency," written in 1956, Frank quotes the line—without attribution—as "to keep the filth of life away.") Playing the part of the Daughter was Irma Hurley, who gave us Bloody Marys that leisurely Sunday afternoon. (Yes, I'm sure it was Sunday, and she probably gave us brunch.) In her early twenties, a high-strung, rawboned slip of a girl with enormous, panic-stricken eyes, she essayed the part with chilling effect, particularly when it came time to utter the line about "the dirt of life," at which point Frank, who tended to get carried away at theater performances, gripped my arm and gasped in admiration. Every so often, for years, he'd quote from the speech verbatim, always exclaiming over Irma's performance.

The night we saw *The Spook Sonata,* I'd not yet met Irma, but Frank had—at a party given by John Myers a couple of months earlier, on which occasion he also met Jane Bowles, who was in New York for the premiere of her luminous, lyrical *In the Summer House;* and unless I misremember what Frank said, Irma was brought to the party by the endearingly eccentric and already legendary writer, the two having become friends during a regional production of the Bowles play, in which Irma had one of the two leads. "If only you'd been in the Broadway production," Frank enthused when we went backstage after *The Spook Sonata,* his voice trailing off—intimating, with his usual flair for hyperbole, that the play wouldn't have flopped if Irma had been kept in the cast.

After we moved downtown a couple of years later, it turned out that she lived near us, in a walkup on East Seventh Street, off Third Avenue, a modest but attractive apartment where she entertained with wit and style, her camp summary of the 1954 Barbara Stanwyck–Ronald Reagan oater, *Cattle Queen of Montana,* being only one of the many off-the-top-of-her-head monologues with which she regaled her friends (almost all male and all gay). Intent on a career in the theater, she stuck by her guns for six or seven years, went her own way, took office temp jobs, made the rounds, struggled courageously with good humor to make a go of it, all the while living her life as though it was complete without a man, which indeed it was. And then, as so often happened with creative women of her generation (I suppose it still happens), the ticking of her biological clock became so deafening that, to put an end to it, she succumbed to marriage and motherhood.

We played with her cat and it fell asleep. "Played with her cat"? How rare for Frank, in a poem like this, to stray from the truth, from what actually happened! Take my word for it, Irma's precious Natasha, a long-haired feline as feisty as she was beautiful, you admired from afar.

Now Frank comes full circle, back to the reference to dykes: (*Are they spelled "dikes"?*) / *People say they are Bacchantes, but if they are / we must be the survivors of Thermopylae.* With these lines, the poem is invested—suddenly, unexpectedly—with a substance that sets it apart from other similarly tenuous and casual poems of Frank's, the sort about which an academic, James E.B. Breslin, made the observation that "O'Hara titled so many of his works 'Poem' [seventy-eight by my count, including those in *Poems Retrieved*] precisely because he was aware that many of his readers would deny them the status of poetry." (Where, I wonder, did Professor Breslin get that—surely not from Frank, who was never defensive about his work. Wouldn't this simple explanation be more like it: when something he'd written didn't suggest a title to him—usually, it was nothing very long or ambitious—he'd call it "Poem" and put it away without another thought.) Now you might think I'm reaching, reading more into the poem than Frank intended, when I tell you what I infer from its final lines, which is nothing less than an espousal of an idea whose time had not yet come: Gay Pride! Yes, I suppose he showed no pronounced signs in his life and work—as, say, Allen Ginsberg did early on—of becoming a future gay activist. Also, I can see what that great embellisher of the truth (and wonderful painter!) John Button was getting at when, upon being asked in an interview how he imagined Frank would have regarded gay liberation, he replied: "Oh, he would have thought it was silly, but he would have *loved* the dances!" No doubt the Frank O'Hara of "At the Old Place" was the one he had in mind when he made his glib prognostication. So only partly conceding his point, I'd suggest that gay liberation was not something Frank *consciously* thought about. Which explains, perhaps, why his pronouncement on the nobility of gays found expression through his poetry, because that was the only way it could have, poetry being the vehicle of the unconscious.

Thus, intending no slur in the use of the word "dyke," he brings to our attention a provocative notion when he suggests that lesbians have an exalted lineage, a thrilling history. "People say they are Bacchantes," he tells us—the Maenads, that is, the Greek women who descended from wild Thrace in the eighth century B.C. Theirs was a Dionysian religion, a magical, dangerous, ecstatic form of worship; it seems they flung themselves into their secret rites with such abandon that terror was struck into the hearts of men. Some scholars maintain that the oppression under which Greek women lived gave rise to their religion, an essentially female form of spirituality that allowed its followers to be goddesses. This leads Frank to conclude that if the Maenads, or Bacchantes, were lesbians, then today's gay men might well be "the survivors of Thermopylae." That is to say, they are as courageous and cunning as that greatly outnumbered army of possibly gay Spartans who, in 480 B.C., defended the narrow pass of Thermopylae and in doing so went to their deaths.

The last line of the poem presents a problem: there were no survivors! Is Frank being ironic? Or is this a slipup comparable to the Keats Cortez/ Balboa blunder? Go figure.

I still say: how prescient our poet appears in view of the mettle shown by homosexuals in the post-Stonewall years! Also, notice that he says *"we* must be the survivors of Thermopylae," thereby proudly identifying himself as gay.

Re: my observation about University Place in the earlier note. Don't take too seriously my grumbling that the neighborhood's "not my idea of the Village," for I set about as much store in our surroundings as Frank did. Certainly, without fail, we managed to have the worst apartments of all of our friends, because when it came to the amenities, we were complacent and unaspiring. But Frank was happy, as he tells us in the poem, and so was I. He was doing a fair amount of writing, and by now it was evident he had a career with a future at the Museum of Modern Art. As for me, somehow it didn't matter that I was getting nowhere, had accomplished nothing, seemed to have no direction. I was floundering and would continue to do so for years to come—right up to the present time, it might be said, since I still hang loose and take things as they come, hoping for the best as I did back then, when, for example, having lost my job at the Holliday Bookshop (it went out of business because its owner, Bob Vanderbilt, was fed up with New York and decided to move to Switzerland), I worried not at all. "Something'll come along," I told Frank. And one evening around Christmastime 1957, just as my severance pay was about to run out, something turned up all right, casually and unexpectedly, over drinks with two new friends from the previous summer. "Joe and I have been seeing a lot of Chuck Turner and Sam Barber whom we both like very much," writes Frank in one of his gossip-filled letters, dateline Southampton, Long Island, August 26, 1957. "They are quite reserved and very interesting and concentrated; Sam is particularly the latter, but he is also finishing the orchestration of his opera *Vanessa* for the Metropolitan's deadline so that may not be an invariable thing." Anyway, it was either Chuck or Sam who said to me, "Gian Carlo's secretary is leaving—maybe you should apply for the job," and the other one agreed it was a good idea, as Frank caught my eye, nodded his approval, then told us, "I was Cecil Beaton's secretary for a couple of months, when I was first living in New York—it was great, I loved it. I didn't meet Garbo, but I met Constance Collier, who was divine."

I had nothing to lose, and if not everything to gain, at least the prospect of having yet another interim job while I continued biding my time, trying to decide what to do with my life. "Yes, I'd definitely be interested," I said; and the handsome, elegant Samuel Barber said he'd put in a good word to his friend and colleague, with whom he shared a house in Mt. Kisco, New York. I had one reservation, which I naturally didn't mention until Frank and I were alone, hailing a cab in front of Sam's pied-à-terre in the East Seventies.

"I don't like his operas."

"Who does?" Frank said.

"Half the world," I answered.

"Don't be a snob," said Frank, who enjoyed all kinds of meretricious music but that of the composer I might be working for no more than I did. And as it turned out, I was hired immediately. My running commentary on what it was like being secretary to Gian Carlo Menotti amused Frank more than anyone, as might be attested by one of my Gian Carlo stories that Ned Rorem mischievously appropriated for his *New York Diary:* "Joe LeSueur, as everyone knows, is Menotti's secretary now. All day long he hears the maestro composing a new opera in the next room. Gian Carlo emerges for a cup of tea and asks, 'Well, Joe, how does it sound?' Joe, at a loss for words: 'Well, mmm, it sounds as though something terrible is going to happen.' Frank O'Hara later adds: 'Something terrible *is* going to happen. He's going to finish it.'"

An imaginative diarist, Ned both improved upon and distorted my story: Gian Carlo never composed while I was around, as I was hired mainly to help him raise funds for the first season of his Festival of Two Worlds at Spoleto, Italy, and we always had plenty to do; I just happened to find him at the piano when I reported to work one morning; and, finally, he would never have solicited my opinion about his music—as if he cared what I thought! *The New York Diary* wasn't published until 1967, and by then Frank was no longer with us. Still, it's safe to say he wouldn't have appreciated his bitchy witticism being made public, since he liked Gian Carlo perfectly well the few times they met.

It was while we were living on University Place that I became one of the many collaborators Frank had over the years, as he was always disposed to joining forces with someone else, the works produced being as diverse as the people with whom he collaborated: poem, song, dance, play, movie, teleplay, musical comedy, lithograph, etching, collage, comic strip, statement for a symposium, an exchange of letters in which the correspondents assumed imaginary personae, simply being the subject of a painting, sculpture, photograph, drawing, or sketch—Frank exulted in all of these forms of collaboration (a term loosely applied here), partly because his collaborators were in most instances friends of his, people he enjoyed spending time with.

I suppose it's unnecessary to add that there was an element of play in all of his creative endeavors, collaborative or otherwise; and yes, I'm aware that the same can be said of the efforts of all true artists, though in Frank's case the play element was so pervasive, so predominant, that it ruled out the possibility of his ever becoming a professional writer (that is, professional in the sense of making a living from one's writing). Thus he gave his poems to mimeographed publications like *The Floating Bear,* wrote art chronicles for *Kulchur,* granted carte blanche to anyone who wanted to do his plays, and was perfectly content to have as his principal publisher the perpetually impecunious John Bernard Myers, who wasn't really a publisher but an art dealer. And had Frank lived to a hundred, he could never have written art criticism for, say, *Newsweek* or *New York* magazine—not that he would ever have been asked, since there was only one way he could write, *his* way, in prose as individual, offbeat, and original as his poetry. As for his collaborative works, they were no more commercial or remunerative than what he wrote by himself.

In the case of *The Undercover Lover,* perhaps it was inevitable that Frank's interest would peter out before he, John Gruen, and Arnold Weinstein got to first base. "I'm tired of getting together with them," he complained to me less than a month after he'd been working with them on the project, a musical comedy for which Frank had only moderate enthusiasm, largely because it was Arnold's idea, his baby, a work that would bear his stamp, not Frank's.

Oddly enough—at least I thought it odd at the time—Frank had no sooner stopped meeting with John and Arnold than he began thinking about writing a couple of teleplays with me. *Teleplays?* Was he kidding? But I was game—indeed, I was excited at the prospect. And as soon as we'd written two half-hour scripts, he had me working with him on a conventional play based on an idea we cooked up together. What could he have been thinking? But I was happy to be swept along by his energy and enthusiasm, only later realizing what he was up to. His strategy worked, too—albeit with dubious results: I went on to write a play that ended up on the tube and then a quickie novel that was brought out by a tawdry paperback house. My sex-obsessed penny-dreadful, schematically worked out so that every other chapter was queer, the other ones being as convincingly heterosexual as I could manage, was called *Always Love a Stranger,* a title Don Allen suggested to me. But the play, first called *The Fifties,* at Frank's suggestion, and then *Cool Wind over the Living,* also his title, was a serious effort. Early on I showed him what I'd written, about a third of the first act, and he said, "I like it—keep writing—but you don't need my help."

JUNE 2, 1958

[J U N E   2 ,   1 9 5 8]

Oh sky over the graveyard, you are blue,
you seem to be smiling! or are you sneering?
under the captured moss a little girl
is climbing, come closer! why it's Maude,
or Maudie as she's sometimes called. I think
she is looking for her turtle. Meanwhile,
back at Patsy Southgate's, two grown men
are falling off a swing into a vat of Bloody Marys.
It's Sunday and the trains run on time. What
a wonderful country it is, so black and blue
airy green, leaning out a window
thinking of the sea and the uncomfortable sand!

t would appear that these dozen lines were an offshoot of "Ode on Causal-
ity," originally entitled "Ode at the Grave of Jackson Pollock" and written
over a period of a month and a half, from May 21 to July 8, 1958. You'll note
that the Green River Cemetery figures in both works, as does a child named
Maude, who appears more prominently in the ode in which she "lays down
her doll, red wagon and her turtle / takes my hand and comes with us, shows
the bronze JACKSON POLLOCK," that is, the plaque bearing his bold signature. Also, it is clear the two poems refer to the same experience, Frank's

visit to the cemetery in Springs to contemplate the much-talked-about giant boulder atop Pollock's grave.

And here's what I learned after doing a little detective work: Maude is the daughter of Peter Fried, Elaine de Kooning's brother; Mike Goldberg and Norman Bluhm are most likely the "two grown men . . . falling off a swing into a vat of Bloody Marys," though it's possible that one of them is Matsumi (Mike) Kanemitsu; and Frank, evidently, leaves the cemetery and joins them at the small, simple farmhouse on Fireplace Road, where Patsy Southgate, the estranged wife of Peter Matthiessen, lives with their two young children and where, on this bright Sunday afternoon, she's entertaining a half-dozen or so people—not including me, however, as I'm elsewhere that weekend. Don Allen is also present, but I can't imagine Frank describing anyone as elegant as Don "falling off a swing into a vat of Bloody Marys."

That's about it—except just now, because of these ruminations, a picture looms inevitably in my mind's eye: Frank seated intently at his humble Royal portable. With "cigarette smoke . . . jetting from [his] nostrils and . . . in a great clatter of keys" (Jimmy Schuyler's felicitous description of Frank under the spell of his muse), he's dashing off a poem that I now imagine to be the dozen lines I've been poring over, lines he filed away and dismissed from his mind like so many other things he wrote that didn't see the light of day until after his death, the present poem being liberated, so to speak, when Maureen, Frank's sister, gave it to Jim Brodey for his fly-by-night *Clothesline* in 1970, all of which makes me think of—yes, the comparison is far-fetched!—those fragments Emily Dickinson scrawled on scraps of paper, tied together with twine and stored in a small box that, after her death, was found among her personal effects by Lavinia, her sister, who saw that the poems were published.

All right, time to move on, you're probably thinking: this isn't, after all, one of Frank O'Hara's major poems. Granted. But it bears an imposing title, as though a significant event is being commemorated. And so it is: "June 2, 1958," the title, the only one of its kind in Frank's oeuvre, marks the time he met the beautiful and provocative Patsy Southgate, whom Mike Goldberg

had just begun seeing. But somehow or other, Frank got the date wrong—
yes, I researched that, too: June 2 didn't fall on a Sunday that year but on a
Monday! Maybe the poem was written, or typed up, the next day at the Modern and dated accordingly? In any event, the date of the poem signifies that
Frank knew in his heart, from the moment he and Patsy Southgate met, that
she would be special to him, would be the next woman in his life, the next
blonde, for I remember his telling me, the moment he got home that Sunday night, "Wait'll you meet the girl Mike's interested in"—"girl" and not
"woman" being what he would have said back then.

I'd come in an hour earlier from my weekend at the Menotti-Barber
domicile in Mt. Kisco, a weekend devoted to Festival of Two Worlds business
prior to Gian Carlo's departure for Spoleto that I wasn't the least interested
in talking about beyond expressing my relief that I'd soon be on my own, left
to my own devices—so after Frank got me out of bed and made us drinks, I
was content to sit and listen as he went on about the great time he had with
Mike, Norman, Matsumi, and Don, and about the fabulous woman he met
over the weekend, a writer who happened to be in the same issue of *Evergreen Review* as Frank, volume one, number three, that appeared the previous year. And now he got it out, showed me: not only were the two of them
in the same issue, their contributions—his three poems and her short
story—were cheek by jowl, as were the photographs of them on the back
cover, Patsy's having been taken immediately after the funeral of her good
friend Jackson Pollock, who was pictured on the front cover, sitting on the
running board of his Model A Ford. Still more: one of Frank's poems, "A Step
Away from Them," touched on the death of Pollock, who was the subject of
a monograph Frank was working on at the time the quarterly came out, while
another, "Why I Am Not a Painter," had to do with a painting of Mike's.

Now surely all these omens, all this synchronism, had to mean something!
And indeed, within a year, by the time Patsy's name turned up again in a
poem of Frank's, she would have become one of our closest friends and, not
only that, she'd be the wife of Michael Goldberg. How could it have turned
out otherwise? This doesn't mean Frank and I sat around pondering how

things would be different now because of their upcoming nuptials, for there was no way we could have imagined the tremendous impact their marriage would have on our lives. Curiously, we thought of the step they were taking only in relation to Patsy, about whom we were beginning to feel protective: Mike could take care of himself, no matter what happened. Didn't he always land on his feet? And being aware of his foibles, we knew that at the very least a marital terra incognita of an unusual character awaited our new friend, whose Katherine Mansfield–like story in *Evergreen Review,* all about a pathetic, middle-aged housewife trapped in a loveless marriage, can be regarded as a foretoken of the feminism she would later embrace and as an oblique, embittered response to her failed first marriage.

None of this was what we divined at first, for she gave no hint of what lay beneath those jewellike, heart-stopping, pale blue eyes, the pent-up rage and resentment that would soon fulminate, perhaps as much to her surprise as ours. Naïvely, we imagined that any woman as warm and alive as Patsy couldn't possibly be unhappy with her lot. And I have to say that it was a long time before we realized that her second trip to the altar was destined to be an experiment of sorts, not only a union utterly unlike her socially acceptable, Paris-based Peter Matthiessen partnership, with ties to Styron, Plimpton, Southern, et al., the smart *Paris Review* crowd that enhanced this couple's attractiveness, made them seem all the more enviable, but—how should I put it? Let me quote Patsy on the subject: "I wasn't just married to Mike," she told me after their divorce, "I was also married to you and Frank."

I knew immediately what she meant, she didn't have to explain: the marriage wouldn't have worked as well as it did, it wouldn't have been such great fun, without Frank and me aboard. A new spin on Noel Coward's triangular *Design for Living,* a quasi ménage à quatre—that's how I've come to think of our arrangement. *Arrangement?* No, that's not the right word, because it was nothing we planned; it just happened, the way one falls in love. Encompassing parties, openings, dinners, movies, East Hampton weekends, bridge, poker, quiet times, riotous times, fueled by a steady flow of booze, yet somehow familial, even wholesome, with Luke and Carey, Patsy's two kids, adored by the four of us, an essential part of the equation—that, I think, sums up the nature of our ménage, which, come to think of it, should be amended to ménage à six.

Now does this setup strike you as bohemian, outré, far-out? We never gave it a thought; to us, it seemed perfectly normal, and it does to me now. But there was, possibly, another aspect to it, one that might, at the very least, sound unusual. Conjecture on my part, it goes like this: Patsy wouldn't have fallen in love with Mike, much less married him, if his rough manner and bravado had not been offset by what his two gay friends embodied, a homosexuality that was gracefully assimilated into straight society without being closeted, a homosexuality that was carefree without being giddy, a homosexuality that was also gentle, amused, and ironic, and a homosexuality that embraced what so many gay as well as straight men abjure, the inner feminine part of the male personality known as the anima, of which my analyst made me aware. Oh, and one more thing, actually what's most important, what I suppose is related to the Jungian concept of the anima, a homosexuality whose proscription of misogyny Patsy could only have found novel and reassuring, a comfort and a boon she'd doubtless never known in heterosexual circles dominated by sexist, egocentric males who thought of themselves as, to use Patsy's most damning epithet, "entitled."

By inference, I might seem to be saying that Frank and I were a model gay couple, at once wise, compassionate, and fun to be with, a gay dream come true for broad-minded straights who want or need to be shaken up. The truth is, when we found ourselves happily entangled in Mike and Patsy's marriage, a bond that endured for almost as long as the marriage lasted, close to five years, we simply rose to the occasion—playing dissimilar roles, of course, mine being relatively uncomplicated, Frank's another matter altogether. I was Patsy's adoring brother and confidant, a straightforward, unencumbered part, and, at the same time, with no effort, I was Mike's champion, pure and simple, while Frank—well, given his impassioned, conflicted nature (to quote from "Four Apartments": "He didn't make distinctions, he mixed everything up: life and art, friends and lovers—what was the difference between them?"), it could not have been easy for him to rein in his feelings, to keep them in check. For his attraction to Mike was as strong as ever and co-existed, even seemed to go hand in hand, with his feelings for Patsy, the bolt-out-of-the-blue yen he would occasionally experience. In both cases, the deep, abiding affection he had for them as friends won out over his amor-phous, romantic longing for what was manifestly beyond his grasp.

A TRUE ACCOUNT OF TALKING
TO THE SUN AT FIRE ISLAND

[J U L Y   1 0 ,   1 9 5 8]

"... And
always embrace things, people earth
sky stars, as I do, freely and with
the appropriate sense of space. That
is your inclination, known in the heavens
and you should follow it to hell, if
necessary, which I doubt.

Maybe we'll
speak again in Africa, of which I too
am specially fond. Go back to sleep now
Frank, and I may leave a tiny poem
in that brain of yours as my farewell" ...

was in the city when Frank wrote his account of talking to the sun, a poem
whose existence I remained ignorant of until Kenneth Koch read it at New
York University's Loeb Center in the fall of 1966. Less than two months
had passed since Frank's death, so the reading was like a memorial. But the
only poem I remember is "A True Account." After Kenneth read the final
stanza—

"Sun, don't go!" I was awake
at last. "No, go I must, they're calling
me."
              "Who are they?"
                                Rising he said "Some
day you'll know. They're calling to you
too." Darkly he rose, and then I slept.

—there was a stunned silence, one that bespoke the shared feelings of grief, melancholy, and mystification among those members of the audience who knew and loved Frank. Kenneth proclaimed (words to this effect, so I'll omit quotation marks): This is the work of a great poet.

And a work Frank never showed to anyone, including Kenneth. Thus, understandably, we were not only moved by the poem but mystified as well. Why had he kept it a secret? That might seem an overstatement, but isn't that substantially the case? While not in the habit of sending out his poems, Frank usually made a practice of showing what he'd written to his poet friends. But with this work he made an exception. Why? When we lived at 791 Broadway, Ted Berrigan was permitted to go through Frank's papers, pore over his poems. Didn't this most avid fan of Frank's come across "A True Account"? Apparently not; if he had, he would certainly have recognized it as a major work and mentioned it to someone. So, for whatever reason, Frank seems to have been reluctant to let anyone see a copy of the poem—or, to put it more provocatively, he must not have wanted us to read it until after his death. For me, the mystery deepens when I cast my mind back to mid-July 1958.

I'd been Gian Carlo Menotti's secretary for the past year and now, with Menotti in Spoleto, Italy, running the festival, I was taking care of New York–related business in a little office I had on West Fifty-seventh Street. Then it was discovered I had nothing to do, so I was given my walking papers and instructed to close the office. This happened toward the end of the week that Frank was spending with Hal Fondren at the Fire Island beach house Hal and his "longtime companion," Jack Shaw, rented each summer.

I wasted no time in getting hold of them. "I'm free! I've been fired!" I said excitedly to Frank, who answered the phone. Hal, the best cook any of us knew, was preparing lunch. "Tell Joe to come out," he called to Frank after he'd been given the news.

This was Thursday afternoon, July 10, the very day Frank communed with the sun and wrote his poem. I dropped what I was doing and was able to make our usual eastbound 4:19 train, except I'd be getting off at Sayville where I'd catch the ferry for Fire Island Pines.

Frank was at the dock to meet me, and Hal must have been back at the house, making hors d'oeuvres for our cocktails. I would have given Frank whatever news I had, and he probably filled me in on what they'd been up to, mainly eating, drinking, swimming, and lying in the sun, all of which is conjecture on my part—plus what we know from the poem: ". . . I stayed / up late last night talking to Hal." The only thing I actually remember concerns a young boy we encountered on the boardwalk as we wended our way to the house.

Not that there was anything unusual about him. He was just an average-looking nine- or ten-year-old with tousled hair, and I wouldn't have noticed him had it not been for the way he acted when he caught sight of Frank. A look of recognition came into his face, while at the same time he appeared embarrassed by their running into each other. Frank smiled and said hello, and the boy nodded back, sheepishly, as he walked past.

"Who was that?" I said.

"A boy from the beach," Frank said.

"And?" I looked at him when he failed to reply. "You're being awfully mysterious."

Later it occurred to me that Frank had so completely empathized with the boy that, out of deference to his tender feelings, he was reluctant to enlighten me about their shared experience. Perhaps he wouldn't even have told me about it had we not run into him.

"It's just something that happened on the beach this morning," Frank said, and went on to explain that he was stretched out on a beach towel, dozing, when he heard distant cries for help. He quickly sat up and saw someone struggling in the surf, caught in an undertow. It turned out to be a boy he'd seen on the beach, an unusually self-possessed child for his age who was always arguing with his mother about going into the water unattended. "Don't worry about me so much!" he insisted. "I know how to swim." And now he was in trouble; the beach was virtually empty, and nobody else was in the water. But Frank, being an expert swimmer, was able to reach him in good time and bring him safely ashore.

"So that was why he acted funny, running into you just now," I suggested.

"He felt chagrined about the whole thing," Frank said. "He came over and thanked me later—at his mother's insistence, I'm sure—and that only made it worse."

With everything that was going on that day, the boy's rescue, my phone call, preparations for my arrival, it was a wonder Frank found the time and solitude to write his poem. Of course it didn't take him long to knock off a poem, and he never needed peace and quiet. But why didn't he show his memorable "True Account" to Hal, particularly since Hal's name comes up in it? Someone has suggested to me that Frank wasn't sure of the poem, that he put it away and forgot about it. I doubt that. But I don't doubt that he was awakened by the sun and thought of Mayakovsky and then recorded his own dialogue, partly in tribute to the Russian poet he admired so much, a sort of gloss on Mayakovsky's poem. The account is described as "true" for good reason, and Frank must have transcribed it right away, on the Royal portable he'd brought with him. But wouldn't his typing have awakened Hal in the next room? Finally, what of his rescue of the boy later that day? In a sense, was it not an extension of the poem, its occurrence as clandestine as Frank's conversation with the sun?

None of my questions needs to be answered. We have the poem, that is what matters. Despite Frank's reticence, his "True Account" shows signs of becoming one of his most popular poems. Just recently, it found its way into the anthology drawn from the Favorite Poem Project of the very energetic poet laureate Robert Pinsky, thanks to Vincent Katz (the writer son of two good friends of Frank's, Alex and Ada Katz), whose felicitous statement accompanies his selection: "This poem catches you in a casual, breezy atmosphere into which the poet injects a beautifully tragic realization of the fleetingness of life, relationships, and desire."

I don't recall the circumstances that brought Frank and Joe Ford together; conceivably, I was the one who introduced them, since I knew Joe first, having met him in 1951 through the scandalous, sex-obsessed, Cinema 16–type filmmaker, sometime-poet, and Wagner College English and American literature professor Willard Maas. It wasn't until five or six years later that Frank got together with Joe. So first, let's get my experience with Joe out of the way.

Greeting me at the door of the cluttered, chaotic, miniature penthouse he and his wife Marie Menken rented for a pittance on Montague Street in Brooklyn Heights, Willard squealed mischievously, "You're in luck, Joe Joy. Eleventh Heaven's here tonight." I was eager to meet him, of course, as Willard had a knack for snagging comely and compliant quasi-hustlers, but I also hoped to see Marie, a good-natured, gargantuan woman who towered over her squat and rotund spouse. You wondered how they ever got together. "I was still straight when I met her," Willard told me once, but that certainly didn't explain anything.

One of the more engaging figures on a bohemian scene the likes of which no longer exists (Paul Goodman, Oscar Williams and Gene Derwood, Judith Malina and Julian Beck, and the Living Theatre crew were among its denizens), Marie was a talented but dilenttantish artist who exhibited once at Betty Parsons and another time at Tibor de Nagy before she concentrated on making grainy, dimly lit experimental films like Willard's. Much to my disappointment, this warm, lusty, vibrant woman, who seemed to thrive on the vicissitudes of a frustrating, anomalous life, was nowhere to be seen, nor was there a female in sight, so I knew immediately what was up: Marie was working the late shift at Time, Inc. (where, by the way, she was known as "The Body"), and that meant she wouldn't be home until dawn—which, in turn, meant that this would be one of her husband's orgiastic nights of booze, boys, and, perhaps best of all, truly wonderful victuals, Willard being a superior cook. As for Eleventh Heaven, he'd been described to me in considerable detail, so I knew I'd immediately recognize him; but now, catching sight of him across the room, I had the immediate impression that he possessed qualities Willard hadn't bothered to mention.

"He looks like he's very nice," I ventured, struck by his docile demeanor and apparent guilelessness—naturally, then, I hoped against hope that my host, never known for his tact, would forgo referring to him as Eleventh Heaven when introductions were made. Instead, he made it worse than I'd anticipated by stage-whispering, as I shook hands with his latest discovery, who could not have been more than twenty or twenty-one, "I hope you get a chance to find out why I call Joe Eleventh Heaven."

In his bearing and physiognomy, there was nothing about the large, hefty, very dark Joe Ford that hinted he'd grown up in a brutal urban environment. But not only was he devoid of a city look and manner, he had the appearance and exuded the aura of a true and noble African—this in spite of his having been born and reared in Harlem. It might be said that he was a miracle—yet he was treated as a piece of meat. But remember, this was the early fifties, before our consciousness had been raised about blacks, a time when those of us who liked blacks had a better chance of making out with them than we did later. For in the wake of the civil rights movement, gay men of both races became self-conscious and ill at ease in each other's company—ironically, or so it might appear, integration drove us apart. At least that was what I experienced: I couldn't make the transition and, gradually my dalliance with blacks came to a close, so that by the early sixties, my interracial sex life was sadly a thing of the past.

It is now some six years later—the summer of 1957, I'm pretty certain—and Frank, somehow or other, has become involved with Joe, who in the years since I met and bedded him, has married, fathered two children, separated from his wife, and picked up where he left off when he got married, which means he's again living it up in various coteries of gay white society. And he's remarkably unchanged, as serene and sweet as ever, though there is one difference—he looks even better. Frank meets him at a party, gets to know him, and has dinner with him. Instead of going to bed with him once or twice, the way the rest of us did, Frank begins having an affair with him, and in no time at all Joe's decided to take Frank home to meet the family— or, more than likely, it's Frank's idea to meet them, the family being Joe's two kids and his widowed mother who's been looking after the kids ever since Joe's wife abandoned them. I'm invited to come along, as it seems there's going to be a party. So up to Harlem we go.

The kids are adorable, so is the mother, and the guests, including several smashing male friends of Joe's, couldn't be friendlier. Frank spends most of the time talking to Joe's mother, with whom he establishes an immediate rapport. Yes, Frank and I are the only whites there, and of course we love it.

The next thing I know—this all happens within a period of a couple of weeks—Joe's joining us in Southampton, where we'll spend the weekend with Larry Rivers, Larry's former mother-in law Berdie, his son Steven, and his stepson Joseph. And they're all crazy about Joe. On Saturday night, Arthur and Bobby—the duo-pianists Gold and Fizdale, equally superlative as musicians and social climbers—are giving a concert at Guild Hall in East Hampton, and we're all expected to go. Which is fine by us, by Frank and me, as their program includes the Poulenc sonata for two pianos, which we're crazy about, plus one of the suites for two pianos by Rachmaninoff. It's during the Rachmaninoff that Joe gets a crush on Arthur. I see it happen with my own eyes: Joe's practically swooning when I look over at him, so mesmerized is he by the metamorphosis that's taking place on stage. For with help from Rachmaninoff, a lot of help, Arthur is transformed into a romantic, mid-nineteenth-century Lisztian figure—why, I almost fall in love with him myself.

In the patio adjoining Guild Hall, there's a reception after the concert, an otherwise ordinary affair partly redeemed by the presence of Larry Rivers, who's wearing one of his wonderfully tasteless outfits; the towering Joe Ford, who puts me in mind of Paul Robeson as the Emperor Jones; and the distinguished houseguest of Bobby and Arthur, the glorioius poet Elizabeth Bishop, whom Frank will later describe in a letter as "the sweetest person in the world." And now he rushes over to meet her, having introduced Joe to Arthur and foolishly left them alone. Indeed, he is so thrilled to be in the company of the best female poet since Emily Dickinson—I think that's how both he and Jimmy Schuyler regarded her—that he seems to lose all control of himself, as he kisses her hands and forearms, something she will mention later when being introduced to Frank's sister Maureen.

"Where is Joe?" he asks me when it is time to leave.

"Don't ask," I tell him.

In dead silence, with Larry at the wheel, we drive back to Southampton without Joe, who doesn't turn up until late the next morning, when Frank and I are in the kitchen getting coffee. Without waiting for me to leave, Joe blurts out excuses for his behavior; and as I'm making my exit, I hear him say something about coming under the spell of the music, after which I hear Frank, without rancor, interrupting to say that no apology is necessary and that he certainly understands about the music. "I love Rachmaninoff, too," he says. It is as if nothing happened, as if Frank doesn't care! Later, when I overhear him consoling Joe, insisting that he did nothing wrong, I am truly at a loss to understand Frank's benign behavior.

I wait until we are back in New York before I try to get him to talk about what happened. About all he says is, "Joe felt bad enough without my making him feel any worse."

I never fully understood how he could have been so calm and collected, and so forgiving. Lately, though, I've been thinking so much about Frank—and now about this incident—that I'm convinced I know why he conducted himself as he did. Not only did he want to spare Joe's feelings, he refused to allow himself to be hurt and jealous, or permit himself to show it—that would have been petty of him, and pettiness, I realized years later when we had our big fight and broke up, was to his mind ignoble, contemptible, the eighth deadly sin. One more thing: while he was furious with Arthur and let everyone know what a poacher he was, Frank never had a bad word to say about Joe Ford—but their affair, such as it was, did not survive the weekend.

Picture, if you will, an evening with a motley assemblage of gay men that included Tennessee Williams, Truman Capote, John Bernard Myers, Yukio Mishima, plus Frank and me, and three or four high-class hustlers, a ratio of about one hustler to every three—you can think of us as johns, if you like. The time: the spring of 1958, the period I've just now been mulling over, which explains why the evening suddenly comes to mind. The scene: an apartment Tennessee rented in one of those nondescript hotellike apartment houses with a switchboard, coffee shop, and maid service, a building whose address, 333 West Eighty-sixth Street, gave me a start when Frank mentioned that was where we were going, for I'd lived there seven years earlier, during my brief, inglorious period as a kept boy—not, by a long shot, one of my fondest memories, due in large measure to the oppressive atmosphere of that monolithic apartment house. "What do they think of us?" I remember asking Paul Goodman, "they" being the Jewish staff that ran the place, the snooty guy at the front desk chief among them, "us" being my keeper and me, a wet-behind-the-ears goy who felt out of place, unwelcome, and patronized. "They think you're a couple of suckers," said Paul, quickly, without having to ponder my question.

While my keeper's modest digs consisted of one bedroom, a sitting room, and a kitchenette—awaiting the availability of a large, sprawling apartment that was also on the Upper West Side, he was encamping here in the interim—Tennessee's place was considerably larger, a two-bedroom suite with a good-sized living room and a bona fide kitchen. Also, by design it was about as tacky as you can get, very Diane Arbus, with beaded curtains, unsightly hotel furniture, cheap knickknacks everywhere, deplorable prints on the wall, and lights so dim you immediately felt you were in some wretched and not terribly interesting den of iniquity. No doubt about it, the place appeared to be pretty much what it was, not the abode of a person of taste and sensitivity—Tennessee never really lived there—but an apartment kept expressly for assignations and shabby little parties like the one to which John Myers got us invited. And it was John, come to think of it, who talked Tennessee into renting the apartment and fixing it up like a brothel. "I told Ten," said John, "that he owed it to himself to take the place, so he could kick up his heels and have some fun." Also, presumably, so he could get away from the man he'd been living with for a number of years, an impression John gave when he phoned Frank and issued his invitation: he said it was going to be "a gay bachelor party; no couples, in other words"—thus, Frank Merlo (Tennessee's lover) was conspicuous by his absence, as were Herbert Machiz and Jack Dunphy, the companions, respectively, of John and Truman. And Mishima, on a visit to the United States, was unattached, traveling alone.

John greeted us at the door, several of the guests were chatting with a couple of the hustlers, and, within a few minutes of our arrival, Tennessee made his entrance from the other room, followed by another hustler. Dressed in a fancy brocaded robe—a djellaba?—and smoking an exotic brand of cigarette through a long, elegant holder, Tennessee parted the beaded curtains and stepped inside the room with all of the grace and dignity of Anna May Wong, thereby establishing the mood of the evening, one of camp decadence that discouraged anything like serious debauchery. That was fine by me, as I had a cold and came for one reason: "Tru will be there," John told Frank, and that was all I had to know. I'd met him before and was eager to witness another of his exhilarating performances. How odd, then, that as clearly as I remember looking forward to spending a couple of hours in his company—I'd still be hard pressed to name anyone I ever met more original and amusing than Truman Capote—I now recall nothing about him that night, so it's possible he didn't show up. In fact, apart from the few details I've already given, all I can exhume from my mercurial memory is this disembodied conversational fragment:

> JOE (*with simple curiosity, not coming on to him, as he's far less sexy and good-looking than expected*): I'm curious about something. Do you like Caucasian men?
> MISHIMA: Am I attracted to them?
> JOE: Yes.
> MISHIMA: Very attracted.
> JOE: For any special reason?
> MISHIMA: Their cocks are bigger.
> JOE (*disingenuous*): That's all a myth, isn't it?
> MISHIMA: Come to Japan, see for yourself.

A True Account of Talking to the Sun at Fire Island · 189

From this, I decided that the gifted Yukio Mishima must be a size queen; and now, thirty-odd years later, cognizant of the direction his life took after 1957, I can't resist considering the possibility, admittedly far-out, that his apparent preoccupation with big cocks was so great that it might provide us with one of the keys to understanding why he did what he did when he returned to Japan after his six-month stay in the United States, a reputedly unhappy time for him. Taking for granted that Caucasians are indeed better hung than the Japanese and that the size of a man's equipment, especially if he's gay, can play a decisive role in shaping his character, personality, and destiny, my scenario goes like this: Mishima's marriage in 1958 was a rueful rejection of his homosexuality, his growing obsession with body-building was a pathetic endeavor to compensate for his Japanese cock, and his embrace of emperor-worship was partly a bitter repudiation of the West, whose male populace he resented for being more impressively endowed than the Japanese—all of which led to his decision to commit hara-kiri, wherein his young lieutenant, his lover, went with him to his death. You think my hypothesis, my scenario, is preposterous, specious, plain crazy? I can just hear Frank: "Yes, this time you've gone too far, Joe."

THE DAY LADY DIED

[J U L Y   1 7 ,   1 9 5 9]

It is 12:20 in New York a Friday
three days after Bastille day, yes
it is 1959 and I go get a shoeshine
because I will get off the 4:19 in Easthampton
at 7:15 and then go straight to dinner
and I don't know the people who will feed me

I walk up the muggy street beginning to sun
and have a hamburger and a malted and buy
an ugly NEW WORLD WRITING to see what the poets
in Ghana are doing these days
                                        I go on to the bank
and Miss Stillwagon (first name Linda I once heard)
doesn't even look up my balance for once in her life
and in the GOLDEN GRIFFIN I get a little Verlaine
for Patsy with drawings by Bonnard although I do
think of Hesiod, trans. Richmond Lattimore or
Brendan Behan's new play or *Le Balcon* or *Les Nègres*
of Genet, but I don't, I stick with Verlaine
after practically going to sleep with quandariness
and for Mike I just stroll into the PARK LANE
Liquor Store and ask for a bottle of Strega and

then I go back where I came from to 6th Avenue
and the tobacconist in the Ziegfeld Theatre and
casually ask for a carton of Gauloises and a carton
of Picayunes, and a NEW YORK POST with her face on it

and I am sweating a lot by now and thinking of
leaning on the john door in the 5 SPOT
while she whispered a song along the keyboard
to Mal Waldron and everyone and I stopped breathing

Almost the first thing Mike said to us was, "Hey, that's too bad about Billie Holiday," and he spoke as if the singer had been someone we knew. Was our train on time that Friday? Probably not; the Long Island Railroad was only slightly more reliable in 1959 than it was in subsequent years. One thing for sure, our good friend Mike Goldberg had taken the usual precaution of bringing a thermos of martinis to the station, because if Frank and I had failed to get seats on the parlor car, the only part of the train that served drinks, he knew we'd need a blast the second the 4:19 pulled into East Hampton—not, incidentally, "Easthampton," the way it's spelled in "The Day Lady Died." Of course Mike brought that thermos for himself as well; if our train was late, he could have a drink while he waited. And in my mind's eye I can see him now, stepping smartly out of his attention-getting yet elegantly understated olive-drab Bugatti, waving to us with one hand and holding a drink in the other—which tells me the 4:19 could not have been on time that late afternoon in muggy mid-July. But where is Patsy? Why don't I see Patsy? Aren't we going "straight to dinner," where neither Frank nor I will know "the people who will feed [us]"? Obviously, there's been a change of plans, because here is Mike meeting us by himself, as he usually does, which means Patsy's back at the house on Briar Patch Road, getting her two kids ready for bed.

192 · The Day Lady Died

DIGRESSIONS ON SOME POEMS BY FRANK O'HARA

"We're eating in, the dinner was called off," Mike explains. He hands us plastic glasses and fills them to the brim. Careful not to spill a drop of our precious potion, we step gingerly into the wildly impractical sports car Mike picked up the previous fall while he and Patsy were honeymooning in Italy, and it's then, as he gets behind the wheel, that he comments on Billie Holiday's death.

Sipping our martinis, we talk about how young she was, just forty-four, and what a rough life she had. But Frank makes no mention of the poem he wrote that day, nor was anything said to me about it on the train. "I've been playing her records all afternoon," Mike tells us. He turns on the ignition and sets the Bugatti in motion, the great tumult from its mighty engine making conversation difficult, so that I have to shout to be heard: "Remember when Billie Holiday sang at Loew's Sheridan? Two years ago almost to the day, wasn't it? The next morning we went on Bob Cornell's boat."

I think of Billie Holiday's one-night stand not because I was lucky enough to have heard her but for the opposite reason. For unlike Frank, Mike, Joan Mitchell, Irma Hurley, and Norman Bluhm—we all went on Bob's boat the next morning, which was a Saturday in mid-July—I wasn't willing to stay up until all hours waiting for the legendary singer to appear. Though the performance was scheduled for midnight, it wasn't until after two that she finally came onstage—looking a little lost, Frank told me the next morning as he launched into an account of the performance. I cut him off, said I didn't want to hear—just shut up about it, I told him—and at that moment it became something I wanted to have experienced, a memory I coveted, and for a while I was so hung up on it that I went as far as to lie to someone about having heard Billie Holiday that night.

I guess it was the last time she sang in public, provided you don't count the time—was it nine months or a year later?—that she "whispered a song along the keyboard" at the Five Spot, "whispered" definitely being le mot juste, since her whiny little voice could scarcely be heard, though the place was half empty and unusually quiet. Well, at least I had that memory to savor, I didn't have to lie about hearing her that time. The odd thing was, I almost forgot about it—that is, I don't remember it being in my thoughts later—and even now, as we talk about this beleaguered woman's death, it doesn't occur to me to bring up the night when I actually heard her sing. But then the occasion only became etched in my memory, and perhaps in the memory of others who were there, because of Frank's poem and its last two lines that encapsulate the way she sang and how we reacted.

And now, I'll tell everything I remember about that night at the Five Spot, the shabby, unimposing jazz club at Third Avenue and Fifth Street, which for as long as five or six years was the watering hole of downtown painters, the place to go when they grew tired of the Cedar and wanted to mellow out and listen to the music of, say, Thelonious Monk, Charlie Mingus, or Ornette Coleman. Joe Tremini, a large and friendly man who seemed to like painters, ran the Five Spot, whose walls he covered with posters and announcements of their shows.

As to who among our friends was there the night Billie Holiday sang, I have only the vaguest memory; Mike Goldberg was probably sitting at the same table with us and maybe Norman was there, too, or Matsumi Kane-mitsu. What I do remember, very distinctly, was the excitement that ran through the place when word got around that Billie Holiday had just come in. The table where she sat with Mal Waldron wasn't far from ours, and I re-member looking over at her and thinking how young she looked. Of course it didn't cross our minds that she might sing; because of a dope conviction, she wasn't allowed to perform anyplace where liquor was served—hence, her pathetic gig at the cavernous, inhospitable Loew's Sheridan. Earlier that evening at the Five Spot, had there been one of those inept poetry readings with jazz that never caught on in New York? Possibly, but not with Frank par-ticipating, as he was never so foolish as to involve himself in such ludicrous San Francisco–type shenanigans, more Allen Ginsberg's thing or Kerouac's than Frank's or John's or Jimmy's. And if there had been a reading, Billie Hol-iday wouldn't have been present, because she slipped into the place later, at about one in the morning, I think. A little later, when I was on the point of leaving, she and Mal Waldron rose from their table and moved to the piano. Aware that she was going to sing, I looked around for Frank. I knew he'd gone to the john, but what was taking him so long? It turned out that I had no cause to worry, for he missed nothing—in fact, the john door he leaned against was closer to the piano than our table was.

To me, Billie Holiday seemed remote, even unapproachable, and it was hard to imagine anyone having the temerity to stare at her or otherwise draw attention to her, much less actually speak to her: it was like being in the presence of—not God but Garbo, whom I actually saw at Ruth Ford's once and could have met had I been bold enough to approach her. Anyway, that was my impression of what it was like to be at the Five Spot that night—a far cry from the recollections of Kenneth Koch; his is a different story altogether, for it turns out he's part of the story, a version trotted out in two parts. Part one came to light in 1983. It was on a panel at the University of Connecticut dealing with Frank's life and work that Kenneth playfully alluded to his (Kenneth's) appearing on the same program with the singer, coyly allowing as to how he never dreamed of such a thing ever happening, and he gave the impression that she was a paid performer that night at the Five Spot, since he seemed not to know she was barred from singing at such places.

Part two, unveiled seven years later, found Kenneth—along with John Ashbery and me—on another panel, when he remembered more details, even quoted what Billie Holiday said to him after his reading. "It's crazy, man," she allegedly told him, referring to his poetry. Oh, would the divine Lady Day really have been that corny, said anything so hackneyed, obvious, and uncool? I hope not. And when someone from the audience asked what song she sang, Kenneth came up with a title without missing a beat, like a magician pulling a rabbit out of his hat. What in heaven's name, I asked myself, will he have remembered by the time of the next O'Hara panel! (The answer: at a subsequent O'Hara-related event he was asked what Billie Holiday sang that night; in response, he reeled off the titles of three songs!) Now what is the truth, what really happened? It is entirely possible that I have a lot of the details wrong. On the other hand, maybe Kenneth wasn't there at all, maybe the night Billie Holiday sang at the Five Spot is for him what the Loew's Sheridan performance was for me.

The Day Lady Died · 195

So we made drinks, Patsy, Mike, Frank, and I, and we sat on the large screened-in porch of the house Mike and Patsy had rented for the summer. Mike put on a Billie Holiday record and Patsy brought out a tray of hors d'oeuvres and Frank said he'd written a poem about Billie Holiday that afternoon and took it out of his pocket and read it.

DIGRESSION ON *NUMBER 1,* 1948
and
JACKSON POLLOCK: A MONOGRAPH

[D E C E M B E R 2 0 , 1 9 5 6 / 1 9 5 9]

I am ill today but I am not
too ill. I am not ill at all.
It is a perfect day, warm
for winter, cold for fall.

A fine day for seeing. I see
ceramics, during lunch hour by
Miró and I see the sea by Léger;
Light, complicated Metzingers
and a rude awakening by Brauner,
a little table by Picasso, pink.

I am tired today but I am not
too tired. I am not tired at all.
There is the Pollock, white, harm
will not fall, his perfect hand

and the many short voyages. They'll
never fence the silver range.

Stars are out and there is sea
enough beneath the glistening earth
to bear me toward the future
which is not so dark. I see.

'm all set to write a note about Frank's Pollock monograph and his Pollock
poem when, to my surprise, I draw a blank—I have nothing to say. Except
this: one Sunday morning in late summer 1959, I was up so much earlier
than Frank that before he'd groggily made his way to the kitchen, I'd pe-
rused the *Times* and the *Tribune,* and had even read, word for word, what a
critic on the *Trib* had to say about Frank's recently published Pollock book.
"Frank, wait'll you read what Emily Genauer says about your book," I called
to him. True to form, he didn't rush over to find out what she wrote, and
what's more, when he finally got around to reading her scathing comments,
all he did was toss aside the paper and say, dismissively, "She's a fool."

Not much for one of my digressions.

I need something to coax my memory. Perhaps the close proximity of the
book will help, will act as a charm. So I put it in front of me, next to my computer, and stare at its cover:

The Great American Artists Series

JACKSON POLLOCK
BY FRANK O'HARA

over 80 reproductions   16 in full color

Inside, embedded in its text, is "Digression on *Number 1, 1948*," and I turn
to it. Lovely poem—but nothing comes to me. I start over, with the book. I
look it over—nothing. I open it to the title page—again, nothing. I glance at
the table of contents—still nothing. I turn to the acknowledgments—
eureka! Something clicks, finally, when my eyes fall upon "It is to Grace Hartigan that I owe an awareness of certain aspects of Pollock's genius, and to
Larry Rivers a particular appreciation of the beauties of *Number 29,* 1950,"

and my memory, as reliable as my computer, promptly calls up an incident that hasn't crossed my mind since it occurred on a midsummer afternoon in 1959, at Georgica Beach, where, in those days, East Hampton artists—accompanied by their friends, lovers, spouses, kids, hangers-on—had picnics at dusk and barbecues after nightfall, but steered clear of the seashore in the middle of the day, never to my knowledge taking time out to lie in the sun or go in the water, their reluctance to leave their studios as invariable as their drinking at the end of the day, in some cases during the day.

Lee Pollock—that was how we all referred to her then—was particularly disdainful of the beach scene, so it must have been closer to twilight than midday when she made her appearance at Georgica. Still, it was a surprise to see her.

"There's Lee," said Frank, who had just come out of the water.

"You serious?" I said, stirring from my sun-induced quasi-dormant state.

He waved to her as he dried himself. "I can't imagine what she's doing here at this hour."

Just that week, he'd received advance copies of the Pollock book, and now he wanted to find out if she'd received her copy. He finished drying himself, then went over to where she was standing, perhaps fifty yards away, while I, for the moment, was content to remain where our beach towels were spread out, confident that Lee was happy with what he had written and that Frank would be happy to hear what she had to say. How could I, or Frank for that matter, not feel confident? While he was working on the book, hadn't he discussed it with her, asked her questions, been told that she went along with his approach, liked his ideas? And as I recall—I could be wrong about this—she was thrilled by the epigraph about Scriabin, even though she may not have known or liked the idiosyncratic Russian's music. But then, it would have been surprising if she hadn't been moved by Pasternak's words (from *I Remember*) and Frank's echoing response that, together, so expeditiously set up his rapturous tribute to her late husband:

> Art is full of things that everyone knows about, of generally acknowledged truths. Although everyone is free to use them, the generally accepted prin-

ciples have to wait a long time before they find an application. A generally acknowledged truth must wait for a rare piece of luck, a piece of luck that smiles upon it only once in a hundred years, before it can find application. Such a piece of luck was Scriabin. Just as Dostoievsky is not only a novelist and just as Blok is not only a poet, so Scriabin is not only a composer, but an occasion for congratulations, a personified festival and triumph of Russian culture.

"And so is Jackson Pollock such an occasion for American culture," Frank audaciously asserts in the salvo that opens his monograph.

That's quite a stretch, from Scriabin to Pollock—and how characteristic of Frank! Then, in another bold stroke, there's his poem about the Modern's great Pollock; he never mentioned it to Lee, so she must have been as surprised by its appearance as she was by the Pasternak quotation.

The poem was written in the year of Pollock's death, and here is my scenario of how it landed in Frank's monograph. He had put the poem away and forgotten all about it until one day, as he was working on the Pollock book and had just reached the section about the paintings between 1947 and 1950, he suddenly thought of a poem he'd never published, his "Digression on *Number 1, 1948*." Why not have his tribute to Pollock, all in prose, burst suddenly into poetry? And while he was at it, did he then decide to quote those lines from his "great predecessor" that border upon, and are subtly relevant to, the paragraphs in which he discusses Pollock's mythic and totemic paintings? While he indicates that the quotation is from Whitman, he doesn't tell us that it is from "Song of the Open Road," the first lines, to be exact, of the seventh stanza:

> Here is the efflux of the soul,
> The efflux of the soul comes from within through
>   embower'd gates, ever provoking questions,
> These yearnings why are they? these thoughts in the
>   darkness why are they?

When Frank's own poem appears a couple of pages later, it's not keyed into the text where you would expect it, when *Number 1* is first mentioned, but instead, like a foretoken, it's inserted two paragraphs before he begins telling us how great the painting is. And surely, it belongs in his book, if only because it strikes the same personal, unacademic note as the text of his paean to Jackson Pollock, a painter whose revolutionary art he regards so highly that he ranks him alongside Willem de Kooning, whom he reveres above all living American artists: ". . . Pollock is the Ingres, and de Kooning the Delacroix, of Action Painting. Their greatness is equal, but antithetical. Because of this, to deny one would be to deny the other."

After the poem comes a marvelous description of *Number 1*'s powerful impact: its "ecstatic, irritable, demanding force" and its "incredible speed and nervous legibility"—"energy made visible," as the subtitle of B. H. Friedman's book on Pollock reminds us. And now that I think about it, Lee must have come to the beach that day with Bob and Abby, because back then, Lee and the Friedmans seemed to be inseparable, were such close friends that the Friedmans named their son after Jackson. I think they must have been as fond of Lee as Frank and I were. "A Jewish dream like Lillian Hellman," a friend of mine pronounced after meeting her, and indeed the two were a great deal alike, both radiant in their craggy homeliness, both formidable powerhouses with a bevy of loyal, loving, long-suffering friends.

All right, you have the picture: I'm lying on the beach, about to go over and say hello, and then—but what's going on? Lee's hands are on her hips, aggressively, and her feet, wide apart, are planted in the sand, as if to hold her ground. In this posture, brooking no interference in her onslaught, she unleashes what is clearly a barrage of angry words; it causes Frank to flinch, as indeed I do, watching the scene unfold, trying without success to catch what she's saying.

Mercifully, the scene is a short one, and that is because of Frank, who offers no riposte; he simply shrugs when Lee has finished and returns to where I'm lying on a beach towel—no, by then I've gotten to my feet, concerned, anxious, curious to know what in God's name Lee could possibly have said to him. Yes, I remember all of this very clearly, but only the essence of the scene, for nothing else comes to mind about it, who else was around or whether the beach was crowded, my memory never more selective, embracing as it does only the two of them, figures isolated on a surreal, empty beach. And if it were a scene in a movie, it would be in long shot and from my point of view—until, of course, Frank appears in medium close-up and I come into the frame. "What was wrong with Lee?" I ask him. "What'd she say to you?"

No answer; Frank lights a Camel to calm his nerves.

"She doesn't approve of the book, she doesn't like it?" I continue. "That can't be, Frank—"

He cuts me off. "It's the acknowledgments," he says quietly, thoughtfully. "She's furious about the acknowledgments."

I'm nonplussed. "The *acknowledgments*?" I say, truly bewildered now. "You thanked her—"

"Along with a lot of other people," he reminds me.

I ask if that's what's bothering her. "Maybe you shouldn't have lumped her in with Clem Greenberg and the others," I say, trying to make sense of her behavior.

"Yes, I'm sure she didn't like that," he tells me. "But it was the mention of two people she hates that infuriated her—that, and the fact that I singled them out from the others."

"Grace and Larry?" I say immediately, but it's more a statement than a question, since I remember they were given special mention and, moreover, I know that they're at the top of Lee's hate list.

Frank nods. "Unbelievable, isn't it?" he says, but without much conviction. He must have felt as I did, that his commendation might have appeared excessive—akin, perhaps, to the way a lovesick person brings up, for no good reason, the loved one's name in conversation. Still, Lee had no right to call Frank to account. How controlling and egomaniacal can you get!—that, as much as I liked Lee, was my immediate response, very close to what I remember telling Frank. But Frank, as I recall, simply shrugged, the way he had when Lee finished her diatribe.

That night, when we saw her at Alfonso Ossorio's, you would have thought her earlier encounter with Frank had not taken place. Willing to let bygones be bygones, as though Frank and not she had been out of line, she promptly brought up the subject of his book and said how much she liked it, then referred specifically to the section that dealt with, among other paintings, the sublime *Lavender Mist,* whose transcendent beauty—for me, the visual equivalent of a delicate perfume—Frank and I feasted our eyes on whenever we came to The Creeks. It hung in one of the larger rooms, with a marvelous Dubuffet nearby, and I believe Lee must have noticed our gazing at it that evening. Yes, that must have been what happened; and, drink in hand, she probably came over and joined us—an ideal opening for her to say something conciliatory to Frank. But all I recall, with any certainty, is Lee telling him how much she liked his description of the painting, which is actually nothing more than a parenthetical reference to the way it "fuses in a passionate exhalation"—and, subito, the incident on the beach was behind them.

"That's it?" I said to Frank later. "You've settled your differences?"

"It looks that way, doesn't it?" he said, with a laugh—and never gave the matter another thought, so far as I know.

And Lee? I can't imagine she suffered any qualms, for it was my impression she wasn't the sort to look back, to regret or question anything she'd done—very much like Frank, if I'm right about her, and maybe that was why he was so quick to forgive her. Also, I can't imagine that this strong-willed woman missed a beat, that she didn't simply go right on to the next dispute, controversy, or confrontation occasioned by the life and work of Jackson Pollock. For, no question about it, this storm in a teacup was at least partly triggered by her obsession with her late husband, an obsession so consuming that she must have felt she owned him, owned his memory as she did so many of his paintings. Though an artist herself, she emerged in the years after Pollock's death as an artist's widow *sans pareil.*

In this instance, however, her conduct was immoderate, as indeed it so often was in relation to her colleagues in the art world. Which doesn't mean she was all that different from her peers, many of whom were as antagonistic toward certain other artists as she was. It's just that Lee cast a wider net— why, she would like to have seen about half of the artists on the scene disappear, or so it seemed to me. And her rancor increased with the years. "Bill de

K. and Elaine de K.," she was given to muttering sometime in the late seventies, punching out their truncated names as though they were epithets. "Now they *both* live down the road," she would complain, in the eighties, when Elaine moved to Springs to look after Bill. Whether she liked it or not, the detested woman was there to stay, ensconced in Bill's sprawling sanctum sanctorum on Woodbine Drive off Fireplace Road, closer to where Jackson's car careened out of control than to the modest Pollock-Krasner house. As for Bill—frankly, I don't know how Lee could have stomached Frank's reference to his greatness being equal to her husband's. Frank, I gathered, was at a loss on that score, too, and perhaps the only possible explanation is that Lee was so preoccupied with the prominent mention of Grace and Larry that the de Kooning passage went right by her. Another thing, Bill wasn't some upstart. Older than either Lee or Jackson, which in itself must have been some consolation to Lee, he'd struggled for years and not had his first one-man show until he was forty-four—a far cry from the circumstances that marked the meteoric rise of Grace and Larry, eleven and twelve years younger than Lee but already, by 1959, far more successful.

RHAPSODY

[J U L Y   3 0 ,   1 9 5 9]

... when I see Gianni I know he's thinking of John Ericson
playing the Rachmaninoff 2nd or Elizabeth Taylor
taking sleeping-pills ...

The title of this poem is an *hommage*, if you will, to the mediocre 1954
movie *Rhapsody,* as is clear from these lines. Vittorio Gassman also
starred in this sentimental, overwrought love story with a European music conservatory setting and a score consisting mainly of Rachmaninoff's
Second Piano Concerto, which modest, touching, but very sexy John Ericson simulated playing, and the Tchaikovsky Violin Concerto (or was it the
Mendelssohn?) "played" by Gassman in the role of the macho, self-centered
violinist. Elizabeth Taylor takes sleeping pills when she's spurned by the violinist and then is nursed back to health by the pianist, whom she realizes she
loves just before the fade-out. Frank, Gianni Bates, and I saw *Rhapsody* together at the Loew's Lexington, when we all lived uptown; they loved it while
I simply wasn't in the mood for its old-fashioned M-G-M gloss, and they
teased me for being such a humorless stick-in-the-mud. And now, five years
later, Frank suddenly remembers the damn movie! Why? Not one to forget
someone of whom he was once enamored, Frank thinks of Gianni because
of their brief affair a year after Gianni and I broke up—an affair, incidentally,
I knew nothing of until after Frank's death, when Gianni casually alluded to
it ("He was like a bird—I didn't realize how frail he was"), and I surprised

myself by feeling pleased, a response that would have surprised and pleased Frank even more.

In *The Norton Anthology of Modern Poetry,* which includes "Rhapsody" along with eight other poems of Frank's, there's a footnote that identifies Gianni as a pianist. Where do you suppose they got that from? Where else but the opening lines of "To Gianni Bates," which Frank wrote around the time we saw *Rhapsody* together: "Like a piano concerto your black / and white eyes, your white face and bright black hair . . ." What resourceful research by the Norton editor! The concerto Frank had in mind was, I suspect, the one for two pianos by Poulenc that Frank and Gianni heard Gold and Fizdale play at Lewisohn Stadium the previous summer.

AT JOAN'S

[J U L Y   3 1 ,   1 9 5 9]

It is almost three
I sit at the marble top
sorting poems, miserable
the little lamp glows feebly
I don't glow at all

I have another cognac
and stare at two little paintings
of Jean-Paul's, so great
I must do so much
or did they just happen

the breeze is cool
barely a sound filters up
through my confused eyes
I am lonely for myself
I can't find a real poem

if it won't happen
what shall I do

Seldom, if ever, has Frank been as immediate and direct as he is in the seventeen lines of "At Joan's." But this is also, for me, a poem that is deceptively simple, since it has more going on in it, or *behind* it, than a casual reader might suspect. As I hope to demonstrate, it sets the scene for what I presume to call the Vincent Warren period, some twenty-two months, from August 10, 1959, to May 20, 1961, during which Frank wrote many of his most beautiful poems, including his love poems to, for, or about Vincent, which are among his finest achievements.

In 1959, Joan Mitchell left us the keys to her studio apartment when she went to live in Paris. That meant we could take turns getting away from the din and grime of East Ninth Street. As I mentioned earlier, her place was downtown, and it was even nearer to us now than when we lived on University Place: all we had to do was walk one block south and a block and a half west, and we'd be at 60 St. Mark's Place, the respectable apartment house where Joan lived from 1952 through 1958. It was after that, after she settled in France, that the place became her American pied-à-terre—and our home away from home when she wasn't in town, which was most of the year.

In 1959, during the summer months, I had access to it one week and Frank had it the next. While I used it mostly for what might be called assignations, I also liked hanging out there by myself for the same reason Frank did, because it was so still and secluded. "Barely a sound filters up" puts it very well, the apartment being on the fourth floor of a well-insulated building in the middle of the street's quiet block. In a few years, St. Mark's would become the ear-splitting hub of hippiedom, but in 1959 it was rather middle class; and Joan's place, that winter and spring and on into summer, offered us much-needed respite from the pandemonium of East Ninth Street. Another thing, in the summer months it was infinitely cooler than our joint, which had no cross-ventilation—oh, it was a wonderful home away from home all right; too bad Joan began subletting a couple of years later.

It was a commodious, high-ceilinged room, its space divided into two areas, the studio being considerably larger than the living area. Every inch of the place was immaculate and in perfect order thanks to our friend's compulsive nature. With infinite care, she had her personal things put away and her large, rolled-up canvases neatly stacked up against the wall, while her kitchen, which she rarely used, was spotless and cockroach free. What the place offered us was the solace and peace and quiet we hadn't enjoyed since our pre–Jimmy Schuyler days on East Forty-ninth Street.

For Frank, the night of July 31, 1959, was not an occasion that could be described in such glowing terms. It was his turn to take the place for the coming week, and he must have looked forward to it. But what awaited him that night "at Joan's" was only misery, doubt, and frustration, all because of what was spread out on the marble top of Joan's sturdy round table, what he would spend much of the night poring over, sorting, tossing aside, grumbling about, sighing over: a smorgasbord of canary-yellow second sheets with occasional pieces of decent white typing paper and Museum of Modern Art stationery interspersed. It was everything he had written since the publication of *Meditations in an Emergency,* along with a lot of earlier, hitherto unpublished poems, and yet there is not one poem he can find that turns him on. "I don't glow at all," he tells us, summing up his mood that night.

It has been two years since Barney Rosset published *Meditations,* and now he has let Frank know that Grove Press would like to bring out another collection of his poems. No contract has been drawn up, so it's up to Frank to follow through. That means deciding what poems to include, phoning and reminding Grove Press of their proposal, making a fair copy of the poems, and getting the manuscript over to them. These boring, time-consuming details would take him away from a lot of things he'd rather be doing. Oh, if only he could be more like Kenneth Koch, his good and loyal friend, a determined and ambitious poet who never tires of pushing his career, he'd have a new book in the stores before the year is out. The trouble is—to begin with— Frank can't find what he confidently feels is a "real poem."

Thus, instead of getting on with it, he stares at two miniature paintings, the only works Joan has hanging in the entire place. Somehow they make him feel inadequate, as though he can never create anything "so great." Highly personal in the sense that they've never been exhibited and are presents to Joan from her lover, Jean-Paul Riopelle, the French Canadian artist who made them, they are indeed "little paintings," something like 12" x 10", very special, one-of-a-kind works that are as extraordinary as Frank suggests, luxuriant tachist paintings created as much by palette knife as by loaded brush, impasto paintings so thick and heavy that it seems a miracle the paint adheres to those two scraps of canvas. Yet however small, they are as vibrant and forceful as the artist's large-scale paintings, works that in recent years have made him famous in Europe. But aren't some of Frank's own small works comparable? Take the fifteen-line poem he wrote earlier that day, the one called "Song" ("Is it dirty / does it look dirty / that's what you think of in the city")—why, it's as terrific as some of his longer, more ambitious poems, and so is "Rhapsody," which he wrote yesterday. Then there's "The Day Lady Died," dashed off after lunch two weeks ago. Wouldn't you think the two little Riopelles would encourage and inspire him? But they don't; he feels dejected, "lonely for myself."

The phrase haunts me; something other than doubts about one's work is suggested. And somehow it brings to mind his coming home one evening—was it two, three weeks before his miserable night at Joan's?—and saying, "I have something to talk to you about."

It was the end of a long day at the museum, the time of day we jokingly called "our cocktail hour"—jokingly, as should be obvious, because of its duration, which was more like three hours than one. In fact, it was that very evening that I decided to do something about the situation. "I want to talk to you, too," I said. "Make our drinks," I went on, seeing that he already had an ice tray out, "and I'll set the alarm clock." He looked at me, nonplussed, and I explained that the cocktail hour should be taken literally. Was I serious or was it a charade? I suppose I was just trying to make a point. In any event, when the alarm went off an hour later, we hadn't started dinner, and how can you prepare a meal without a drink handy? So my temperance campaign was nipped in the bud, aborted also because we laughed uproariously when the alarm went off. I guess it was the only time I ever tried to do something about—I started to say *our* drinking but it was really Frank I was thinking of, as he usually had two drinks to my one.

"Shall we have another drink or should we start dinner?" I said. It was

DIGRESSIONS ON SOME POEMS BY FRANK O'HARA

then, as I began taking things out of the fridge, that he reminded me he had something on his mind. "Why don't we sit down," he said. "Something the matter?" I said, following him into the living room. When he turned off the radio, which was playing a terrific piece of music, I knew it had to be something serious.

"As long as we're living together," he began, "there's no way either of us is ever going to have a serious love affair."

Right away I started to interrupt—I hated what he was saying, dreaded what he was going to say—but he wouldn't let me get a word in as he went on to describe our relationship as frustrating and incomplete. "We're neither lovers nor mere friends, and we're certainly not ordinary roommates," he said. Then he wanted to know how I felt.

This was the first time either of us had alluded to the ambiguous nature of our relationship, and I certainly didn't want to talk about it now, or at any time, my philosophy being that if you don't admit you have a problem, then none exists. I took things as they came, I didn't worry unduly.

"Have the past four years really been so terrible?" I said at last, hoping to put him on the defensive.

"You know that's not how I feel," he said. "You also know what I'm talking about."

The truth of the matter was, our arrangement suited me fine; I couldn't imagine not living with Frank, and my love life, a fairly rapacious one of sex with attractive strangers, sometimes with guys I actually got to know, was a source of continuing excitement.

We sat for a while in silence, until I finally came right out and asked if he thought we should split up.

"You don't think we should?" he said, as though that was exactly what was on his mind.

"No," I said. "I like our life together—why would I want us to separate?" I told him that we could have had an affair but eventually it would have come to an end, as all affairs do, and what we had together, what we had now, need never end. "I don't want it to end, I would be unhappy without you," I concluded.

At Joan's · 211

"All right," Frank said, getting to his feet, "we don't ever have to talk about this again."

From all of this, it is clear that I was no longer thinking of Frank's well-being as I had in the past, when I couldn't be happy unless I thought he was happy. Of course I was fooling myself, but at least I was thinking of him. Certainly, given his refusal or inability to depersonalize sex, there was no way he could ever have been content with our arrangement. But did that occur to me? No, it did not; I thought only of myself.

So now, forty years later, I reproach myself; and taking into account the emotional context in which "At Joan's" was written, I can only conclude that Frank's unhappiness, his discontent, was at the root of his dissatisfaction with his poems. For if he was lonely for himself, it was because he missed some-one—someone unknown to him, someone he might never meet. Then there is the phrase "if it won't happen to me," which surely refers not only to his fear of not writing another decent poem but also to his fear that he will never again find love. No wonder he writes, "I don't glow at all." But in the next two poems, we'll see an opportunity opening up for him and we'll then see him making his move, taking advantage of that opportunity.

ADIEU TO NORMAN,
BON JOUR TO JOAN AND JEAN-PAUL

[AUGUST 7, 1959]

It is 12:10 in New York and I am wondering
if I will finish this in time to meet Norman for lunch
ah lunch! I think I am going crazy
what with my terrible hangover and the weekend coming up
at excitement-prone Kenneth Koch's
I wish I were staying in town and working on my poems
at Joan's studio for a new book by Grove Press
which they will probably not print
but it is good to be several floors up in the dead of night
wondering whether you are any good or not
and the only decision you can make is that you did it

yesterday I looked up the rue Frémicourt on a map
and was happy to find it like a bird
flying over Paris et ses environs
which unfortunately did not include Seine-et-Oise which I don't know
as well as a number of other things
and Allen is back talking about god a lot
and Peter is back not talking very much

and Joe has a cold and is not coming to Kenneth's
although he is coming to lunch with Norman
I suspect he is making a distinction
well, who isn't . . .

From the date of this poem, we see that a week has passed since the night Frank doubted he had a "real poem" in him and then proceeded to write one. Now it is Friday, August 7, and plans have been made for Frank and me to spend the weekend with Kenneth and Janice Koch in Southampton. The last weekend with them, we went home with Mike and Patsy after a wild party on Friday night and didn't see Kenneth again until late Sunday evening when, en route home on the 7:56 from East Hampton, he met us at the Southampton station where he handed us our weekend bags. Somehow, that doesn't bode well for the coming weekend. Besides, I have a cold and would rather spend the weekend at Joan's, alone. So is this note going to be about me? Well, inasmuch as I figure in the poem's gestation—indeed, caused it to be written!—it is appropriate that I take center stage for a while . . .

This is a pleasant period in my life. Each morning when I awake, which can be any time I like, I feel happy just by being able to remind myself that I am jobless and collecting unemployment insurance. I have the day to myself—I can do whatever I please. And while it isn't my nature to feel guilty when idle, I am happy in the knowledge that my time isn't being wasted: I'm reading Proust and trying my hand at writing poetry when I'm not working on the play I began at University Place. But the morning of August 7, I am up earlier than usual so I can finish my poem on the occasion of Norman Bluhm's departure for Paris. I get right to it, because we're meeting him for lunch at Larré's, and I want to give it to him there. It's a very simple poem, based on a dream I had a couple of nights ago, and I finish it an hour and a half before I'm due to meet Norman and Frank. Then I decide to phone Frank at the museum. "You're the poet," I tell him. "You're the one who should be writing him a poem. I feel funny giving him something if you don't."

"Are you suggesting that *I* write him a poem?"

"You have time, don't you?"

"Are you serious? It's almost twelve and we're meeting him at one. If I had an idea, it'd be different."

"You'll get one. Try."

We ring off. I read over my poem, full of doubts about it:

TO NORMAN, EN VOYAGE

For the first time
Norman appears in a dream
which is rather like
an appropriate epigraph
to a very long novel.
But about the dream
I remember very little.
Only that his mother
is with him,
a young, cranky woman.
We are traveling together,
the three of us.
"She looks younger than you,"
I tell him.
"I could marry her,"
he answers.
"Noblesse"
is all I say to that,
and Norman understands.

And now it is Friday, August 7th.
I am awake,
Norman is going away,
his mother is in Chicago, I think,

and I will remain here,
in New York.
What did the dream mean?
Should I go back to analysis?
There is so little
one understands about life,
or dreams,
which I confuse with life,
that it is nice to be able
to cling to something
simple and real
like missing someone.

Not bad, I tell myself—and good enough, it turns out, to land in the posthumous *Poems Retrieved,* a misreading corrected in the revised 1996 edition (at the time of Frank's death, the manuscript was in the possession of Norman Bluhm, who sent it to Don Allen when he was assembling Frank's poems).

Oddly, I remember nothing about the lunch except that Frank arrived late, in a very good mood, and said to me, almost immediately, "Do you want to read your poem first?" Years later, wondering if my memory was playing tricks, I mentioned the two poems to Norman and asked what he remembered. He was no help; all he knew was that he had copies of two poems and both, he assumed, were written by Frank. Well, I'll stick to my guns. Not only did Frank not have time to write two poems, he wouldn't have written anything like "Should I go back to analysis?" since he never went to a shrink, and besides, he didn't remember his dreams the way I did.

No matter: the other poem is the one that matters. And what a remarkable piece of writing it is! Having no idea for a poem, he must have immediately begun typing away in that brisk hunt-and-peck way of his the minute he was off the phone. He simply set down what was happening at the moment and waited for a poem to emerge.

Although Vincent's name isn't mentioned, he's in the poem as far as I'm concerned, indirectly, by implication, so that I'm tempted to regard it as the first poem of the Vincent Warren period—on account of one line, just one line: "and Joe has a cold and is not coming to Kenneth's." To which Frank could have added, "and Vincent is coming instead," which I only learned that morning when he casually apprised me of his plans.

I couldn't have been more surprised. Unlike several others of us who had our eyes on the winsome and radiant young dancer—he'd joined us for a couple of TV evenings at John Button's—Frank had not expressed any special interest in him. "Sly fox," I said when he explained he'd seen Vincent somewhere recently and then decided to call him last night. "How convenient," I added, "that I came down with a cold."

It was no wonder he was in such a good mood at lunch, since in a couple of hours he would be meeting Vincent at Penn Station, where they will be "entraining to Southampton in the parlor car with Jap," Jap being Jasper Johns, who's spending the weekend someplace else, not at "excitement-prone Kenneth Koch's." On Friday or Saturday, as I remember, Anne and Fairfield Porter were having a lawn party, and the other night there was going to be a buffet given by Mary Abbott and her husband at the time, Tom Clyde, who in those days entertained frequently, lavishly, and very successfully. If that weren't enough to give me second thoughts about staying in town, the forecast was for perfect weather right through the weekend. But this would probably be my last chance to sleep at Joan's; she and Jean-Paul would be using the apartment during their stay in New York, and then, before they left, she might not think to give the keys back to us. (She didn't.)

> I wish I were staying in town and working on my poems
> at Joan's studio for a new book by Grove Press
> which they will probably not print

Frank tells us in the poem he gave Norman at lunch. Well, don't believe any of it, as I think our poet is being facetious: it was improbable that Barney Rosset would turn down any manuscript Frank submitted (Barney said as much recently when I asked him about it); Frank couldn't have stayed at Joan's even if he wanted to, since it was my turn to have the place; and it was highly unlikely that he wanted to risk having another miserable night working on his poems when he could be with the lovely person he'd lined up for the week-end. So he's happy to go away for a couple of days, just as I'm content to stay in town, where I can nurse my cold in the comfort of Joan's apartment, lie around and read more Proust, and clean the place up for Joan and Jean-Paul, who will be arriving first thing Monday.

JOE'S JACKET

[A U G U S T   1 0 ,   1 9 5 9]

. . . and soon I am rising for the less than average day, I have coffee
I prepare calmly to face almost everything that will come up I am calm
but not as my bed was calm as it softly declined to become a ship
I borrow Joe's seersucker jacket though he is still asleep I start out
when I last borrowed it I was leaving there it was on my Spanish plaza
    back
and hid my shoulders from San Marco's pigeons was jostled on the
    Kurfürstendamm
and sat opposite Ashes in an enormous leather chair in the Continental
it is all enormity and life it has protected me and kept me here on
many occasions as a symbol does when the heart is full and risks no
    speech
a precaution I loathe as the pheasant loathes the season and is preserved
it will not be need, it will be just what it is and just what happens

am "still up and we talk / only of the immediate present and its indiscrimi-
nately hitched-to past." And it's as though Frank and I haven't seen each
other for at least a month, we have so much to say to each other: the weekend was wonderful, he is crazy about Vincent, my cold is better, I finished
Swann in Love, Jasper didn't ask after me or wonder where I was, Patsy was
upset when she saw Frank arrive at the Porters' lawn party with someone
other than me, Kenneth read aloud the libretto he's writing for Virgil Thom-

son, and yes, I tell him, I cleaned Joan's place, put everything in order. One of us brings up another practical matter: the rent—it has to be paid by the tenth, which is tomorrow, and we always make sure that the disgruntled, homophobic super gets our check at the last minute, just as he's sitting down to dinner. One of us writes out a check, and then we turn in. And the very next day, possibly that morning, maybe as soon as Frank is seated at his desk at the museum, the outpouring of poems begins: first, of course, the superlative and moving "Joe's Jacket," followed by—but now we're moving into the Vincent Warren period, and we don't want to get ahead of ourselves, so let's zero in on "Joe's Jacket."

It was seersucker, from Brooks Brothers. I picked up my first one in 1949, for $25.00, which is all they cost in those days. I was fresh from Los Angeles and somewhat ashamed of it, and I wanted to be taken for a preppie—how pretentious I was! You'll recall my wearing it to the Oak Room of the Plaza. Back in the fifties and early sixties, we wore them every summer until they were too shabby looking and then it was time to buy another one. Frank and I often wore each other's clothes, as we were about the same height and build, so his borrowing my jacket was not unusual. And it became the title of his poem. Why? What does the jacket represent to him?

Marjorie Perloff's reading in *Frank O'Hara: Poet Among Painters* hits the mark, I think. It is, she writes, "the talisman that protects Frank from daily misfortunes; as a synecdoche, it stands, of course, for Joe's love. But Frank also resents its protection ('a precaution I loathe'), and in a second, ironic sense, Joe's jacket is his straitjacket. 'Entraining' with Vincent, he ultimately returns to Joe. The jacket is, then, an ordering principle which the poet alternately needs and resents."

Picking up from there, I would add that Frank in his resentment (which may be too strong a word) is beginning to feel the urge to free himself of the "precaution I loathe" symbolized by the jacket. Ambivalent about me—how can it be otherwise, given the ambiguous, less than satisfying nature of our relationship?—he wants something else and realizes, in Vincent, that he may have found it at last. In other words, he wants the unattainable: happiness.

DIGRESSIONS ON SOME POEMS BY FRANK O'HARA

I am not, however, so audacious as to delve into the singular depths of this poem. And academic critical analysis I of course leave to others. But I would like to explore something that comes up a number of times in Frank's poetry—glancingly elsewhere, here painstakingly and with great seriousness: his excessive drinking. With intense self-awareness, he tells us:

> I drink to smother my sensitivity for a while so I won't
> stare away
> I drink to kill the fear of boredom, the mounting panic of it
> I drink to reduce my seriousness so a certain spurious charm
> can appear and win its flickering little victory over noise
> I drink to die a little and increase the contrast of this
> questionable moment

In all the years I knew Frank and all the times I saw him drink more than any of the rest of us, I witnessed his passing out—I mean, literally collapsing—only once, the time Norman and Cary Bluhm came to dinner not long before they were married, Norman wanting his beautiful, elegant fiancée to become better acquainted with Frank, the apple of his eye, and Frank, exhausted from too much work at the Modern and too much drinking before the modest dinner we sat down to in our dreadful digs on East Ninth Street, got through the meal all right, indeed succeeded in reducing his "seriousness so a certain spurious charm / [could] appear," but after dinner, desirous "to die a little," he suddenly did a quick jig, bent over, dropped his pants as if to moonlight, and spread his cheeks before keeling over, as Norman moved to break his fall. He was out, truly out, and it was a wonder he was able to perform his improvisation before being blown away. When Cary showed no signs of being shocked or offended and instead was delighted, it became clear to me, as I'm sure it was to Norman, that he had found the right woman to share a life that would undoubtedly incorporate such goings-on.

Perhaps that was partly why Frank drank so much, because, thanks to his friends' permissiveness, he could overindulge with impunity. He was almost encouraged to do so. I don't remember hearing anyone ever say anything

Joe's Jacket · 221

remotely like, "Frank, you've had enough." The fact is, he couldn't get enough—enough of life. Not only capable of utterances like, "If I had my way, I'd go on and on and on and never go to sleep," he also meant what he said and truly felt that way—hence, understandably, he wanted to dull his senses, exhaust himself, make sleep possible. And the times when the workaday world closed in on him—how did he stand all the paperwork at the Modern?—he would drink "to kill the fear of boredom, the mounting panic of it."

THE VINCENT WARREN PERIOD

[1 9 5 9 – 6 1]

YOU ARE GORGEOUS AND I'M COMING

Vaguely I hear the purple roar of the torn-down Third Avenue El
it sways slightly but firmly like a hand or a golden-downed thigh
normally I don't think of sounds as colored unless I'm feeling corrupt
concrete Rimbaud obscurity of emotion which is simple and very definite
even lasting, yes it may be that dark and purifying wave, the death of boredom
nearing the heights themselves may destroy you in the pure air
to be further complicated, confused, empty but refilling, exposed to light

With the past falling away as an acceleration of nerves thundering and shaking
aims its aggregating force like the Métro towards a realm of encircling travel
rending the sound of adventure and becoming ultimately local and intimate
repeating the phrases of an old romance which is constantly renewe by the
endless originality of human loss the air the stumbling quiet of breathing
newly the heavens' stars all out we are all for the captured time of our being

The deluge began immediately after "Joe's Jacket." Which is to say, right af-
ter Frank spent the weekend with Vincent. "You Are Gorgeous and I'm
Coming," "Saint," "Poem" ("Hate is only one of many responses"), "Poem"
("I don't know what D. H. Lawrence is driving at"), "Personal Poem,"
"Post the Lake Poets Ballad," and "Naphtha" were written in the subsequent

three weeks, and that was only the beginning. For over the course of the next twenty-one months, Frank's output continued apace, steady and unbroken, with the exception of a couple of unproductive months when he was so frantically busy with a traveling exhibition that he could hardly think of anything else. Take a look at the *Collected Poems*, pages 329 through 406, and my case is made, for these marvelous poems testify to what finally came together for Frank, what he at long last experienced, love and the reciprocation of love—physical, sexual, romantic love, fully and deeply realized.

Who was this person who inspired Frank to write such incandescent love poems? Not yet twenty-one when he met Frank, Vincent Warren was guileless, unworldly, even naïve, and he was a dancer, not a poet or a painter or an intellectual. Was he, then, an unlikely love object for Frank? I had the feeling some of Frank's friends thought so. But what did they know about Vincent, beyond what was apparent? Yes, he was gorgeous, with thick eyelashes, a perfect profile, a ballet dancer's great body—but there was a lot more to him than that. And friends of Frank's who took the trouble quickly learned how true that was, how bright, quick-witted, and well-informed he was. Not that Frank cared what anyone thought. For example, I suspect he sensed Grace's reservations, and there was no way he could not have detected Earl McGrath's irritation when he arrived for drinks, chez Earl and Camilla, with Vincent in tow.

An autodidact, Vincent always seemed to be reading something, either a classic or some obscure book like the Mary Desti autobiography that inspired Frank to write the delightful "Mary Desti's Ass"; and he knew a lot about various and sometimes unexpected aspects of the arts, and about antique furniture, the history of the ballet, the nineteenth-century novel, old movies. Then, too, since he was as voluble as Frank and by no means inarticulate, they always had a great deal to say to each other—too much to suit me, as many a night I lay awake as they chattered away in Frank's room, Vincent's voice higher pitched than usual, or so it seemed at that late hour, and I remember wishing they'd make love and go to sleep instead of making love and getting more revved up. Which is my only complaint about Vincent, who made Frank happy and inspired him to write so many wonderful poems.

DIGRESSIONS ON SOME POEMS BY FRANK O'HARA

They are among Frank's finest works, and the poems I find most moving. Yet, interestingly, they elicit few personal responses from me. But I suppose this isn't surprising. How can an evocation of old memories be triggered by love poems that by their very nature are private and enclosed, essentially between two people? I am not part of these poems anymore than I was part of Frank's relationship with Vincent. And though Frank was in the habit of taking me into his confidence—he always had in the past, about everything—he never once spoke to me about Vincent. What his feelings were toward him, the problems they might have had, the whys and wherefores of their breakup—about all of this, he was uncharacteristically reticent, even secretive.

In Frank's lifetime, a number of the poems for, about, and inspired by Vincent were published under the Tibor de Nagy imprint in a slender volume called *Love Poems (Tentative Title)*. Significantly, Vincent's name never appears in any of the poems, though his initials are part of the title of the dedicatory poem, "Poem V (F) W," which was actually the tenth of the love poems Frank wrote. So what about this cryptic reference to Vincent's name—does it rub any of us the wrong way? Gay activists who espouse outing might very well object to it, since there's nothing in the entire sequence of poems that gives the show away, nothing that's overtly gay or homoerotic; and apart from two instances, references that merely imply the sex of Frank's lover ("your orange shirt" and "the faint line of hair dividing your torso"), the object of his affection is undefined, could be male or female.

Frank would like to have had it otherwise: it was what Vincent wanted, and not because he objected to his name being associated with the poems. The reason, in a word: Mother.

Operating on automatic drive fueled by a high-octane homosexual guilt, Vincent had it in his head that there was every chance his mother might one day run across the book of poems written for him, so naturally he couldn't allow his name to appear in it. Think about it a minute: that slim volume was an edition of fewer than five hundred copies, not one of which found its way into a bookstore; Vincent's mother wasn't a devotee of the arts or a reader of poetry; and—get this—she would have had to come all the way to New York, from wherever she lived, and happen into the Tibor de Nagy Gallery in order to set eyes on the aforementioned pamphlet of poems, which was not, as I remember, conspicuously on display. Incredible, isn't it? Not really: to live in fear of matriarchal disapproval, all you have to be is gay and not necessarily young and naïve to boot. We all know about E. M. Forster and his mom, and then there's the more recent case of Roland Barthes, who waited until his mother's death, in 1978, to make a gesture toward coming out: he promptly wrote, and allowed the publication of, a preface to Renaud Camus's sexually explicit, outrageously gay *Tricks*—then died himself, poor guy, just two years after his ancient mother bit the dust.

While Frank wouldn't have been judgmental, he would surely have rolled his eyes in consternation, as he did upon learning that I, at age thirty-five or thereabouts, still put up with my mother's fantasy that one day I'd get married—to a nice Mormon girl, no less. "Why do you persist in deceiving her?" he demanded. "I don't deceive her," I said, "I just don't contradict her. I let her think what she wants to think." Frank then took another tack, one he recognized as being part of my oedipal-induced gay guilt, that is, the religious baggage Mom had saddled me with since as far back as I could remember: "And what about those Mormon friends of your mother's who looked you up when they came to town?" he fumed. "They asked if you went to church, and what did you say—did you tell them it was none of their business? No, you didn't! And why not?" I shrugged; he had me there. Not that it was any excuse, but I wish I'd thought to remind him that I wasn't that unusual, since almost all of our gay friends, at one time or another, suffered under the yoke of matriarchal tyranny, a tyranny based solely on a voluntary and craven obeisance to one's mother.

At this point some readers—straight readers—might be wondering about Dad's role in all of this. Well, only rarely does he figure in the scheme of things—it's Mom who casts her long, intimidating shadow over our lives. And it's been my observation that the greater an albatross one's mother is, the better she's treated by her gay son. Hence, by that rule of thumb, Frank should have been the most obliging and self-sacrificing of sons: that he was

DIGRESSIONS ON SOME POEMS BY FRANK O'HARA

quite the opposite is a tribute to his strength of character and allegiance to what he felt was fair and just. Which means, he treated his mother even-handedly. That she was widowed in early middle-age he did not, I'm sure, disregard, and no doubt he would have accepted her becoming a drunk if she hadn't endangered the welfare of his young sister. And for that, he could never forgive her. Also, unlike his younger brother Philip, he didn't get all teary-eyed over her. He wept buckets over the Lana Turner remake of *Madame X*—it was about the last movie we saw together—but when it came to real life, to his own mother, he eschewed the sentimentality that attaches itself to the concept of motherhood, perhaps to the point of being unreasonably hard on the poor woman.

I met her once, over drinks at the Stork Club on an August afternoon in 1960, the occasion being a get-together celebrating the marriage of Frank's sister to Walter Granville-Smith. And how did I fit in, how come I went? It was, after all, a family affair, one I thought I shouldn't attend, I told Frank. But it was just like him to insist upon my presence, though not for the reason he gave, as indisputable as I knew it to be ("Maureen's very fond of you—she'd be hurt if you didn't come"). No, I'm convinced he instinctively saw it as an opportunity to remind people, in this instance his family and Maureen's new in-laws, that he was gay and that he didn't want anyone to forget it. And indeed, when I appeared with him at the wedding party, what else could be assumed but the obvious, that we were a couple of queers? As I said, it was the sort of thing Frank was always doing, and I'm sure it was a conscious part of his modus vivendi, of the way he lived his life as a homosexual. For if he was going to be adamantly opposed to the gay ghetto principle as exemplified by Cherry Grove on Fire Island, Lenny's Hideaway downtown, the Bird Circuit uptown, any gay gathering where straights were excluded or not wanted—in other words, a way of life that promoted compulsive cruising, misogyny, and homosexual separatism—he must have felt it necessary, as a point of pride and as a moral obligation, to hammer home to straight people the clear, unmistakable message that he was an uncontrite, arrogant queer who was not about to sing *miserere* or fall on his knees to anyone, a message

Grace Hartigan failed to comprehend, hence her odious insensitivity in regard to his bringing Vincent around to straight social functions.

So, of course, what could I do but agree to accompany him to the Stork Club on that hot summer afternoon, and I remember his being as grateful as he was on those rare occasions when he and Philip, the latter in town on business, had dinner together and I'd join them at Frank's insistence, because my presence kept them from quarreling. But on this occasion, things didn't work out so well. To begin with, Frank hadn't counted on my sitting next to his dark-haired, hazel-eyed, good-looking mother, whom he barely acknowledged as he took a seat at the other end of the banquette. "There was no place else for me to sit," I apologized to him later. "But did you have to turn on the charm?" he demanded. "And don't think I didn't notice," he said when I tried to look innocent. "All right, I was charming," I admitted. "But what could I do? She was charming to me."

And seductive, I could have added. When the waiter, taking orders for drinks, came up to where we were seated, Mrs. O'Hara looked at me doubtfully, then demurely allowed that she might have a Scotch and water, an order she promptly amended in a voice so hushed that only the waiter and I could hear what she said—"Would you make that a double, please," she murmured and then gave me an intimate, conspiratorial smile. If she was trying to win me over, she was certainly succeeding, since it actually occurred to me that she might not be as bad as Frank made her out to be, her selfish, irresponsible, boozy behavior notwithstanding.

Abruptly, when we'd been there only long enough for one drink, Frank caught my eye and said it was time to go. "I have a prior engagement," he explained to the others. It was the first I'd heard—and my look of surprise did not go unnoted by Katherine O'Hara, who whispered to me, striking just the right note of bravery infused with sadness and resignation, "It's all right, I understand." Then, as Frank and I got to our feet, she cooed these parting words: "Francis, you must come for a visit soon. And bring your Joey," she added sweetly, offering me her hand. We were hardly outside the Stork Club when Frank lit into me. "Thanks a lot for being so nice to my mother," he said bitterly, as we headed for the nearest bar.

Four years later, pretty much the same thing happened when we were living at 791 Broadway. On that occasion, I was caught red-handed on the phone with Mrs. O'Hara. "I'll tell him you called," I remember saying just as I heard the front door being shut; and as I went on to say, "It was nice talking to you," echoing Mrs. O'Hara's pleasantry, I looked over and saw Frank standing stock-still, glowering. Did I get any credit for having the presence of mind not to let on that he'd just come home from work? None at all. "That was my mother, wasn't it?" he said accusingly. I looked away. "How dare you be so pleasant to her!" he shouted.

And here is a sample of the way *he* spoke to her: "Why don't you go fuck yourself!"—not terribly original, but that's exactly what he said on one occasion when she happened to get him on the phone. Also, I'm convinced those were his very last words to her, as the conversation in which they figured was described to me immediately after it was concluded, early in the evening two or three weeks before the accident that ended his life—oh, Frank couldn't wait to get me on the horn to tell me about it! (By then, I should explain, we were living apart.) "And do you think my outburst gave her pause?" he said. "Oh no." With amusement and grudging admiration, be repeated what she said: "Is that any way for a Harvard graduate to talk to his mother?"—her final words to him as well, for once she'd uttered them, Frank laughed, replaced the phone in its cradle, and dialed my number. "I guess she had the last word," he observed. And I said, "It makes you almost like her, doesn't it?" "No, it doesn't," he said decisively.

It occurred to me then, as it had before and would again, that at one time in his life, in his childhood no doubt and perhaps in his youth, he must have loved her a great deal.

And now I am perusing "Post the Lake Poets Ballad" and wondering again how it found its way into *Love Poems*. The poem's not about, for, or addressed to Vincent, and it ends with the words, "am I Joe." Well, I suppose Vincent's the reason Frank could assert, "but I'm happy anyhow." Still, that doesn't qualify it as a love poem, so how come it's in the book? For what it's worth, here's my scenario, based not on conjecture but on information found in Alexander Smith's bibliography. Frank gave John Bernard Myers, his editor at Tibor de Nagy, a folder of typescripts labeled "Poems: Frank O'Hara," and John, on his own, made the selection that ended up as a sequence of love poems—to the surprise of Frank, perhaps? In any event, it must have been John's decision to include the poem in question, just as he selected all the other poems and arranged them in an order showing, in John's words, "the beginning of a new love, its middle period of floundering, the collapse of the affair with its attendant sadness and regret"—an artificial arrangement that had nothing to do with the order in which the poems were written. And yes, Frank was that indifferent about the fate of his poems, about what happened to them once they were written. Same with his plays—much to the exasperation of Taylor Mead, to whom *The General Returns from One Place to Another* was dedicated: "I hated his attitude toward the play, the way he let everybody do whatever they wanted with it," Taylor told me in 1979, still hot under the collar fifteen years after its production (in which he played the lead).

Now John Myers was no dumbbell, he knew his stuff—so, the question, at least as I see it, is this: Instead of "Post the Lake Poets Ballad," why didn't he select two poems that would have been far more suitable, that indeed could be thought of as love poems, namely "Vincent" and "Vincent (2)"? Copies of those two poems would have to have been included in the aforementioned folder. But they weren't, according to Alexander Smith's bibliography, and that begs the question: Were they held back because Vincent's name was boldly proclaimed as their titles? And maybe, too, that was why the poems weren't published in Frank's lifetime. Which, I suppose, brings us full circle, back to Mother. How sad, pathetic, and disheartening it is to contemplate all of this!

And what about "You Are Gorgeous and I'm Coming," the very first poem inspired by Vincent Warren? Now, I can see why a copy of "Steps," one of the best of Frank's love poems, wasn't sent to John Myers—it had already been published in *Lunch Poems;* but "You Are Gorgeous" had only appeared in an anthology, Don Allen's *New American Poetry.* Surely it wasn't withheld because it's an acrostic poem, because Vincent's name is spelled out! It's a love poem, damn it, and it should be the first thing in the book—whose selection, come to think of it, I was never that wild about.

> I've advised Maxine what to get you
> what will I give you myself
> it's already given
> I'm having a beer
> I'd like to start with the Prado
> I'd give you open-faced Rome or wall-eyed Toledo

are the opening lines of "Flag Day," and somehow they remind me, more forcefully than other poems of this period, of how little I was in Frank's life at the time: I remember nothing about Vincent's birthday, I wasn't part of the celebration . . . Of far greater significance, this wonderful poem written on the occasion of Vincent's twenty-second birthday on August 30, 1960, heralds the beginning of the end for Frank and Vincent, for it was then that the Vincent Warren period began to wind down as the young dancer's career repeatedly took him out of town and out of Frank's life—which is to say, there were fewer and fewer poems written during the last phase of their affair.

And then there is "Early on Sunday," which I feel is significant for its omission of Vincent's name, as though Frank is preparing himself for the time, not long off, when Vincent will be living permanently in Montreal. Without question (I can see the two of them in my mind's eye), Vincent is in bed with Frank when

> Joe stumbles home
> pots and pans crash to the floor
> everyone's happy again

Happy again? Not this drunken queen; I am miserable, a detail not in the poem. Also missing is my mumbling "degradation, degradation," as I make my noisy entrance, knocking over pots and pans in the kitchen, for the memory of the previous night—I was rejected by a cute, sexy guy who led me on—

still pains me. And I remember Frank and Vincent laughing uproariously at my antics as they snuggled contentedly in bed, so at least *they* were happy.

Though not for long: three weeks later, on May 20, 1961, comes "St. Paul and All That," the last of the Vincent Warren poems. And after that—well, after that comes Bill Berkson.

THE BILL BERKSON PERIOD

[1 9 6 0 – 6 2]

EMBARRASSING BILL

Bill is sounding so funny there in the bathtub like a walrus
he is very talkative and smelling like a new rug in a store window
how pleasant it is to think of Bill in there, half-submerged, listening
and when he comes to the door to get some more cologne he is just like
   a pane of glass
in a modernistic church, sort of elevated and lofty and substantial
well, if that isn't your idea of god, what is?
in these times one is very lucky to get a bath at all, much less
have someone cheerful come over and help themselves to one in your tub
I like to have all the rooms full and I just hope that Bill will get bigger
and bigger and bigger and pretty soon I'll have to get a whole house
or I could always find a pedestal with central heating perhaps
in case he wants to write his poems standing up
                       now, Bill, use your own towel

t is late fall, one of our weekday evenings when we are eating in and not
planning to go out later, though there is always the possibility of our slipping over to Loew's Commodore, and it doesn't matter what movie is playing, as witness what we sat through a couple of months earlier in that seedy
Second Avenue theater, which in a few years would be Fillmore East and

then, in the seventies, a glittering gay disco called The Saint—*The Horse Soldiers,* a truly uninspired John Ford / John Wayne Civil War concoction that evokes this complaint from Frank in "Post the Lake Poets Ballad":

> and then we eat and go to
> *The Horse Riders* and my bum aches
> from the hard seats and boredom

A truly forgettable movie; no wonder Frank got the title wrong. But on the night in question, there is no chance of our catching a movie, for by a quarter to nine there is still no sign of my wayward roommate who hasn't called to say he'll be late and I've been home more than two hours from my ignominious new job at the sleazy Scott Meredith Literary Agency, where manuscripts are read for a fee and where Allen Ginsberg says he worked less than a week before quitting out of disgust and shame, because he couldn't bear being a party to hoodwinking naïve, untalented, would-be writers—which doesn't mean I'm heartless for being capable of dashing off letters of encouragement to them, it's just that I need the work, my unemployment insurance having run out.

By nine, I've had it. I took a nap that went on too long and now I'm disgruntled and in no mood to start dinner, and it's then, as I suspend my disinclination to drink alone and resignedly get out the Jack Daniel's, that Frank sweeps in and immediately announces, without a word of apology, "I just met the most heavenly young poet!"

"I'm so happy for you," I say disingenuously, feeling at the same time truly happy to see Frank, and eager to sit and drink and talk.

He elaborates, supplies me with details, doesn't let me get a word in, and I know immediately, I *sense,* that the student Kenneth Koch arranged for him to meet—it seems that the three of them went to a bar near the New School after Kenneth's poetry workshop—is no passing fancy but the exact opposite, someone destined to become yet another integral part of his crowded emotional life. And a couple of months later, by which time Frank is seeing his new friend maybe three or four nights a week (in other words, when he's not seeing Vincent), I boast how I foresaw what would happen.

DIGRESSIONS ON SOME POEMS BY FRANK O'HARA

"And no," I insist when he gives me a skeptical look, "this isn't hindsight." Which is the truth. But as smart as I am, I fail to take note of a coincidence that would have added another dimension to my clairvoyance: the parallel between Frank's announcement that night and words of my own, when I told Gianni Bates on New Year's Eve 1951, "I just met the most terrific person!"

Nor was my prescience so great that I intuited that my place in Frank's life would be altered, that henceforth I'd be odd man out, a third wheel. I suppose I figured that since Vincent was causing me no grief, I'd certainly have nothing to fear from this student of Kenneth's, who was as straight as they come, Frank informed me the night they met, making it sound as if being heterosexual were a virtue, a notion that came naturally to gay people in those downtrodden days of low self-esteem—yes, I believe that Frank, even Frank, as defiant and secure as he was, experienced some of those feelings of inadequacy society ingrained in us. "Isn't he lucky," I commented dryly. "But how come you're so sure he's straight? And if he is, why should that stop you?"

Frank didn't bother to reply and I attached some significance to that, realized even then that questions were out where this new person in his life was concerned. Thus, in the weeks and months that followed, I never asked what his feelings and intentions were, never asked if he'd fallen in love, never inquired into how he found it possible to sustain—to *juggle*—his uninterrupted love affair with Vincent Warren and his absorbing, time-consuming romantic friendship with handsome, talented, articulate Bill Berkson, who disliked me on sight, I could tell, and I naturally responded in kind. After Frank's death, we made our peace—not immediately but eventually, and, a matter of some importance to me, he was the first to read "Four Apartments." While he was extremely complimentary, he seemed bemused by the way I worked his name into my account of what transpired in the watershed year of 1959: "Vincent Warren entered his life and right after that began the invasion of younger poets, spearheaded by Bill Berkson." Later, when it was too late to make any changes, I decided I didn't like my wording, either—I had tried to be clever, which was bad enough, and I ended up being glib, not to mention inaccurate and misleading. For Bill stood apart from the other

The Bill Berkson Period · 235

young poets and had nothing to do with paving the way for their entry into Frank's life—if anything, he would have liked to set up a roadblock.

A few sentences back, I made a reference to romantic friendship. I don't know what else to call it. Very English, a throwback to *Brideshead Revisited* and earlier, all the way back to Shakespeare and the youth who inspired the sonnets—except in such cases weren't both males heterosexual? That was the point. And now, without trying to surmise what Bill's feelings were, since that's for him to disclose if he so chooses, I propose to tell how I saw the whole thing—mere conjecture, to be sure.

Knowing Frank as well as I did, I feel confident that he essayed his straight role flawlessly; and what helped make that possible, what kept him from being frustrated, was the sexually satisfying thing he had going with Vincent. Even so, it might be wondered if there were not on Frank's part an element of masochism in his romantic friendship with Bill. There usually is when an older man hangs out with a younger man for whom he has a letch, whether the beloved is straight or gay being beside the point. As a friend of mine wisely counseled me when I was hung up on a dry hustler: "Masochism without sex is a bore." Well, whatever went on between Frank and Bill, Frank's being bored or made uncomfortable or worse wasn't part of it, because, in the first place, there was no masochism. How could there have been? He was Lucky Pierre; he had Vincent for a lover and Bill for a friend—I doubt that he'd ever been happier.

In April 1960, while Frank is in Paris on business for the museum, Bill is there at the same time. They have known each other for about six months, but not until now does Bill make his debut in Frank's poetry—in two poems, one after the other: first, in a minor capacity in "A Little Travel Diary" when all we get is "the back / of the head of Bill Berkson, aux Deux Magots," while in the second one, "Embarrassing Bill," written the following day, he is center stage, having come to Frank's hotel room to take a bath.

Interestingly, never again will a poem of Frank's place Bill in such an intimate context; and the reason for his debut at this time seems obvious enough—it's because Vincent's in New York and Frank's in Paris, where Bill happens to be. Meanwhile, the Vincent Warren period shows no signs of letting up, as is borne out by what Frank writes upon his return to New York: after all his wonderful travels, he lets Vincent know that "having a coke with you / is even more fun than going to San Sebastian, Irún, Hendaye, Biarritz, Bayonne . . ." Still, those two Paris poems in which Bill appears augur the beginning of the Bill Berkson period, which will eventually overlap and co-exist with the Vincent Warren period, just as these two young men, as dissimilar as the poems they inspire, will continue sharing Frank. From 1959 until his death in 1966, they represent the two biggest influences on his poetry; and as Bill moves into the ascendancy and circumstances nudge Vincent out of Frank's life, we'll see an extraordinary change in the kind of poetry that's produced. But the full emergence of the Bill Berkson period doesn't come about until the final Vincent Warren poem has been written—until, in other words, Vincent has left the city to settle in Montreal, where he will become a Canadian citizen.

"Drifts of a Thing That Bill Berkson Noticed," written on June 19, 1961, a month after that final Vincent Warren poem, signals the beginning of this new phase, whose climax is reached, quite obviously, with "Biotherm (For Bill Berkson)," completed on January 23, 1962. That means the period lasted approximately the same length of time as Vincent's. But Frank's creative life during that time was, like his everyday life, almost totally dominated by Bill—it was pretty much Bill Berkson all the way, with very few detours away from the FYI poems and the like, whereas Vincent merely exerted an *influence* on Frank's writing, a salutary, magnanimous influence that was the wellspring of poems other than the love poems.

Thus Frank's poetry undergoes a change that can be clearly perceived if we restrict ourselves to the love poems on the one hand and the Bill Berkson poems on the other. In the former, we are in the recognizable world of going to the movies and the ballet, drinking too much coffee and smoking too many cigarettes, sharing a coke with someone, eagerly awaiting the arrival of someone, deciding on a birthday present for someone, and, above all, having strong feelings about someone, while in the latter—well, make of it what you will, page after page of disparate thoughts, images, ideas, quoted remarks, antic wordplay, private jokes, and occasionally eccentric typography. I'm referring mainly to the work I have just now read through again, the ultimate Bill Berkson poem, "Biotherm," which I'm prepared to believe is terrific. I put it that way because I am not a poet or a literary critic or an academic, and this strikes me as poetry concerned with poetry, poetry written for other poets, clever, dry, experimental, obscure, arcane, inaccessible, no lines to cherish and commit to memory, nothing to move and stir the reader. At least not this reader.

Let's go back to "Embarrassing Bill," take another look. It's light and gently amusing, but there's also something private going on—Bill, in the first line, is described as "sounding so funny there in the bathtub like a walrus," and in the last line he's admonished by Frank to "use your own towel." As I suggested earlier, we won't see anything like it again in any of the Bill Berkson poems, which become increasingly abstract the longer Frank and Bill know each other. You would think it would be the reverse. So hold on to the thought, as I believe it's one of the keys to understanding what's going on with Frank in his life and in his poetry, now more than ever one and the same, the tone and thrust of his poetry a reflection of his life, the love poems to Vincent Warren reflecting emotional and sexual fulfillment, the Bill Berkson poems reflecting something quite different—but what? Whatever it was, it meant a great deal to both Frank and Bill, and I would say it had to do with intellectual camaraderie and poetry and art and music and ballet and an older man with a younger man, their feelings and ideas about life meshing so wondrously, their sensibilities being so compatible, that they were sufficient unto themselves. But even without the corroboration of the poems, there's no question in my mind that Frank found their friendship so consuming—far more than he did his great love affair with Vincent—that it became the center of his life, and as a result he grew increasingly indifferent about me, until finally he didn't like having me around. I'd never known him to be so enamored of anyone as he was of Bill, in the sense that he craved Bill's presence, simply his presence—that was enough for him; it was not about sex, it was beyond sex. For I now firmly believe, having looked closely at the poetry, that Frank did not have a letch for Bill—not for the long haul, only at first. This is what I see in the poems. I could be wrong, but I doubt that I am. However,

DIGRESSIONS ON SOME POEMS BY FRANK O'HARA

far from downgrading Frank's attraction to Bill and his obsession with him, I mean to do just the opposite; and to understand why Frank felt as he did, why he was so enraptured, you have to keep in mind the sort of person Bill was in those days, the figure he cut, the impression he made, and, most important, what lay beneath the surface. While there's no question that he was polished, poised, graceful, and charming—the ideal extra man, you might say—he was also a young man of integrity, wit, and intelligence, someone who had good sense and the right values. What more could anyone want? And I couldn't stand him, anymore than he could me. That was at first; later, we got along and even liked each other for months at a stretch, then we'd suddenly rub each other the wrong way and be right back where we started. Frank seemed oblivious, above it all—as indeed he was, since he occupied the catbird seat. The worst time for me was when they were getting to know each other: Bill would leave his mother's fancy Fifth Avenue digs, come downtown, and talk with Frank over drinks in our dreary, depressing place on East Ninth Street, and I'd be sitting right there with them—but I might as well have been on the moon. Bill would not look at me, even on those rare occasions when he addressed me; and Frank followed suit, as though nothing out of the ordinary was taking place, as though this was an acceptable way to treat someone you lived with.

Obviously, I should have had it out with Frank, I should have told him to stuff it; but I didn't, so I guess Joan Mitchell was right when she said, years after his death, "You were a fucking masochist, Joe—admit it." Okay, I admit it; she was right as usual, the bitch. And remembering all this, being confronted with these memories on my computer screen (how official and indisputable the words look!), I find my servility at that time loathsome and unforgivable, and for that reason I'm angry with myself, with the person I once was, not with Frank or Bill, who were so wrapped up in themselves that I should have known better, should not have expected them to consider my feelings. When Frank and I broke up, Bill said to me, not unkindly, "It's a good thing, Joe; now you can find your own identity." Yes, it must be said that Bill had a point.

The Bill Berkson Period · 239

PERSONAL POEM

[AUGUST 2 7 , 1 9 5 9]

Now when I walk around at lunchtime
I have only two charms in my pocket
an old Roman coin Mike Kanemitsu gave me
and a bolt-head that broke off a packing case
when I was in Madrid the others never
brought me too much luck but they did
help keep me in New York against coercion
but now I'm happy for a time and interested

I walk through the luminous humidity
passing the House of Seagram with its wet
and its loungers and the construction to
the left that closed the sidewalk if
I ever get to be a construction worker
I'd like to have a silver hat please
and get to Moriarty's where I wait for
LeRoi and hear who wants to be a mover and
shaker the last five years my batting average
is .016 that's that, and LeRoi comes in
and tells me Miles Davis was clubbed 12
times last night outside BIRDLAND by a cop

a lady asks us for a nickle for a terrible
disease but we don't give her one we
don't like terrible diseases, then

we go eat some fish and some ale it's
cool but crowded we don't like Lionel Trilling
we decide, we like Don Allen we don't like
Henry James so much we like Herman Melville
we don't want to be in the poets' walk in
San Francisco even we just want to be rich
and walk on girders in our silver hats
I wonder if one person out of 8,000,000 is
thinking of me as I shake hands with LeRoi
and buy a strap for my wristwatch and go
back to work happy at the thought possibly so

dd what some readers can seize on in a poem, as for example what David
Lehman came away with, after poring over "Personal Poem," in *The Last
Avant-Garde: The Making of the New York Poets.* The lines that stood
out, caused Lehman to ponder their significance, were the tenth and
eleventh lines from the end of the poem: ". . . we don't like Lionel Trilling /
we decide, we like Don Allen . . ." After commenting on how "comically one-
sided" the antithesis is ("the Columbia eminence . . . versus the little-known
Grove Press editor"), he wonders at length about the whys and wherefores
of the matter, and asks himself, quite seriously, if Frank's apparent disapproval of Trilling could be traced to Diana Trilling's bitchy *Partisan Review*
piece about Allen Ginsberg's triumphant return to his alma mater, "The
Other Night at Columbia." Wisely, Lehman dismisses this possibility.
O'Hara, we're assured, "was perfectly capable of distinguishing one Trilling
from another," and besides, "O'Hara's own relations with the Beats had come
under strain earlier that year when Kerouac was rude and Corso gauche at a

reading O'Hara allowed himself to be talked into doing"—none of which is true. The reading, at the Living Theatre, was a benefit to raise money for LeRoi, who had hepatitis, and Frank did not have to be talked into participating; Kerouac's rudeness—he interrupted Frank's reading by shouting, "O'Hara, you're ruining American poetry"; Frank countered with, "That's more than you could ever do," and left the stage—had no effect on Frank's friendship with the Beats, including Gregory Corso, who was no more gauche that night than he usually was. Also, Frank and the boorish Kerouac soon made up, their admittedly shaky reconciliation occurring at the Cedar when Kerouac sidled up to Frank and blubbered, "I thought you liked me, O'Hara," to which Frank retorted, "It's not you I like, it's your work I like," which naturally pleased Jack no end, so much that he was forever after playing up to Frank . . . More than likely, Lehman goes on, "one may discover the key to this literary mystery" in something else by Mrs. Trilling, *The Beginning of the Journey,* a portrait of her marriage in which she states that "for Lionel seriousness, not happiness, was the goal worthy of an intellectual life," a creed that goes counter to Frank's "quiet but incessant pursuit of happiness." Frank couldn't have read Trilling's book, since it wasn't published until after his death—but forget that. My point is, what's any of this got to do with "Personal Poem"?

Look who's talking! Why am I so rough on this very good writer? Well, that's exactly why, because he's a good writer, one whose work I usually admire, I can't help but feel that in dealing with Frank's work he could have dug a little deeper and maybe done as well by him as by the other poets in the book—Ashbery, Koch, and Schuyler.

With that off my chest, I can now bask in the warmth that radiates from this poem, which is indeed personal but no more so than the majority of Frank's works. So let's forget Lionel Trilling, about whom Frank had no strong feelings that I know of—ditto James and Melville—and celebrate the sweet, gentle, diminutive Mike Kanemitsu, a wonderful artist with an exciting history; LeRoi Jones, in the years before his transformation into the angry, combative Amiri Baraka, as warm, outgoing, and engaging as anyone on the downtown scene; and the poets Maxwell Perkins and Don Allen, the latter of whom wore a cloak of restraint, irony, and elusiveness that failed to conceal his generous nature. It is their presence in the poem that makes it warm and personal, and lends support to Frank's hope that at least one of New York's eight million is thinking of him as he heads back to work, "happy at the thought possibly so."

On Sunday afternoon in the spring of 1959, Frank and I and several others were at Norman Bluhm's studio for an informal viewing of his new paintings, and at some point Mike Kanemitsu took Frank aside and pressed something into the palm of his hand. I waited until later, on our walk home, to ask him about it. "You and Mike looked awfully conspiratorial," I said. "He gave you something—what was it?"

"An old Roman coin for luck," said Frank, handing it to me.

I examined it with admiration; it looked old all right, and seemed to glow with history, or so I imagined. "If it could only talk," I said.

Frank laughed and said, "I love Mike Kanemitsu."

Later at home, over dinner, I began thinking about the old Roman coin. "It should bring you luck all right," I said, "if it was responsible for any of the wonders in Mike's life."

Frank reminded me that Mike hadn't been all that lucky. "Look what happened to him when war broke out," he said. "Of course he didn't have his good luck coin back then."

"He told you that?"

"Yes. He said it was passed to him ten years ago, by a friend it had brought luck to."

"Would that be before or after Frances Farmer?"

"Well, you wouldn't associate Frances Farmer with good luck, so Mike must not have had it then."

Of all the things about Mike Kanemitsu, that was probably the most amazing part of his history, even more amazing than his being born in the Mormon town of Ogden, Utah, growing up in a suburb of Hiroshima, returning to the United States and enlisting in the army, being arrested and sent to a detention camp after Pearl Harbor, serving as a hospital assistant in Europe when he was released from surveillance, and, after the war, studying at the Art Students League and becoming friends with de Kooning, Kline, and Pollock. "I can't imagine it," I remember Frank telling me after Mike's casual disclosure that he'd once been married, ever so briefly, to the magnificent and beautiful Frances Farmer, the legendary actress whose life was so tragic. "Oh, I don't know," I said. "I can just visualize Mike with a very drunk Frances Farmer clinging to him, her hair all a mess as they're leaving a Hollywood police station. It's as vivid to me as a photograph in *National Enquirer*."

We never did find out if there was any truth to his Frances Farmer story. He was awfully playful; maybe he dreamed it up to titillate us, knowing we were such big movie fans. As for the old Roman coin, I asked J.J. Mitchell about it after Frank's funeral. "I don't really care that much about the Motherwell watch," I said, referring to the Tiffany wristwatch Motherwell had given Frank at the time of his show at the Modern, a keepsake J.J. and Maureen decided I should have. "What I'm interested in," I went on, "is an old Roman coin. Was that among his things? Did he have it on him at the time of the accident?"

"A good luck charm?" J.J. said; and he looked disconsolate when I nodded. "He must have left it at home."

> . . . *in the summer of 1959 . . . began the invasion of younger poets, spearheaded by Bill Berkson . . . Frank Lima, Tony Towle, Ted Berrigan, Jim Brodey, Kathy Fraser, Allan Kaplan, Ron Padgett, Aram Saroyan, Peter Schjeldahl, Steve Holden, Joe Ceravolo, David Shapiro . . . —his extraordinary rapport with them rivaled his deep friendship with painters.*
> ["Four Apartments"]

What could I have been thinking? Why didn't I mention LeRoi Jones, the future Amiri Baraka? Twenty-four at the time Frank met him, he belongs on the list of younger poets as much as, say, Ted Berrigan, whose year of birth, 1934, is the same as Roi's. What's more, Frank was closer to Roi than he was to Ted or any of the others, Bill Berkson excepted. In fact, so great was Frank's affection for Roi that "Personal Poem," which has nothing to do with

Vincent and a lot to do with Roi, was written at the outset of his affair with Vincent, when he was writing virtually nothing except love poems.

Is it possible that I omitted Roi's name intentionally, out of spite, because I felt he didn't sufficiently value Frank's friendship? I remember feeling that way, but I believe—I like to think—that it was an honest oversight, and I imagine it had something to do with Roi's having been unusually mature and accomplished for his age, also with the fact that as founder and editor of *Yugen*—with his wife, Hettie—and as co-editor of the mimeographed *Floating Bear*—with his mistress Diane Di Prima—he was one of Frank's publishers. Thus, from the beginning of their friendship, Roi was a colleague of Frank's and never, like some of the other budding poets, a disciple, or in future years, after his death, what I called an O'Hara freak, as in Jesus freak, dear Ted being Frank's number-one fan, champion, and posthumous groupie.

When I met LeRoi Jones, what struck me was how at ease he seemed to be with himself and the world, a white man's world of poets and artists in which he was the only black. Was that comparable to being the only gay in a straight gathering, a social situation not unknown to me? To some extent, yes. For while Roi, in effect, was passing for white, I enjoyed the same privileges of assimilation, my sexual orientation, like his ethnicity, being disregarded. That meant we were accepted as equals, with a catch: he didn't exist as a person of color any more than I did as a gay person. Once in a while, in certain situations, I felt like a mascot—did Roi ever feel that way, I wonder? Possibly he did, since he would later write about the indignity of being a "token nigger." (I should mention that the predominantly black jazz scene, of which Roi was a part, did not intersect with the downtown art and poetry world.)

Is there a connection, I wonder, between Frank's meeting Roi and his writing "Ode: Salute to the French Negro Poets"? It was summer, we were still at University Place, and Frank was impressed with the young black poet who didn't seem to either of us like an American Negro, perhaps because of his small frame and delicate features. Well, I suppose we had a stereotyped idea of the American Negro. The ode is dated July 9, 1958, which was around the time Frank met LeRoi—at the Cedar, I believe.

Neat, compact, physically appealing, conservatively dressed, clearly intelligent, obviously gifted, son of a New Jersey postman—here was a young black man who seemed to harbor no anger or resentment, so that his easy smile, sparkling eyes, and courtly manners quickly won over everyone he met in the downtown art and poetry community of the late fifties, which was when Frank became friends with him and he'd drop by, first when we were living at 90 University Place, later at East Ninth Street, sometimes staying over and sharing Frank's bed, while I, the very soul of discretion, was in my own bed, minding my own business, never asking questions, never saying a word to anyone later about what I thought might be going on, Roi being a married man, a father, a stud, a sexist, a *heterosexual*! And how am I repaid for that discretion, keeping to myself what I could dine out on? Almost twenty years after Frank's death, I picked up a copy of *The Autobiography of LeRoi Jones/Amira Baraka* and found my answer when I came upon a passing, altogether irrelevant reference to me as Frank O'Hara's boyfriend, with a compliment thrown in about my movie-star good looks, which by no means assuaged my pique. The passage, which I'm unable to quote, smacked of a veiled homophobia and was utterly disingenuous, inasmuch as he knew that Frank and I weren't lovers.

And strange as it might seem, considering what happened later, there was grumbling behind his back, mild complaints about his being—well, not exactly an Uncle Tom, but too placid, easygoing, and conservative, not as radical in his politics as his liberal white friends would like him to have been. I should mention that there was one other black on the scene, Kynaston McShine. A colleague of Frank's at the Modern and his sometime lover, he was so elitist and apolitical as to make Roi seem a firebrand in comparison. However, this elegant, snobbish, handsome, mellifluously voiced recent graduate of Dartmouth hailed from Trinidad and had not become a U.S. citizen, so he wasn't expected to identify with American blacks and he was let off the hook, unlike poor Roi: "Why isn't he more like Jimmy Baldwin?" protested Patsy Southgate, a friend of Baldwin's from their Paris days in the early fifties. That was the sort of thing that was said.

Nonetheless, Roi's charm was taken at face value, as a sign of simple affection for his white friends, and only later did we suspect that it must have masked deep feelings of resentment—so deep that Roi was no more aware of what was going on than we were. As for his metamorphosis, from mild-mannered, assimilated Negro to embittered, out-of-control revolutionary, it can be equated, in some respects, with the transformation of certain gays after Stonewall in 1969, gays who went from being tight-lipped and defensive about their sexual orientation to dealing with it openly, with anger and resentment. I won't push the analogy beyond suggesting that Roi and those hitherto docile gays became extremists partly for the same reason: rudely awakened from their apathy, they felt an urgent need to make up for lost time and to compensate for what they guiltily perceived as their disgraceful past, years of kowtowing and swallowing their pride. "How loud does fate have to shriek in your face before you pay attention?" Paul Monette finally asked himself near the end of the painful odyssey limned in *Becoming a Man: Half a Life Story.* So it was with LeRoi Jones, who came to his senses, divorced his white wife, fled to Harlem, converted to Islam, changed his name, and became the literary lion of black militancy, just as Monette became a spokesman for the gay liberation movement.

What happened next, in the community of artists and intellectuals who had taken LeRoi up, was inevitable, I suppose: they felt they'd been stabbed in the back. As witness, for example, one night at the Dome—was it before or later that this St. Mark's Place disco was the Electric Circus?—when Frank ran into Leonard Bernstein, whom we used to see at Morris Golde's parties that were straight for the first several hours and then turned gay when the straights left (Lenny would hang back with the queers, of course). Anyway, here Lenny was slumming with Lauren Bacall and Jason Robards, and eager, as always, to be liked and regarded as egalitarian, which is to say, he waved to Frank and asked him to sit at their table. This would have been the fall of 1964, because it was then that Robards was electrifying audiences with the O'Neill one-act play *Hughie,* which Frank and I had just seen, and now he showered Robards with compliments so excessive that Bacall went into a sulk. A prima donna himself, Lenny reacted by immediately changing the subject: he suddenly launched into a diatribe against Roi, whose recent behavior he characterized as a betrayal of his friends, and what, he wanted to know, did Frank think about it? "So, what'd you say?" I asked when Frank related all of this over coffee the next morning, knowing that he wouldn't have countenanced criticism of Roi from anyone, even from the world-famous, and therefore automatically intimidating, Leonard Bernstein. "I told him," Frank said, "that Roi was someone I loved and I couldn't possibly discuss anything like that with him." And how did Roi repay Frank for his loyalty? Fortunately, it didn't get back to Frank what I was told by a black playwright and founder of a Negro theater group: "I asked Roi how he could have accepted Frank and Joe's hospitality all those years, and he said, 'I was just pissing in their beer.'"

VARIATIONS ON SATURDAY

[DECEMBER 10, 1960]

> . . . In Joe's Deli the old lady
> greets me Sonny   the man with
> the rolls is my son, Sonny, how
> are you today in the cold out? fine
> and coffee too and Camels
>
>   well
> a saucepan smells of eggs soft sour
> Tanya   the Barone Gallery
> tomorrow   the light broke
> before I even got out of bed
> and then it got put together again
> you discard your jacket
>
>   and go
> sweatered into the afternoon
> wait for me
>   I'm staying with you
> fuck Canada . . .

This poem is about, for, and to Vincent, whose career will take him out of New York, away from Frank—to Canada, as we surmise from "fuck Canada." But in my usual fashion, I gleaned from the poem something unrelated; poring over its fourth stanza, my attention was arrested by the first five lines: *Joe's Deli . . . the old lady . . . Sonny . . . the man with the rolls . . . coffee . . . Camels . . . eggs . . .* The words spring from the page, co-alesce, form whole sentences, bring alive an entirely new scene, situation, set of circumstances, a modest narrative locked within the lines of Frank's poem and now liberated by me! And like "Variations on Saturday," the digression it prompted is in six parts—as a sort of homage to Frank's poem:

1

Joe's Deli was almost directly across the street from us at 441 East Ninth Street and just a few doors from the singularly ugly Garfinkel's Pharmaceu-tical Supply Company, which also found its way into a poem of Frank's. An old Ukrainian couple owned the place, a hole in the wall, badly lighted, with nothing much to offer. Frank made a point of buying his Camels there and I bought as many practical staples as I could espy in their meager stock: Fol-ger's Coffee, a quart of milk, a can of Campbell's soup, once going so far as to buy a loaf of Wonder Bread, wherein I learned it was true what I heard said as a child, that a slice could be rolled into a disgusting little wad—"No won-der they call it Wonder Bread!" I exclaimed. Another time I bought a half-dozen eggs; two or three of them were rotten, and I was going to take them back. "Don't you dare," Frank said.

2

There was only one reason we patronized Joe's Deli, which wasn't a deli-catessen at all since they had no cold cuts: it was because Joe and his wife were so damn nice—always cheerful, as though their life together in that dim, grimy little store was all they ever wanted. They called both of us Sonny. One time Frank came in and Joe's wife said, "Your brother was just here. You don't have to buy no milk." Their son, who lived in New England somewhere, visited once; they were very proud of him, because he'd made a success of himself in some sort of business. I didn't get to see him, but Frank did, as I'm reminded by the poem. "He's kind of sexy," he told me, "a big muscular man, right out of an Eisenstein movie"; but by the time I got over to Joe's Deli, he had left.

3

One evening, returning from work—this would have been when Frank and I were still very close, in the days before Vincent and Bill—I stopped off at Joe's Deli for something we needed for dinner. I found Joe's wife by herself, looking very low. I was taken aback; I'd never seen her that way, and I immediately wondered where Joe was. "Are you all right?" I asked.

"Not so good," she said. "Joe died last night."

It was an awkward moment. I didn't know what to do or say. We weren't close, after all; I didn't really know her—Frank and I didn't even know her name. I mumbled something, got what I'd come in for, and left as quickly as possible without seeming too abrupt, and heartless.

4

I gave Frank the news as soon as he got home. He looked stricken. "Is she over there alone?" he asked.

"Well, yes," I said.

We had a couple of drinks and ate dinner. We were unusually quiet. "I've got to go out for some cigarettes," Frank said, getting up from the table.

I was in bed reading when he came back, more than an hour later. "I was wondering what happened to you," I called out.

"I decided to take a walk," he said.

5

A few days later, I strode into the deli not knowing what I would buy. Joe's wife greeted me warmly, the way she always did: "Sonny, how are you?"

I still felt awkward in the face of Joe's death; vaguely, I thought there was more I could have said or done. "How are *you*?" I asked. "Are you all right?"

She nodded and smiled. "Ah, your brother," she said. "So kind, so nice. He made me feel better."

Then it came out—I got it out of her with no difficulty; she wanted to talk about it. Frank had come over to express his condolences, and they got to talking—or, rather, she did, I gathered: about the old country and coming to America. She was just closing up when Frank came in, and she asked if he'd like to join her for a drink in the back room where she and Joe lived. So Frank and Joe's wife sat together and had a nice long talk over several glasses of sherry. "My son couldn't come," she told me. "But your brother made it all right, Sonny."

6

When Frank came home that evening, I waited for the right moment and then told him I'd dropped by Joe's Deli. "I heard about your going to see Joe's wife the other night," I said.

"Oh, yeah," he said. "She was very nice."

"*You* were very nice."

He shrugged, as if to say it was something one did.

THREE POEMS

[A P R I L   2 5 ,   1 9 6 1]

DANTE

I could guide you into depravity but I'm not sure I could lead either of us back out.

MASTURBATION

It's a pause in the day's occupation known as the children's hour.

TELEPHONE   *(to Patsy Southgate)*

I sometimes wonder how we all get through this soap opera that is our life.

t was the least he could have done," said Patsy when I told her that one of Frank's facetiously titled "Three Poems" had been dedicated to her.

"Yeah, and it's pretty unusual," I suggested, "dedicating something to the person who thought it up."

"I didn't think it was that funny to begin with."

"If it was really funny, he wouldn't have used it."

"Meaning what?"

"It's the nature of wit in poetry, isn't it? If a poet wrote something really funny, he'd be suspect; he'd be thought of as a writer of light verse."

"Like Dorothy Parker, you mean."

"Or Ogden Nash. Real poets are never funny."

· 253 ·

"Are you sure about that?"

"No," I admitted. "You were always saying things that broke Frank up. I remember another day he got off the phone with you, when he repeated that thing you said about having a penis."

"About having a penis?"

"Yes. You said, 'If I had a penis, I'd really wield it.' I wonder why he didn't use that somewhere."

"It's certainly unfunny enough," Patsy said.

This exchange transpired one morning over the telephone in the winter of 1968. I'd just gone downstairs and found the latest *Paris Review* in the mailbox, and of course I couldn't wait to tell Patsy that "Three Poems" and a couple of other things of Frank's were in the issue.

Oddly, she didn't know about "Telephone" and its dedication to her, anymore than I knew beforehand that

> Wouldn't it be funny
> if the finger had designed us
> to shit just once a week?
>
>> all week long we'd get fatter
>> and fatter and then on Sunday morning
>> while everyone's in church
>
>>> ploop!

was going to be in the volume of poems he dedicated to me, the delectable *Lunch Poems* that came out in 1965. "I assume you're not planning to include this in your next book," I quipped after he yanked the yellow second sheet from his Royal portable and showed me the deathless lines he'd punched out—on a Sunday morning in 1959, when I reminisced about going to Sunday school and acknowledged how the memory lingered, how those childhood days of Mormon rectitude still glimmered grimly from the past when Sunday morning rolled around: Was this what prompted Frank to write what might be thought of as his scatological *hommage* to the Sabbath?

Well, it was around the time of Patsy's "Telephone" remark that she concocted, no doubt with the same nonchalance that induced the mots Frank found so beguiling, her absurdist playlet called "Freddy," whose situation centered on a ménage à trois involving a married couple and their horse Freddy. Published in *Evergreen Review* with drawings by Alex Katz, it was performed one East Hampton summer in the spacious backyard of Anne Roiphe when she was still Anne Richardson. With Jim Dine and Clarice Rivers as the husband and wife, and with a wonderful wooden horse that was built by Bill King, it was offered as a curtain-raiser to Frank's "Try! Try!" that starred Larry Rivers, Syd Solomon, and Shirley King. A professional, Gaby Rodgers, directed these nonprofessionals in an exhilarating evening enlivened by the arrival of cops drawn to the premises by a deafening sound system Jerry Lieber insisted on installing.

Before she agreed to a production of "Freddy," Patsy read it to Frank and me to see what we thought. "It's heaven!" Frank said. "Yes, it's terrific," I agreed, "but I don't think it's long enough. Can't you make it into a real play, a one-act play?" That got Frank's back up; he hated it when I played the critic, and we almost got into a fight. "What are you talking about?" he said. "It's perfect the way it is." And he made Patsy promise not to add a word to "Freddy." But years later, long after his death, she took my suggestion and fleshed it out. Of course it didn't work. Frank was right, as usual.

THE PREVALENCE OF KENNETH KOCH

[1 9 5 2 – 6 1]

ON A BIRTHDAY OF KENNETH'S

Kenny!
Kennebunkport! I see you standing there
assauging everything with your smile
at the end of the world you are scratching your head wondering what is
    that funny French word Roussel was so fond of? oh "dénouement"!
and it is good

I knew perfectly well that afternoon on the grass when you read Vincent
    and me your libretto that you had shot out of the brassière factory
    straight into the blue way ahead of the Russians (what do they know
    now that Pasternak is gone) and were swinging there like a Strad
And that other day when we heard Robert Frost read your poems for the
    Library of Congress we admired you too though we didn't like the way
    he read "Mending Sump"
and when Mrs. Kennedy bought your drawing that was a wonderful day too

but in a sense these days didn't add up to a year
and you haven't had a birthday
you have simply the joyous line of your life like in a Miró
it tangles us in your laughter

no wonder I felt so lonely on Saturday when you didn't give your annual
   cocktail party!
I didn't know why

His name is like a leitmotif, a recurring theme, a tune Frank can't seem to
get out of his head; and perhaps it serves Frank as a charm, a talisman, a
mantra. Leaf through the pages of the *Collected Poems* and you'll see
what I mean: his name will appear when you least expect it, but not as
often as it might seem—by my count, in a mere seventeen poems. Sometimes his name is trotted out, the way a great star pops up in a cameo role, or
it will be mentioned in passing, usually by his first name only, as though that
is enough to identify him, and indeed it is. At other times he is the subject of
the poem, or one of its subjects, and he even has a poem dedicated to him.
In his penultimate appearance, it is a poem in celebration of his birthday, and
in his last, his name plays second fiddle to his mother, which is to say, it is in
the possessive case, just so Frank can fit her into his delightful ditty, "Mary
Desti's Ass," which I swear was inspired by the rousing anthem in Cole
Porter's *Kiss Me Kate* ("we open in Venice . . . "). And as if all of this were not
enough, the name of Frank's ubiquitous friend is the title of a play he wrote
with Larry Rivers!

So what is going on here? Why this prevalence of Kenneth Koch in
Frank's oeuvre? The answer, *my* answer: implausibly, Frank was crazy about
this bumptious, blustering, irrepressible, and never-at-a-loss pundit, peda-
gogue, wit, egomaniac, and impossible human being, a friend of Frank's
unlike any other of the many people who entered his poetry and whom
he counted as an intimate. *Kenneth, an intimate?* Not really; and that was
what set him apart from all the others, because what he had with Frank
was a literary friendship enlivened by joshing, ribbing, a playful war of
words. Good-naturedly, Frank made sport of Kenneth, a contrivance that
spilled over into his poetry, as in these lines from "3 Poems About Kenneth
Koch":

He never, Kenneth, did an effortless thing
in his life, but it pains us to send him into the world
in a hurry, he might stumble and commit a series!
Under the careful care of our admiration his greatness
appears like the French for "gratuitous act" and we're proud
of our Hermes, the fastest literary figure of his time.
Are you sitting down to write outside the delicatessen?
Get up, man! come home! Who do you think you are?

Or have I missed something, have I got it all wrong? Well, my characterization of their relationship is based on what I observed and heard and felt, it is merely my impression of what these two highly dissimilar individuals shared, a friendship that seemed to have had nothing to do with exchanging confidences, discussing love and sex, getting down to the nitty-gritty, the quotidian, the prosaic.

And here is how their literary friendship ends up. Upon getting the terrible news of Frank's death and hearing that people have gathered at my place for an impromptu wake, Kenneth arrives with two suitcases that elicit from me a wan joke, "Have you come to stay with me, Kenneth?" The suitcases are for Frank's poems, he explains; he doesn't want anything to happen to them. "Nothing will happen to them; Maureen will see to that," I tell him; but I get the keys to the apartment I shared with Frank until a year and a half ago, and Kenneth goes off, gathers Frank's manuscripts, and later, with the help of Maureen and her husband, Walter Granville-Smith, who have everything copied at the advertising agency where Walter works, Kenneth ensures the integrity of Frank's oeuvre. From then on, with great generosity, expecting and wanting nothing in return, Kenneth does everything in his power to promote Frank's poetry. Is this not the appropriate culmination of their literary friendship? But Frank always did bring out the best in Kenneth.

THE RACHMANINOFF POEMS

[1 9 5 3 – 6 3]

ON RACHMANINOFF'S BIRTHDAY #161

1

Diane calls me so I get up
I wash my hair because
I have a hash hangover then
I noticed the marabunta have walked into the kitchen!
they are carrying a little banner
which says "in search of lanolin"
so that's how they found me!
crawling crawling they don't know
I never keep it in the frigidaire the little dopes
there's something wrong with everyone
that's how we get by at all keep going
and maybe you'll find it you little creeps

2

Darkness and white hair
everything empty, nothing there,
but thoughts how awful
image is, image errrgh
all day long to sit in a window

and see nothing but the past
the serpent is coiled thrice
around her she is dead

3

How are things on the stalinallee
behind the façades is there despair
like on 9th Street behind the beer
and all that life that must be
struggling on without a silence
despair is only the first scratch
of death on the door and a long wait

t is of no great moment, I suppose, but Frank seems to have been confused about or uncertain of what day and month the great Russian composer-pianist's birthday fell on: four of his seven "On Rachmaninoff's Birthday" poems were written in July of 1953, July of 1961 (two that year), and July of 1963, while three of the manuscripts have April dates. I don't know what to make of this—do you? Maybe he knew but kept forgetting that Rachmaninoff was born March 20 (old style) or April 1 (new style), his year of birth being 1873. In fact, the manuscript dated April 2, 1959, indicates that he was aware of these vital statistics; he's only a day late, according to the new style, and he accurately computes how old Rachmaninoff would have been that year ("It is your 86th birthday," he observes in the poem's first line). It is, of course, the poems written in July that really throw me; with those four, he waited three months before he got around to observing Rachmaninoff's birthday. And what an odd way he had of honoring a musician he admired so much, cluttering his tributes with anything that came into his head. Here are notes I made on a couple of the poems:

I noticed the marabunta have walked into the kitchen! brings to mind a corny but entertaining movie with a South American jungle setting, the 1954 *Naked Jungle* in which the marabunta, an army of ants, lays waste to everything in its path, threatening even the insipid Eleanor Parker, who plays a mail-order bride who has a hard time warming up to stolid, humorless Charlton Heston. "They're like the marabunta," Frank said of the cockroaches at Squalid Manor, and that was how we thought of them in the coming years, for they seemed to follow us from one wretched apartment to the next.

they are carrying a little banner / which says "in search of lanolin" / so that's how they found me! is yet another reference to lanolin, which Frank, as of 1961, was still applying to his skin—to what end I never learned.

It's terrible under Kay Francis's armpits (from "On Rachmaninoff's Birthday & About Arshile Gorky") is what Gorky said to de Kooning as they emerged from a movie starring the great lesbian. She appeared in melodramas and tearjerkers of the 1930s, the most famous of which was *One Way Passage* (she had a fatal illness in that one). If you ever saw her—she wore black, slinky evening gowns—you would know what Gorky meant by his comment on her armpits: there was something nasty and dank about what they seemed to conceal.

O Willem de Kooning, you are a very great man / for saying what you said about him and I love you refers not to de Kooning's repeating the armpit comment but to his moving tribute to Gorky's sweet character. Another thing about Kay Francis: she had an incredible lisp (her *r*'s sounded like *w*'s) that amused both de Kooning and Gorky, and Frank, too, as we know from his imitation of her delightful speech impediment in a short untitled poem dated July 28, 1960 ("I wather think I can").

Why do gnats always get into white wine? is something Frank, Mike, Patsy, and I observed and wondered about one East Hampton weekend in the summer of 1963, the last summer the four of us would be together.

In the second of the Rachmaninoff poems (April 1954) Frank wears his heart on his sleeve, unashamedly acknowledging his feelings about this most soulful and romantic of Russian composers:

Blue windows, blue rooftops
and the blue light of the rain,
these contiguous phrases of Rachmaninoff
pouring into my enormous ears
and the tears falling into my blindness

for without him I do not play,
especially in the afternoon
on the day of his birthday. Good
fortune, you would have been
my teacher and I your only pupil

and I would always play again.
Secrets of Liszt and Scriabin
whispered to me over the keyboard
on sunny afternoons! and growing
still in my stormy heart.

Only my eyes would be blue as I played
and you rapped my knuckles,
dearest father of all the Russias
placing my fingers
tenderly upon your cold, tired eyes.

I truly believe that Frank's early desire and ambition to be a pianist remained with him throughout his life, not in any practical or realistic sense but as a dream or fantasy one stubbornly clings to, knowing all the while that what one longs for has always been out of reach, never obtainable. On an out-of-tune piano that Mike and Patsy had in their Springs house, Frank would sometimes play those gorgeous opening chords of Rachmaninoff's Second Piano Concerto—and that was all; like his thwarted career in music, his performance would end before it got started. Other times, to my irritation, he would enlist the assistance of his great collaborator, Bill Berkson, and together they would bang out a crudely improvised, hideously cacophonous, and utterly shapeless one-movement sonata that was supposed to sound like Prokofiev, and perhaps it did to Frank, whose imgination knew no bounds.

DIGRESSIONS ON SOME POEMS BY FRANK O'HARA

And now with my vast collection of CDs, dispensing hours upon hours of music at any time of the day or night, I cannot help but think of Frank—and of myself, too—getting by on the meager music offered by our tinny radio, and I especially think of Frank when I feast upon the late-nineteenth-century piano concertos (some written in the twentieth century!) that in recent years have been released on CD, decadent, excessive works that Frank never had the opportunity to hear, thrilling virtuoso pieces lush with chromaticism and displaying no great creative range to interfere with their exuberant pianism—these are the piano concertos of Balakirev, Medtner, Scriabin, Alkan, Henselt, Rimsky-Korsakov, Moszkowski, Rubinstein, Arensky, and, above all, Sergei Eduardovich Bortkiewicz, my latest discovery, whose dates (1877–1952) parallel those of Rachmaninoff (1873–1943), his compatriot, and whose Piano Concerto Number 1 in B flat, opus 16, would have wowed Frank with its one truly great theme, as seductive and lovely as any melody dreamed up by Rachmaninoff, plus an orchestration that makes Max Steiner and Erich Korngold sound restrained by comparison. Oh, Frank, if only you were here to wallow in all this luxurious, rapturous music!

POEM

[F E B R U A R Y   9 ,   1 9 6 2]

Lana Turner has collapsed!
I was trotting along and suddenly
it started raining and snowing
and you said it was hailing
but hailing hits you on the head
hard so it was really snowing and
raining and I was in such a hurry
to meet you but the traffic
was acting exactly like the sky
and suddenly I see a headline
LANA TURNER HAS COLLAPSED!
There is no snow in Hollywood
There is no rain in California
I have been to lots of parties
and acted perfectly disgraceful
but I never actually collapsed
oh Lana Turner we love you get up

never missed a poetry reading of Frank's unless it was out of town, and
even then, as on the occasion of his reading at Wagner College, I'd seriously consider making a special effort to get to it. What a loyal fan I was!
The evening of February 9, 1962, a Friday, was raw and dismal, but that

· 264 ·

didn't stop me from joining Frank and Bill Berkson at the Staten Island ferry. On the ride over—should it be called a voyage?—I drifted away from Frank and Bill, who clearly wanted to be alone. "Are you Edward Albee?" It was Robert Lowell, standing suddenly beside me at the rail; he'd be reading with Frank that night, and earlier, as we were coming aboard, they'd briefly exchanged greetings. I suppose Lowell thought I might be the sensational new playwright because of Edward's association with the Wagner College writers conference. I confessed I wasn't Albee, and that ended our conversation.

I liked to hear Frank read his poems, and I think a lot of other people did, too. Even with a voice that was nasal, lacked resonance, and had a curious Yankee twang to it, he was a consummate reader who had no trouble holding his audience. Sam Barber, the possessor of a beautiful tenor voice and elegant diction, could not reconcile Frank's voice with his being a poet. "How can you be a poet with a voice like that?" he said incredulously, out of the blue—it was the summer we got to know him in Southampton. But it is entirely possible that Sam didn't think much of Frank's poetry, either. I know that he lost or misplaced the "Dee Dum" poem Frank wrote on the occasion of his fifty-second birthday. (See the next note on that very poem.)

I think there's been a misunderstanding about Frank's attitude toward Lowell; he didn't like the guy's poetry but he had nothing against him personally. Thus, and I'm quite sure about this, at their joint reading he didn't try to show Lowell up or tweak his nose in public by reading the Lana Turner poem he'd written on the way to the reading. It's simply not the sort of thing Frank would have done. Also, too much shouldn't be made of his writing a funny poem about Lana Turner. It has no big significance; Frank was merely responding to a *New York Post* headline—impulsively, unpretentiously, with humor. And isn't it just plain dumb of John Updike to get worked up over it? He has let it be known that he thinks the poem is Frank at his "silliest and emptiest"—this from someone who writes light verse that bears no relation to poetry!

In recent years, the poem has been set by at least two composers. There's

DIGRESSIONS ON SOME POEMS BY FRANK O'HARA

a nice recording, on the Musical Heritage Society label, of the Christopher Berg setting by a fine young tenor named Carl Halvorson. Ned Rorem's setting of Paul Goodman's earnest and sobersided "The Lordly Hudson" comes just before the campy Lana Turner song—oh, if only Paul had lived long enough to hear the two songs, one after the other!

POEM

[M A R C H   9 ,   1 9 6 2]

Dee Dum, dee dum, dum, dum, dee da
here it is March 9th, 1962
and JJ is shooting off to work
I loll in bed reading *Poets of Russia*
feeling perfectly awful and smoking

hey wait a minute! I leap out of bed
it's Sam Barber's birthday and they
are going to play *Souvenirs*! turn it up!
how glad I am I'm going to be late that's
starting the day with rose-colored binoculars!

The first line mirrors the melody of the opening waltz movement of Samuel Barber's almost unbearably sweet and charming *Souvenirs* for four-handed piano. The composer advises: "To be played with amused tenderness, not with irony." Were his hands two of the four negotiating this not terribly difficult work, Frank would have found those words unnecessary and, what's more, he would have disregarded the qualifying "amused," so shamelessly touched was he by music this simple-hearted and nostalgic. (Had they enough practice time, I can imagine that he and Alvin Novak could have pulled it off.) Frank loved salon piano music like *Souvenirs,* anything for piano by Fauré (he never tired of the Marguerite Long recording of the *Ballade*), and most especially Poulenc's gorgeous *Soirées de Nazelle,* which Jimmy Schuyler brought to his (and my) attention. If Frank couldn't start the day with music, he was just as happy opening a book upon awakening. He'd light a Camel and pick up where he left off with, say, the latest Gertrude Stein released by Yale University Press, each volume remaindered almost as soon as it was published; but from the beeline Frank made for the Eighth Street Bookstore, you would have thought it was the latest best-seller, not just another arcane work from the Gertrude Stein estate. I don't remember *Poets of Russia,* no doubt an anthology, but I do remember giving him the new Nabokov translation of *Eugene Onegin,* which he could not have liked since he never said a word about it later.

. . . *JJ is shooting off to work*—to Grolier's, a boring encyclopedia job where he met Stephen Holden whom he then brought into our circle. No, J. J. Mitchell had not just left Frank's bed but mine; the switch over would come later, after our move to 791 Broadway.

. . . *turn it up!* That's where I come into the poem—Frank was talking to me; obviously, I was already up and about, though I had no place to go, no job I had to report to, since I hadn't finished running through the money I made from my paperback original, *Always Love a Stranger,* and from my play on TV, *Cool Wind over the Living.* Now I was writing another paperback original, *You Die with Your Eyes Open.*

So what else is in this poem, what other associations can I ring from it? Not surprisingly, it is the incidental mention of J.J.'s name that causes my memory to take flight: I can see him slipping from my bed, dashing through our tiny living room to the john where his ablutions are quickly attended to and just as quickly he puts on pants, shirt, tie, coat, spurns the coffee I've just made, and is out the door, already fifteen minutes late to work.

I met him a year and a half earlier, at a small dinner party I gave. Chuck Turner brought him as a "mystery guest," and probably lived to regret it. I took one look and thought: I want him. (Don Bachardy to someone who complained about my lack of scruples when it came to making out: "I would trust Joe with my life but never with a boyfriend," which I mention as a cards-on-the-table confession, not as a boast.) Rapacious, sexy, sociable J.J. was

DIGRESSIONS ON SOME POEMS BY FRANK O'HARA

trouble from the start, so perhaps I, more than Chuck, lived to regret my enticing his new young friend back to my place after a Halloween party later that night at Kenward Elmslie's.

The first thing you noticed about J.J. (for John Joseph) was his smile, because it was always there, his natural expression, daring you not to find him attractive. Great white teeth, perfectly even, and his mouth that curled at the edges seemed to have existed for the sole purpose of setting them off. Years later, at the Bronx, a gay bar on the rue Sainte Anne in Paris, he boldly approached Mick and Bianca Jagger, who were slumming, no doubt amused by all the queers, and J.J., with barely a glance at Mick, chatted up Bianca, with reminiscences about the days when she went out with Bill Berkson, until their one-way tête-à-tête was abruptly ended as Mick, with his index finger, clicked J.J.'s great white sparklers. "Nice teeth, kid," a bum's rush that actually amused the unflappable J.J.

Legendary, too, was his great chest—actually, the nipples on his chest, since that was what you zeroed in on when you saw him nude for the first time; they seemed to be an extra sex organ, so indecent, overripe, and inviting were those two proudly androgynous nipples. A great swimmer's body. Curly, sandy-colored hair. Perfect cock. And blue eyes that had seen everything. One of two ne'er-do-well sons of an admiral and a saintly but ineffectual mother, he was also athletic (swimming and tennis), intelligent, and well-educated (Harvard and Choate, as mentioned earlier); but after years of institutional living (boarding schools, Choate, a brief stint in the navy), he was unprepared for life on the outside. A sex addict and an alcoholic, he was in such great shape when he started out in New York, at the time I met him, that it was ten years before he was burned out, a shell of the gorgeous Adonis he once was.

Here is a poem I ran across in *The Times Literary Supplement* of February 14, 1997, that needs no comment from me, though I might explain that "BAR on 2nd Avenue" was J.J.'s last hangout. The author of the poem, the estimable Thom Gunn, has kindly granted me permission to reprint it.

FAMOUS FRIENDS

Could never place him.
But I'd go into
BAR on 2nd Avenue
and there he was, face
lighting up, helpful
silly and eager, yes,
jump-started again
and now unstoppable
on an expressway of talk, fast
and funny, but after half an hour
I'd edge away.

J.J.,
he said, J.J.,
that's my name.
Talked, that time,
of getting something published
—So you write, I said!
Why, didn't you know,
his smile triumphant,
I was
Frank O'Hara's last lover.

Didn't see him again.
It was like having met
—years afterwards—
Fanny Brawne
full of bounce, or
Degen, the conceited
baker's boy.

No, it wasn't.

Rather, it was like having met
Nell Gwyn,

on the way down,
good-natured, losing weight,
still chatting about spaniels

With that wonderfully evocative poem, I have gotten ahead of myself inasmuch as it describes the J. J. Mitchell who came later, the J.J. who evolved in the years after Frank's death, from golden boy to derelict, a meta-morphosis with the makings of a cautionary tale that will inevitably inform my reckoning of his downfall. If I'm beginning to sound moralistic, *tant pis*—and check this out for sermonizing, not my usual mode:

"Why don't you do what I did and what I'm still doing," I suggested to him early on in our affair, which stumbled along for a miraculous run of two years. "Try different jobs, don't get in a rut, keep looking for something you might like to do," I went on. And then I said something that—I realize only now—summed up my philosophy, a prosaic belief that has kept me going lo these many years: "It doesn't matter whether you succeed or not, because the search is what matters, that becomes your life." J.J. listened to what I had to say, but there was nothing he could do. For he was exactly like a convict in-carcerated over many years and then set free: he hadn't the foggiest notion how to begin, what to do, where to look. I never knew anyone who found work, or any sort of effort, so out-and-out repugnant. "I'm paralyzed," he said many years later, when I suggested he try to do something, *anything*, to save his life; but he was paralyzed back then, years earlier, as soon as he was out of Harvard. And in the succeeding years, until 1967 or thereabouts, he barely held down his undemanding research job at Grolier, while conserving his nonstop energy and considerable verbal gifts for the only thing that mattered to him: the pursuit of pleasure.

"He's fine the way he is," Frank said when I broached the subject of what to do about J.J.

"I know. I have no room to talk. But don't you think he shouldn't drink so much?" I actually had the nerve to say that to Frank!

Of course he didn't dignify my question with an answer. Meanwhile, I paid no heed to the growing camaraderie of my roommate and my lover, saw it merely as a boon, an asset to my love affair: it kept J.J. interested in me, kept him coming around—not that I saw the situation in such crass terms. But Alvin Novak did. "You're a package deal," he told me, cheerfully. Abashed, I took umbrage. Yet I didn't believe it was true—it *couldn't* be true, not with all I had to offer on my own. Why, then, have those withering words dogged me through the years?

Coinciding with the gradual rift between Frank and Vincent, my far less committed affair with J.J. ended abruptly one fine day when my restless paramour, who possessed the terrible virtue of honesty in sexual matters, confessed he had to have his freedom. I knew what he meant, he didn't have to explain. As much as he cared for me, he was all too aware of the enticing studs awaiting his attentions in the vast New York sex arena.

LUNCH POEMS

[1 9 5 9 – 6 5]

Often this poet, strolling through the noisy splintered glare of a Man-
hattan noon, has paused at a sample Olivetti to type up thirty or forty
lines of ruminations, or pondering more deeply has withdrawn to a
darkened ware- or fire-house to limn his computed misunderstanding
of the eternal questions of life, co-existence and depth, while never
forgetting to eat lunch his favorite meal . . .

n no uncertain terms, this collection of poems demonstrates how averse
Frank was to publication, so averse that some people might be tempted to
describe his attitude as capricious, inscrutable, neurotic, or self-destructive.
I look at it another way.

You'll recall Frank going through his manuscripts at Joan's. How bleak
and unrewarding he finds the chore! He wrote the damn poems—isn't that
enough? He has better things to do than sit by himself and decide which ones
should go into a book whose publication, he tries to convince himself, no
longer interests Barney Rosset.

At the same time, Frank would obviously like to have it over and done
with: "I wish I were staying in town and working on my poems" he asserts—
meaning, he wishes he *wanted* to stay home, etc., because in fact he is looking forward to the weekend with Vincent, who hereafter will be so important
to him that he won't hesitate to put his new book of poems on a back burner.
With nobody from Grove Press breathing down his neck—Barney is preoc-

cupied with his heroic court battles to change the country's obscenity laws while Don Allen is presumably busy editing *The New American Poetry* anthology—he eventually abandons the project altogether.

That is how I remember the situation: I could be wrong about what Barney and Don were up to at that moment. In any event, when Lawrence Ferlinghetti, on a visit to New York that fall, looked Frank up and suggested they do a book together, Frank apparently had no qualms about going along with Ferlinghetti's proposal, particularly since the San Francisco–based City Lights Books was a modest operation, the kind of independent publishing house he liked. Then, too, I'm sure he regarded the size and format of Ferlinghetti's pocketbooks as the ideal showcase for some of the short poems he'd written over the past six or seven years.

From the beginning, it was agreed that the title would be *Lunch Poems,* which Frank generously credited Ferlinghetti with having thought up while Ferlinghetti has said that it was probably Frank's idea. From what I remember Frank having told me, I believe they hit on the title jointly, in somewhat this manner: when Frank explained that most of the poems were written on his lunch hour, Ferlinghetti said with a smile that they were Frank's lunch poems, which prompted Frank to rejoin, "Maybe that should be the title."

That was in the latter part of 1959, and it wasn't until the end of February 1965 that Frank finally had in hand his copies of this pocket-size paperback measuring 6¼" x 5" and numbering a mere seventy-four pages, an occasion followed within a few weeks by a glorious party in his honor at Morris Golde's garden apartment on West Eleventh Street. We were all exceedingly impressed that it took so long for such a small book to be edited, printed, and published—so long, in fact, that half of the poems selected were written after Frank agreed to be number nineteen in Ferlinghetti's Pocket Poets series.

"Have you decided what poems to send?" I'd ask every few months; and then, once the poems had been selected, "Have you sent Ferlinghetti the manuscript?" Oh, what Frank put me through! And he was aware of it, I'm sure. For on the dedicatory page of my copy, he drew an arrow-pierced heart that encircled my name ("To Joseph LeSueur," reads the dedication), and inside the heart, in a great scrawl, he let me know he appreciated my seeing him through close to five years of anguish, boredom, and indecision. "How could it have gotten done without you," he wrote, sans question mark, as if to say there were no question about it.

Yes, I gave him support and encouragement, but there was no way I could have helped him with the selection of the poems or convinced him that a decent book could be made from them. That was where Kenneth Koch came in: he got the job done. Also, at some point Don Allen advised Frank what poems should be included. Meanwhile, funny postcards would arrive from Ferlinghetti—"I'm hungry for lunch," they'd say, or "When will lunch be ready?" To the end, Frank did everything he could to forestall publication— for example, by insisting that the title would have to be changed because of its similarity to *Naked Lunch,* whose publication created a sensation in the early sixties. So Frank then decided to call the book *To Joseph LeSueur.* Though I thought he was making a mistake, I so liked the idea of being the title of a book that I kept my mouth shut; but Kenneth, thank heavens, convinced him that *Lunch Poems* was a perfect title and that he should forget about the Burroughs book.

Was anything else bothering Frank that might hold the book up? Yes. Suddenly, he changed his mind about a couple of the poems. "Kenneth knows what he's talking about," I said, "and if he says they're right for the book, I'm sure they are." Then Ferlinghetti made the mistake of asking him to write the jacket copy. What he must have wanted, I thought, was a straightforward, fairly conventional blurb, nothing resembling what Frank obliged him with in one quick typewritten draft, dreamed up while he was on his second or third drink before dinner one night. "*Lunch Poems* is never going to come out," I said in despair after he showed me what he'd written.

At the time—by now it was 1964—I was an editor at a conventional trade publishing firm, so maybe I'd gotten a little square. Besides, it turned out that Ferlinghetti had nothing against—perhaps even wanted?—an irreverent, tongue-in-cheek blurb, since he immediately decided to go to press. Incidentally, it is Frank's facetious reference to his pausing "at a sample Olivetti to type up thirty or forty lines of ruminations" that led later commentators to assert that he sometimes wrote his poems on an Olivetti show-room typewriter. The dumbbells—didn't they know when they were being kidded?

So, the die was cast—we could all relax; Frank's new collection was coming out. As to his being indifferent about publication, it made perfect sense: it allowed him to embrace life, not careerist concerns, and it was through his everyday experiences that a poem might come to him, not through reading over, thinking about, admiring, or castigating something he'd already written, something he was finished and done with.

Exactly when this jewel of a book was published is open to dispute, as Alexander Smith's bibliography makes clear: Ferlinghetti claims it was brought out in 1964, but Frank didn't receive his copies until February 28, 1965, while April 3, 1965, is the publication date on the copyright application. This confusion is fitting, very much in Frank's spirit: it's a wonder *Lunch Poems* ever saw the light of day.

THE SENTIMENTAL UNITS

[1 9 6 4]

1

If only more people looked like Jerry Lieber we would all be a lot happier, I think.

2

It is May 17th, 17 is a strangely sonorous number, and I haven't made out my income tax yet.

3

There is a man going by with his arm in a sling. I wish men could take care of themselves better.

4

Mahler is great, Bruckner is terrible.

5

Listen, I have to go out and get food. If you want some cigarettes, I'll go out with you.

6

Where they've come from. We're not even up to 23rd Street yet. Sings a little song in middle. "I hate driving."

7

There are certainly enough finks in the world without going to a German restaurant.

8

Listen, I have to go on foot. Would you mind lending me your snow (hic) shoes?

9

I saw T.S. on the telly today. I find that he is one of the most intelligent writers of our "day."

10

If you have to see *Sporting Life* it helped to make sense out of that movie. Read *Radclyffie,* he said.

11

Part 9 is an imitation of Joe Brainard.

12

It was Jerry's eyes, one brown and the other blue, that elicted from Frank this excessive testimony to the attractiveness of the lyricist of the team of Lieber and Stoller. But was it Frank or Jerry who first said, "He does what I can't do and I do what he can't do"? Jerry was the one who told me, many years after Frank's death, that "that was what we said about each other," but I imagine the remark originated with Frank—it would have been so like him. Never a snob, always the egalitarian, not the sort of poet who would look down on a pop songwriter, he clearly recognized in Jerry Lieber a kindred talent. In Jerry's case, it might be said that his was a God-given talent. The story goes that one day, at a precocious age, he said to himself, after listening to a pop song he admired, "Hey, I can do that." And found that he could. Which is to say, no training or apprenticeship was needed—it came that naturally to him—so that over the next dozen or so years, ingenious lyrics for the likes of Elvis Presley and Peggy Lee poured out of him, set to music by Mike Stoller.

I can only guess how Frank and Jerry became acquainted; it was probably

DIGRESSIONS ON SOME POEMS BY FRANK O'HARA

through Virgil Thomson, who seemed to know everyone. As to how, where, and when I got to know Jerry, it would have been in East Hampton during the summer of—well, I'm not sure when; sometime in the mid-fifties when he was part of the crowd we ran with, he and his wife, Gaby, whose promising stage and screen career was cut short when she bore him two sons. And now that I've broached Gaby's name, it occurs to me that a special entry should really be devoted to her, and that could have been accomplished earlier, if I'd been alert, by citing a wonderful untitled Vincent Warren love poem from 1960:

> So many echoes in my head
> that when I am frantic to do something
> about anything, out comes "you were wearing . . ."
> or I knock my head against a wall
> of my own appetite for despair and come
> up with "you once ran naked toward me / knee
> deep in cold March surf" or I blame it
> on Blake, on Robert Aldrich's *Kiss Me,*
> *Deadly,* on the "latitude" of the stars
>
> but where in all this noise
> am I waiting for the clouds to be blown
> away away away away away into the sun
> (burp), I wouldn't want the clouds to be
> burped back by that hot optimistic cliché, it
> hangs always promising some nebulous
> healthy reaction to our native dark
>
> I will let the sun wait till summer
> now that our love has moved into the dark
> area symbolizing depth and secrecy and mystery
> it's not bad, we shall find out
> when the light returns what the new
> season means / when others' interpretations
> have gotten back up onto the pedestals

The Sentimental Units · 279

DIGRESSIONS ON SOME POEMS BY FRANK O'HARA

> we gave them
> so long as we are still
> wearing each other when alone

It is the reference to *Kiss Me Deadly* (no comma in the title, Frank) that summons to center stage the spontaneous, original, irrepressible, surprising, wonderfully attractive—I could go on, and so could Frank if he were still with us—Gaby Rodgers. Yes, I'm quite certain that when *Kiss Me Deadly* loomed in Frank's ever-fertile imagination and landed in his poem, he had in mind not only the director, as witness Aldrich's name conspicuously before the title, but also Gaby of the close-cropped blond hair and alluring Dutch accent that were so indelibly a part of that trailblazing film noir. Vicious, violent, and hard-hitting, it was based on a Mickey Spillane pulp novel and boasts scores of unsettling images, like that of the divine Gaby going up in flames when she opens a Pandora's box of nuclear fission, which of course is the last we see of her—in *any* movie, come to think of it. Hollywood wasn't meant for this stage-trained actress who had worked with Henry Fonda, Fredric March, and other luminaries, and who would star thirty years later in a Robert Wilson puzzler, *The Golden Door*, at the Brooklyn Academy of Music.

"Don't listen to those boring *Partisan Review* friends of yours," Frank advised Gaby, pointedly raising his voice at a party not long after the 1955 release of *Kiss Me Deadly*. We were at Harold and May Rosenberg's, I believe, and the stodgy intellectual who had just ridiculed Gaby for appearing in a trashy Hollywood movie must have heard Frank. I just wish I could remember who it was. In any event, poor Gaby—then as now, a sensitive and impressionable soul—was made to feel defensive about the movie until she was set straight by Frank, who prophetically praised it as a brilliant film of corruption and paranoia, and Gaby's appearance in it as the movie debut of the year. I began to say something about the male lead, Ralph Meeker, whose career we'd been following after seeing him in William Inge's *Picnic,* a so-so theater experience redeemed by his sexy good looks, great physique, and sterling stage presence; but I was cut off by Frank, who explained later that

280 · *The Sentimental Units*

he was afraid Gaby would get the idea Meeker was actually the reason we were crazy about *Kiss Me Deadly*.

Mahler is great, Bruckner is terrible. For all the years I knew Frank, our disagreement over the comparative merits of Mahler and Bruckner persisted, and I think he wrote this Unit to reproach me. Also, perhaps because I'd made sure it got back to him what Jimmy Schuyler confided to me: "I've been listening to Bruckner, Joe, and you're right—he's great."

If you have to see Sporting Life *it helped to make sense out of that movie. Read* Radclyffie, *he said. This Sporting Life*, the movie made from David Storey's novel, we had seen sometime before I brought home from work his third novel, *Radcliffe*, which my employer, Coward-McCann, was bringing out in one of their offset editions from British plates, a cheap way of publishing for that exceedingly cheap company. Maybe you saw it. A gritty evocation of the brutal world of Rugby football, it drew from me a predictable response. "Wildly homoerotic," I remember asserting as we emerged from the theater. Since Frank looked doubtful—"You would say that," he scoffed— I naturally felt vindicated when I had the opportunity of bringing to his attention Storey's latest novel, a dark, depressing Lawrentian story about the passionate relationship between two butch men that features a shit sandwich (literally) and ends with one of the men murdering the other. "Get a load of this," I said, tossing the bound galleys to him at the end of a work day. He gave it a quick read that night and, over coffee the next morning, agreed that Storey had pulled out all the stops and taken the violent, sexually repressed world of *This Sporting Life* to its logical conclusion. And was this Unit, like the one about Bruckner and Mahler, written with me in mind? Well, perhaps in the back of Frank's mind—with, you'll note, the title of *Radcliffe* so perversely misspelled that it surely could not have been through carelessness. A commentary on me, David Storey, the novel, or the title character? Your call.

Part 9 is an imitation of Joe Brainard. He stammered, he barely spoke, he kept his own counsel. He was also sweet, kind, and modest, and so laid-back as to seem ineffectual. Yet, along with the egregious J. J. Mitchell, though as blameless as J.J. was remiss, he was from my jaundiced point of view instrumental in causing the end of my partnership with Frank O'Hara . . .

In my mind's eye, I can summon my first glimpse of him—in Greenwich Village on an evening in early 1964, during the intermission of an Al Carmines musical. Edwin Denby is standing beside me, somewhat apart from the small crowd of young people milling in front of Judson Church. Unlike my ascetic companion, who is merely observing the scene, I am shamelessly on the prowl, as becomes evident when I make a pleasurable sound that causes Edwin to glance at me and follow my gaze to a gangling, bespectacled kid with dark, curly hair. How indelibly that first glimpse of Joe Brainard is etched in my memory!

Actually, it is his red nylon jacket that first catches my eye, a jacket so like the one famously worn by James Dean in *Rebel Without a Cause* that I wonder: Any connection? (Maybe so, I will decide many years later when, perusing Joe's magnum opus, *I Remember*, in the Penguin edition published after his death, I come across "I remember James Dean in his red nylon jacket," which will elicit an "I remember" of my own, how Joe once spoke to me of having shared Frank's passion for the actor.) Something else: the jacket—Joe's, not the one worn by James Dean—is badly torn, ripped all the way across the back. (Could it possibly have been the same garment Joe refers to when he remembers "going to the ballet with Edwin Denby in a red car coat"? Again, maybe so.) And solely on the basis of that pitiful jacket, I assume—correctly, as it turns out—that its possessor is as indigent as he is thin. An apparent newcomer on the scene, he also looks touchingly out of place, a rube who, I will soon learn, hails from Oklahoma—Tulsa, to be exact.

"Who is he?" I ask Edwin. He reads me perfectly and answers, with cold-blooded finality: "Not for you, Joe"—meaning, he's too young or unavailable or possibly not even queer. Edwin persists in thinking I should never have broken up with Gianni and feels, too, I'm sure, that all I have in mind is bedding this innocent youth, which of course is the truth.

The evening ends uneventfully, without my meeting Joe or even learning his name. (If Edwin knows it, he isn't saying. Has he already taken Joe to the ballet?) Then, a few weeks later, Ted Berrigan introduces us; and when Joe and I finally get together, he tells me that Ted, after being apprised of Joe's interest in me, said with great confidence, as though he were an intimate of Frank's and mine: "Forget it, he's Frank O'Hara's lover"—more of the conspiracy, it would appear, to keep us apart.

"I remember learning to play bridge so I could get to know Frank O'Hara better"—again, from *I Remember*. So much for the reason *I* thought Joe agreed to be a fourth with Tony Towle, Frank, and me. And our card playing was all that went on during those first two or three evenings—that and conversation: "I remember playing bridge with Frank. (Mostly talk)," Joe notes in the entry immediately following the one just quoted. "Mostly talk" refers accurately enough to Frank, whose volubility could not be dampened by a silly game of cards. Still, it's not as if bridge can be played by two people! Was Joe's an extreme case of hero-worship? Judge for yourself: "I think often of the way Frank O'Hara was. If I have a hero (I do) it is Frank O'Hara"—that's a quote from his diary in the 1970 *Selected Writings*. Also, it is worth noting that in the highly selective Penguin *I Remember*—I am tempted to add "bowdlerized" on account of the exclusion of a couple of Joe's raunchiest homoerotic fantasies—Frank is featured more often than anyone else.

And what did Frank think of his latest admirer? After the first couple of times Tony brought him by, Joe having recently moved in with Tony, into the wretched apartment on East Ninth Street we'd abandoned, Frank said he couldn't understand what I saw in anyone that skinny. "And he's too quiet," he added. But here is what he wrote to Larry Rivers in a letter dated April 18, 1964: "Now I am making some cartoons with Joe Brainard, a 21-year-old assemblagist genius you will like a lot . . ."

Around the time of that letter, Frank also mentioned Joe in one of several marginal works he wrote during the last years of his life, the curiously titled "Sentimental Units" that is the starting point of this digression. "Part 9 is an imitation of Joe Brainard," we're told, the ninth Unit being a parody of an intriguing stylistic quirk of Joe's, his droll use of quotation marks: "I saw T.S. on the telly today. I find that he is one of the most intelligent writers of our 'day.'" I think Frank put Joe in this work—it was the last entry—right after he read something of his for the first time, and I remember Frank's being as surprised as I was that besides creating artworks like nobody else's, notably assemblages with gaudy religious decorations, our new friend also wrote faux-naïve prose poetry as original as his art. "How did Joe come to write the way he writes?" I wondered aloud. Frank's answer (words to this effect): It wasn't something he learned, it was something he started doing one day. And what is that, I now cannot help thinking, but a kind of genius, one that encompasses even more exceptionally the hundreds of glorious collages he created in the 1970s.

Well, when Frank pointed out that Joe was too skinny, I let him know in no uncertain terms that I didn't care. "I'm still mad for him," I said. Frank thought for a moment and then suggested I invite Joe to dinner by himself, without Tony. "There'd just be the two of us?" I said. "Wouldn't that be too obvious? Why don't you join us, then make yourself scarce?" "Which wouldn't be too obvious?" Frank laughed.

In one of the two sequels to the original *I Remember,* neither of which I have been able to lay my hands on, Joe wrote that he remembered "how much Frank O'Hara liked Joe LeSueur's chili," which didn't make it to the Penguin edition. Or is that an "I remember" from my imagination, dreamed up out of an eagerness to occupy at least a subordinate slot in Joe's memory vault? Could be. Anyway, chili was definitely what I made that night, chili with more beans than meat preceded by lots of drinks and followed by the three of us adjourning to Frank's bedroom to watch the Norma Shearer–Leslie Howard *Romeo and Juliet* on his newly acquired TV, the first set either of us had, not counting the hand-me-down Norman Bluhm gave us.

"I remember my first lover (Joe LeSueur). I don't think he'll mind"— there it is, Joe's acknowledgment of our affair in the original *I Remember,* which I have just unearthed after a long search among all the chapbooks and poetry magazines I accumulated over my thirty-odd years on the New York poetry scene. Oh, if only I could say to Joe now: No, I don't mind being described as your first lover—on the contrary! And would you mind, I'd add, if I gave an account of what happened that first night? Joe's guileless confessional writing answers that question: of course he wouldn't mind . . .

For the longest time, the situation doesn't look promising. Joe, I told myself, is going to be a hard nut to crack; if only he weren't so shy, he'd meet me halfway. Later, when I got to know him, it became clear that he was deceptively shy, in his quiet way assertive and headstrong, someone who knew exactly what he wanted and went after it. But at the moment, not yet aware of the nature of his shyness, I foolishly respond in kind, eschewing my usual aggressive approach in sexually charged situations.

Frank tunes the TV to *The Late Late Show* and stretches out on his bed, a drink in hand, as Joe and I fetch chairs from the living room, a routine we will fall into over the next couple of months. On one such occasion, Joe makes a mental note that will find its way into the original *I Remember* six years later, further evidence of his hero-worship: "I remember seeing Frank O'Hara write a poem once. We were watching a western on TV and he got up as tho to fix a drink or answer the telephone but instead he went over to the typewriter, leaned over it a bit, and typed for 4 or 5 minutes standing up. Then he pulled the piece of paper out of the typewriter and handed it to me and then lay back down to watch more TV. (The TV was in the bedroom.) I don't remember the poem except that it had some cowboy dialect in it." I don't remember the poem either—yes, I'm sure I was there—but it might have been "At the Bottom of the Dump There's Some Sort of Bugle." Written when we first knew Joe, it refers indirectly to a Western starring the gorgeous but minor movie star Joel McCrea, whom Frank adored and whom I dubbed, much to Frank's irritation, "the poor man's Gary Cooper" because of the B pictures he made—like the 1947 *Ramrod*, which is possibly the very movie we saw that night.

Another of Frank's many "movie" poems, the wicked and irreverent "Ave Maria" of 1960, I somehow failed to take note of earlier, in its proper sequence, and now is an appropriate time to make amends. Written out of Frank's love of old movies and his experience of seeing them years later on TV, it is more autobiographical than one might think. Surprisingly, the almost Swiftian impulse behind the poem can be related to Frank's childhood—specifically, to his not having been allowed to see Dietrich and Garbo movies, something he revealed on one of the few occasions he reminisced with me about his childhood. Of course I'm only guessing, but I think the idea for the poem occurred to him when he finally got to see one such "forbidden" movie, a Garbo melodrama called *The Painted Veil*, at one of John Button's TV evenings. So what we have here, in "Ave Maria," is the grown-up Francis Russell O'Hara of Grafton, Massachusetts, ruefully recalling his childhood as he admonishes the "mothers of America" to "let your kids go to the movies!" lest there be grave consequences like those cited in the poem's concluding lines: "so don't blame me if you don't take this advice / and the family breaks up / and your children grow old and blind in front of a TV set / seeing / movies you wouldn't let them see when they were young." There is, however, a bright side to all of this: Frank's beloved great-aunt Elizabeth, of whom he kept a small framed picture in our Forty-ninth Street apartment, took him to a matinee of a Dietrich vehicle, *The Devil Is a Woman*, without his mother's knowledge. At the time of his death, I think he was still hoping to see that delicious piece of claptrap again—on TV, naturally.

Where were we? Oh yes, watching M-G-M's bloodless *Romeo and Juliet*. The instant John Barrymore's plump, over-the-hill Mercutio is run through by Basil Rathbone's sneering Tybalt, who also looks long in the tooth, Frank says he's seen enough. "Barrymore's the only good thing in the movie," he explains, and suggests that I take the TV to my room. Well, from "To the Film Industry in Crisis," we know that its author had a weakness for Norma Shearer, no matter that her manner was cloying, her eyes tiny and slightly crossed, and her age too advanced for a credible Juliet, particularly when she got to the balcony scene, which Frank surely had in mind when he wrote the line, "and moonlike, too, the gentle Norma Shearer"—indubitably, then, he made a great and noble sacrifice in forgoing the rest of the movie.

"Maybe I sh-should . . . go . . . home," Joe stammers. Too late; I've already begun wheeling the TV to the rear of the loft where my bedroom is, and it is no time before we are lying on my bed together, with the TV glowing in the dark but almost immediately ignored. "Frank doesn't mind?" he whispers when I make my move. It is then that I put him straight.

Having gone this far in my account of that long-ago night, I should be able to forge ahead; instead, I am undecided what tack to take, whether to skip the intimate details or give some idea what happened after I drew Joe into my arms—"It's none of our business!" That's Frank, invading my train of thought, as he so often does: it is the retort he flung at me back in 1959 when I mildly complained that Pasternak didn't describe the physical love experienced by Zhivago and Lara. "What happened was between them, all right?" he went on, heatedly. You would have thought they were real people, not mere characters in a novel! "You don't have to be so fucking sanctimonious about it," I shot back. Later, wondering why he was so sensitive about the Pasternak novel, I thought it might have been because Harold Brodkey got his goat a couple of days earlier when he teased him about his laudatory piece in *Evergreen Review*, "About Zhivago and His Poems"—how infuriating the detestable Brodkey was as he smirked that the novel had too many coincidences, too much inept plotting, to be taken seriously! On the other hand, Frank was hardly one to brood over insults or slights, so I could be mistaken that his fly-by-night lover at Harvard was involved in any of this. One thing is plainly evident, though: Frank is with me as I write this roundabout account, and it is in deference to him that I have decided on a discreet fade-out. Still, I would like to add something that Frank, I feel, would not find unworthy: on the night in question, it became dazzlingly clear to me that Joe's recumbent demeanor concealed a finely tuned sensuality and a responsive, passionate nature. I had the feeling he had waited all of his twenty-one years for what we conspired together.

Thus, with a nudge from Frank, my affair with Joe Brainard was finally launched—and an affair was all it could ever be, one destined from the outset to be the sort of dalliance I invariably sought. As for the unworldly boy I bedded, he would know soon enough that he wanted something else, something permanent, though not with me, as I would learn to my chagrin—chagrined, I confess, even if I wasn't available for, interested in, or capable of a long-term commitment. So what was with me, what was my problem? No problem; I just wasn't the sort to plan for the future, a fantasized future with a certain someone at my side, so I had no need or desire to emulate the mat-

ing ways of straight people. And in Joe's case, it was all to the good: we became close friends, and remained so to the end of his life.

It was, of course, my attachment to Frank that ruled out my forming a lasting romantic relationship with any of my boyfriends—his presence in my life
was that encompassing. Even as late as the spring and summer of 1964, only
months before it was decided we could no longer be together, I found living
under the same roof with him a solace and a pleasure, an *anchor*, in spite of
our not being as close as we once were. Resignedly, I knew there was no way
we could be, not with Bill Berkson and Vincent Warren occupying places in
his heart I could never fill, and, in the latter part of 1964, not with Kynaston
McShine, Stephen Holden, Jim Brodey, and I don't know who else making
themselves available to him, in some cases at the behest of a middle-of-the-
night phone call he'd make when he was in his cups after an evening out on
the town—oh, Frank went too far all right, landing a bed partner in such cav-
alier fashion, as though he were ordering Chinese takeout, for God's sake!
But I said not a word to him, because what he did in that instance, or in any
other instance, was no more my business than the penchant I had for picking up strangers was his. And just as he said nothing about my embrace of
marijuana in lieu of down-to-earth boozing, I never questioned the way he
now started the day, taking his orange juice laced with bourbon. Our habits
and private lives, particularly as they involved sex, were never a source of
trouble between us—not yet, anyway.

It just occurred to me that I may have given you the idea that those late-
night phone calls typified what life was like at 791 Broadway during all of
1964. Actually, half of that year could be described as a hiatus in the whirlwind life Frank pursued in his final years. He drank less than usual, he stayed
home two or three nights a week, he took pleasure in at last having a decent
place to live. He must have missed Vincent, but I suspect he was optimistic
about the chances of working things out with him, which I suppose would
account for his equanimity at that time. Then there was Joe, my frequent
bed partner, who would sometimes join us for dinner: being quiet and
unassertive, he did not intrude upon the everydayness of our lives. In some

ways, those six months were like it was in the beginning, the easygoing time before Jimmy Schuyler's return to Squalid Manor.

It was also during that period that I found myself drawn into the orbit of Andy Warhol, whose fabled Factory I visited on several occasions, once to appear in one of his dumb home movies. The footage must be somewhere: I am filmed eating a banana—that is all I do. Actually, on the occasion of that visit, the first of three or four, I had come by not to appear in a movie, which was a spur-of-the-moment improvisation, but to follow up on an idea I'd drunkenly proposed to Andy at one of Kenward Elmslie's parties. "For a change," I said, "why don't you make a really long movie?" Never one to dismiss an idea, Andy exuded enthusiasm in his usual zombielike fashion. "A really long movie?" he echoed softly, looking off. "Yes," I said, "with something happening." "Hmm," he murmured. "Do you have any ideas?" "Oh yes," I lied, "I have several ideas." This, by the way, was before his first feature-length films, the Empire State Building footage, which was interminable and static, and *Chelsea Girls*, which went on for a mere three hours, as I recall, and, in a murky sort of way, actually had something going on. Anyway, Andy said just enough—intoning the word "super," no doubt—to convince me he was interested.

When I told Frank of our plans—it was understood that I would provide the scenario—I wasn't the least surprised by the bored, skeptical look he gave me. For one thing, hadn't he stated categorically, "It won't last beyond this season," when I asked what he thought of Pop Art? And there was the time Andy approached him about doing his portrait. "I don't like posing," Frank told him. "You pose for Larry Rivers," Andy said. "You're not Larry Rivers," Frank snapped, a riposte whose irony he would not live long enough to appreciate. But as indifferent as he was in regard to Andy and his kind of art, he agreed to write a segment for our omnibus movie, whose dozen or so episodes would be written by poets I knew on the downtown scene. But apart from Frank, who collaborated with Frank Lima on an utterly uncinematic script entitled "Love on the Hoof," which you'll find in Frank's *Selected Plays*, only Edwin Denby and Ron Padgett came through with something before both Andy and I lost interest in the project. Actually, I doubt that Andy was ever serious, though it was hard to tell with him.

But something from our nonexistent movie has survived: its catchy title. Unless I misremember, it was Bill Berkson who thought it up and offered it to me, and many years later, in 1997, I came upon it in *The Farewell Symphony*, Edmund White's gossipy roman à clef about New York's gay literary scene in the age of AIDS. "I'm going to write the story of my friends and call it *Messy Lives,*" announces a character named Tom who is described by the narrator as "my droll friend who was the poetry editor of a famous magazine."

A related matter is a discovery I made while ransacking my attic in search of the original *I Remember* and its two sequels. Seemingly from nowhere, a letter of Frank's addressed not to me but to Mike Goldberg found its way into my hands—yes, like wheat from chaff, it truly appeared to have separated itself from the other papers and printed matter; and while I wondered how the letter got into my attic, I blithely brushed aside this mystery, so caught up was I in the prospect of reading a letter of Frank's, a letter whose postmark, November 28, 1964, only enhanced my inquisitiveness, that date being just a month before we broke up!

Am I making too much of this? Are you still with me? Ordinarily, Frank typed everything, his correspondence as well as his poems, on dirt-cheap canary-yellow second sheets, but on this occasion he had decent stationery at his disposal, courtesy of the museum—thus, the two-page letter he'd written Mike, then enduring a "messy life" of his own as a patient at the Psychiatric Institute at Columbia-Presbyterian, was not parched and faded but in pristine condition so that it appeared to have been written and mailed just the other day, and had somehow gone astray, making me the recipient. I had unwittingly intercepted it!

Unable to wait until I was downstairs and had decent light, I made myself as comfortable as possible, squinted to bring Frank's words into focus, and then—well, what happened then was miraculous: the years fell away, Frank came alive, and, to my relief, I was soon basking in the warm, supportive message he'd composed for Mike. I felt I'd been granted a reprieve: there were no words of disapprobation concerning me. Then this on the next page, and I was abruptly embroiled anew in the gay soap opera that unfolded at 791 Broadway some thirty-odd years ago:

> As for my love life, I seem to be having a kind of double one, which means probably that I will soon be totally alone and able to write you even longer and more frequent letters. I don't want you to mention this to Patsy, because I think she sometimes gets either over-fond [of] or over-irritated with Joe and spills the beans (as I do) to prove a theoretical point, but it seems right now to be equally divided between JJ and Kynaston, both of whom I am crazy about, though not necessarily happy because of. However, that is not a complaint, since I have long since given up the idea of being happy for the idea of being active, or engagé, or whatever it is the French tell us we ought to be and Walt Whitman seems to back up. I just reread this and it is a little too cagey, but I'm sure you understand my every thought and inference and which way the land lies. I have also been having some interesting fights with Joe because he is pompous, hypocritical, egoistic, jealous and doesn't deliver phone messages unless they are from Kynaston, a little trick that may cost him plenty since Kenward has moved into his scene in no uncertain terms . . .

I stopped reading and threw the letter to the floor, suddenly overcome with the urge, the irrational, impossible urge, to get Frank on the phone and tell him how stung I was . . .

I picked up the two slips of paper; I gazed at them, stupidly; I pondered. Then, and only then, did it begin to dawn on me that I had seen the letter before, in another context, in another life—but where? when? Seven, eight years ago—in Brad Gooch's *City Poet,* of course! There it had no meaning, no reality, not within the pages of Brad's cold, deadly account of Frank's life. The letter became real only when it was palpable, when I could hold it in my two hands.

Now I am back at my computer, ready to follow through on J.J.'s suggestion that I relate the story that even in its abbreviated form, as provided herewith, has as rightful a claim as any to the title MESSY LIVES.

DIGRESSIONS ON SOME POEMS BY FRANK O'HARA

Where to begin? Why not with Vincent Warren's departure from Frank's life and Joe Brainard's entry into mine? They occur simultaneously and provide the basis for the mess that will ensue. In the weeks after my first night with Joe, Frank and I have dinner parties—exclusively gay, I might add: this will be Frank's final gay period, the analogue of the summer of 1955 commemorated by "At the Old Place," "All of a sudden all of the world . . . ," and the James Dean poems, except no comparable works will emerge this time. Joe often has dinner with Frank and me, just the three of us, and sometimes we watch TV together, usually old movies. Then Joe shares my bed. I am very cold to J.J. when I run into him. He knows about Joe and me, seems piqued that I've made out so soon after our breakup.

"I think I should tell you that I've been seeing Joe Brainard," says Alvin Novak, who is ordinarily evasive and irritatingly discreet. (Why tell me this? When I made out with a friend's lover, my friend certainly never heard about it from me!) A few weeks later, I see J.J. at John Button's and we go off together at the end of the evening, to his place. This unexpected reunion occurs on the night Frank is in Princeton for a reading he's giving with several other poets, including Joe Brainard, who ends up *chez nous,* in Frank's bed. (I found this out from Frank himself, his admission a simple statement of fact when I asked how the evening and the reading went. I did not experience any jealousy. Why not? Maybe because I spent the night with J.J.) Kenward Elmslie is interested in Joe Brainard. But I knew that a couple of weeks ago when he took Joe and me to his Westhampton beach house for the weekend.

Jim Brodey spends the night with Frank, Steve Holden spends the night with Frank, Kynaston McShine spends the night with Frank—not quite but almost in tandem, one night after another.

Kenward finally makes his move. (How did I know? Joe told me himself: I had become the repository of confessions.)

Frank is collaborating with Frank Lima on an episode for *Messy Lives.* I come home; drunken laughter draws me to Frank's room, and there the two of them are, buck naked, fooling around with each other. "What the hell are you two doing?" I ask in astonishment.

In May 1964, Frank writes a poem called "The Green Hornet" and dedicates it to J.J. (I learned about the poem later and decided that it foreshadowed the moves Frank would make that fall.)

Getting home at three in the morning from a ships-passing-in-the-night tryst—no, I am not being faithful to Joe; we have no understanding—I run into Jim Brodey at our downstairs door, about to ring the bell. "Oh, good," he says, "you can let me in—I won't have to get Frank out of bed." "I bet his phone call got you out of bed," I tell him, opening the door. Jim is a heavyset, mildly attractive twenty-year-old student of Frank's at the New School. Just the other day, I heard Frank tell him, "Stop writing like me! That's not what I have to teach you." (Jim could be very irritating, and I complained about him more than I did about any of Frank's boyfriends. "If you ever met his mother," Frank said, ever-permissive and nonjudgmental, "you'd forgive him anything." But was he straight or gay? Frank didn't seem to care, and neither did Jim.)

One morning, as I'm making coffee, I hear voices from Frank's room and, as I am wont to do, I look to see if the clothes and shoes outside his door are Kynaston's or Jim's and quickly surmise they are Jim's. "Frank," I call, "are you and Jim ready for coffee?" Kynaston's head pops out: "Bitch!" (Frank berated me later, even though it was an honest mistake. I had the uneasy feeling, then and on other occasions, that I was beginning to get on Frank's nerves.)

What happened to Alvin? He is out of the picture and Kenward is very much in it. But since I am making out with others besides Joe—for example, a fuck buddy named Dennis, someone I never see socially—I have no room to complain, and I don't. (Dennis, I soon learned, was in the habit of calling J.J. when he felt horny, which was quite often, and if J.J. wasn't available or wasn't interested, usually the case with the younger, better hung, and more popular J.J., the fuck buddy would then call me. "Expect a call from Hungry Dennis," J.J. would alert me by phone on those occasions when the pecking order reached me.)

Joe tells me how much he dislikes J.J., and I decide he must be jealous because of my affair with J.J. (Years later, when he finally landed J.J., it would become clear that all along he was simply attracted to my sexy ex-boyfriend.)

The Sentimental Units · 293

"I went over there a couple of times when Joe wasn't there, and Frank came over a couple of times to his old apartment on East Ninth Street where I was living with Tony Towle. A dozen times at the most, probably. I think if Joe had known I was seeing Frank on the side he would have been jealous." Joe Brainard, as quoted by Brad Gooch. (When I came upon this statement in *City Poet*, I didn't know what to make of it. A manifestation of Joe's hero-worship of Frank, assignations that never took place, or could Frank actually have made room for Joe with all the others? Also, I was always home; I think it was a fantasy of Joe's.)

Jim Brodey appears to be out of the rotation, and I'm not sure Steve Holden will be coming around again, so the field is now open to Kynaston McShine. (Or so I thought: the biggest jolt was yet to come.)

That jolt comes when I am making coffee one morning and J.J. emerges, stark naked, from Frank's room. "Hi," I say coolly, disguising my surprise, shock, outrage. "Hi," he says back to me, with extraordinary aplomb, and slips past me to go to the shower off the kitchen. Frank appears, comes into the kitchen, shouts above the sound of the shower: "How do you like your coffee, J.J.?" Not missing a beat, I say: "One sugar, Frank." (How else was I supposed to play this scene, if not as Miriam Hopkins to Frank's Bette Davis?)

Days go by. Kenward is seeing a lot of Joe, I assume, because I'm certainly not. Out of the blue, as though we're back to being confidants and the best of friends, Frank tells me: "I am beginning to prefer J.J. to Kynaston, because when Kynaston comes over he's always gloomy and there's nothing I can do to change his mood. With J.J. it's different; he lights up when he sees me. I feel I've changed his life. That never happens with Kynaston." (I don't know why I didn't ask: Why are you telling me this? This was the last time Frank took me into his confidence—about anything.)

Kynaston, aware that J.J. is winning out, complains to me about his neme-sis: "He never reads anything. He's empty—there's nothing to him." (Some complaint. Like Joe Brainard, Kynaston was attracted to J.J. and eventually, years later, he would also make out with him.)

DIGRESSIONS ON SOME POEMS BY FRANK O'HARA

It seems I failed to let Frank know J.J. phoned when Frank was out. The inevitable happens: Frank gives me my walking papers. He's brutal about it but also generous: he suggests I take the New Mexico landscape John Button gave us as well as a Norman Bluhm gouache we shared. Our two cats will remain where they are.

OEDIPUS REX

[A P R I L   7 ,   1 9 6 6]

*He falls; but even in falling he is higher than those who fly into the
ordinary sun.*

hese words—I suppose they can be regarded as his final lines of poetry—
comprise the sole entry in a journal of Frank's, an attractively designed
notebook he picked up on one of his trips to Europe. The notebook was
among his things at the time he was run down on the beach at Fire Island
Pines; no doubt he thought he might write something in it over the weekend.
Oddly, his name as scrawled on the cover is not in his immediately recognizable hand. Did Frank consciously change his signature, and if so, why? Make
of that what you will. What interests me is the epigraph recorded in the journal and what it brings to mind, what I remember in connection with it.

What I remember, first of all, is having lunch with Frank in the spring of
1966 and his telling me about a commission Larry Rivers had received and
accepted, that of providing the decor and costumes for Stravinsky's *Oedipus
Rex*, an opera oratorio with a text by Cocteau. It was going to be part of a
Stravinsky festival that summer at Lincoln Center, with Lukas Foss con-
ducting the New York Philharmonic. Though unacquainted with the work, I
knew it to be something of a hybrid, one bound to pose problems for the most
experienced stage designer or artist. "It'll be interesting to see what Larry

dreams up," I remarked. Frank nodded, noncommittally. I had no idea then, or later, whether he was aware of the hijinks Larry had planned for his mis en scène. Anyway, it was around the time of our lunch—on April 7, as we know from the journal—that Frank made his *Oedipus Rex* entry.

About two and a half months later, I ran into Frank and Larry on Second Avenue. It was early in the evening; they were going off to dinner, to some-place downtown, and Frank asked me to join them. I remember saying, "I've got nothing better to do," and we laughed. It was suddenly like old times, when Frank and I lived together and we'd sometimes have dinner with Larry.

When we finished eating—at Sing Wu or some other dreary haunt of ours—Frank asked Larry, "Do you want to read it or should I?" and then ex-plained to me that they had to go over a statement Larry had written for the *Oedipus Rex* program. I think he had to turn it in the next day, as the concert was just a couple of weeks off.

Larry read what he'd written in a big, confident voice. I don't remember the gist of the piece, what he was trying to get across, but I do remember the way it was written, in a hip, casual, vernacular manner, in a style not all that different from the way he and Frank wrote some of their things. Also, as one would expect from Larry, there was the impression that he was anything but overwhelmed by being involved with the New York Philharmonic in the per-formance of a work by Stravinsky.

Frank blew up. As best I can remember, his tirade went something like this: "Picasso, Nijinsky, Auden, and Balanchine are among your predeces-sors, great artists who had the distinction of working with another great artist, *Igor Stravinsky*! . . . and you write something like that, as though what you're doing is no big deal!" Frank paused for effect. Larry tried to say some-thing, but Frank cut him off. "You're not showing the proper respect. It's as though you're unaware that you're involved in a creative capacity with the greatest composer of the twentieth century." He shook his head despair-ingly; this was Frank O'Hara at his best—passionate, incisive, uncompro-mising. "What you have written is inappropriate and totally unacceptable.

It just won't do, Larry. Now," he concluded, after taking a deep breath, "we will go back to my place and put together a statement that is worthy of you."

As I watched Frank and Larry heading toward Broadway and Tenth Street, with Frank resolutely leading the way, I suddenly became aware of the weather. It was especially beautiful, almost balmy, and since it was still the shank of the evening and I felt horny—nice weather always had that effect on me when I was younger—I saw no reason why I shouldn't go cruising.

I was lucky; I made out. I know that not because I remember anything about the experience but because of the brief exchange I had with Larry when, some three hours later, I ran into him in front of the Gem Spa on Second Avenue. Poor Larry! How beaten and haggard he looked!

"My God, what happened to you?" I said.

He shook his head, wearily. "That Frank. He wouldn't let me leave until we had something he thought was acceptable." He looked at me. "And what have you been up to all this time?"

"I've had a wonderful time since I left you."

"Guess I don't have to ask what you did. See you." And he trudged off into the night.

Try to imagine the spectacle that greeted the audience at Lincoln Center's Philharmonic Hall on the evening of July 20, 1966 (to jog my memory, I have consulted Larry Rivers's "unauthorized autobiography," *What Did I Do?*, which he wrote with the assistance of Arnold Weinstein).

The members of the orchestra, in shirtsleeves, and the one hundred and fifty members of the chorus, in sleeveless undershirts and dark glasses, take their places; the soloists—the Oedipus of the evening dressed as a boxer, the Jocasta in a wild plastic number, the narrator in blue cashmere sweater, white boating shoes, and pastel-colored pants—then make their entrances, followed by the informally attired conductor. As for the set and decor, the action takes place in a boxing ring and there is a backdrop of cutouts of spray-painted insects representing the plague that besets Thebes—this I remember without having to refer to Larry's book, since he later presented me with a mock-up of three of the insects that I had framed and still have hanging where I live. What else? Oh yes, at the climax of the piece, the audience is drawn into the proceedings when a bank of lights, a thousand watts each, is trained on them, thus blinding them so that they experience what Oedipus endured.

Well, I don't think I have to tell you how the notoriously conservative Philharmonic concertgoers responded. After polite, respectful applause for the musicians and soloists, there was vigorous booing for Larry as he was brought onstage and recognized as the culprit. Larry, I must say, took it all very well, as we knew he would if things didn't go well. Frank and I, by the way, had excellent orchestra seats, courtesy of Larry.

In the *Times* the next morning, its chief music critic, the tradition-bound Harold C. Schoenberg, echoed the sentiments of the unforgiving first-night audience. After characterizing Larry's set and costumes as "low camp . . . [and] patchy things hastily thrown together" and the performance of the piece as "falling into the spirit of the occasion"—Lukas, it seems, "did his best to destroy" the score—he concluded: "If these bright boys would only keep their hands off the art works of their betters the cultural scene would be a good deal healthier."

Virtually everything I remember about the evening involves Frank; everything else is a blur. Why that should be so is easy to understand: it was our last time together, an occasion that brought us full circle, the *Oedipus Rex* concert being an analogue of the Town Hall concert at which John Ashbery introduced us fifteen years earlier. But that is a mere conceit of mine, an afterthought. What matters to me is my recollection of the evening of July 20, 1966, whose fleeting moments I cleave to some thirty-odd years later.

Moving down the aisle to take our seats, I catch sight of Richard Howard and Sandy Friedman getting seated and, as Frank sensibly moves on, with an easy smile and nod in their direction, I foolishly and unnecessarily call out, "Have you come to see what Larry's done?" which draws from one of them, haughtily, "We've come to *all* the Stravinsky concerts."

Oedipus Rex · 299

Frank, getting seated, is miffed with me for not having a comeback: "Why didn't you tell them you were listening to Stravinsky before they knew who he was?"

As Jason Robards appears on stage, I can't resist saying: "To think Cocteau was the narrator at the premiere—what a comedown!" which elicits from Frank a reminder that gently puts me in my place: "Remember how great Robards was in *Hughie*?"

We are unusually attentive during the performance. I don't know how Frank feels but I want desperately to like Larry's contribution. Always looking for something positive, Frank grips my arm at a powerful moment in the music.

It is now intermission. I say to Frank, "Let me buy you a drink." He sees Camilla McGrath, knows Earl is in London, realizes she is here alone, and says, as he moves to greet her, "And a drink for Camilla." I say, "Of course," thinking: Frank's always so thoughtful and generous, even with other people's money. I am not yet aware—I will find this out at the end of the evening—that he hasn't enough money on him to buy himself a drink, let alone enough for the three of us.

When we return to our seats, Frank mentions that he's been reading my theater reviews in *The Village Voice*. "You're so mean, Joe," he tells me. "But those off-off-Broadway things are terrible," I explain. "What am I supposed to do?" His solution: "Don't write anything."

When the performance is over, Frank and I applaud enthusiastically. Our neighbors look at us as though they think we're out of our minds.

The next thing I remember, we are in a cab heading across town to drop off Camilla at her place in the East Sixties. We chat about everything but the concert. Camilla looks particularly beautiful. Frank comments on that. When we get to her place, he is his usual gallant self: he hops out of the cab and walks her to the door, kisses her good night, waits until she's safely inside before he gets back into the cab.

We proceed downtown. Frank's is the next stop, mine the last. We are unusually quiet, as though we have nothing to say to each other. Well, we don't share each other's lives anymore. I don't even know what he's doing for the weekend—surely, he's going somewhere with J.J. And I suddenly feel left out. Frank turns to me, as though aware of my mood: "Everything going all right for you?" "Sure," I answer. "You're awfully quiet," he says. "So are you," I tell him. And we fall silent again.

As we're nearing the four-story building at Broadway and Tenth, opposite Grace Church, which is all lit up and looks quite grand, I quickly thank him for the evening. "It was nice of you to take me," I tell him, without adding what is implicit: "Instead of taking J.J." Frank says, "This was your sort of thing. I thought you should come." I tell him thanks again. This, however, is not a moment for an emotional display—there never is a chance of that anymore—and Frank sits forward and instructs the driver where to let him off.

And now, as he alights from the cab, he reaches into his coat pocket and turns back to me. "This is all the money I have," he says amiably, and showers me with pennies, dimes, nickels, maybe a quarter, then closes the door before I can say a word.

What happens next, as the cab pulls away, I will remember more clearly than anything else that evening. As though reverting to a childhood habit of mine—after kissing my mother good night, I'd turn to look at her before leaving the room, thus framing a picture I'd forever hold in my mind in case she died during the night—I now turn to look out the rear window so I can watch Frank as he walks briskly to the building at 791 Broadway.

Saturday morning, three days after the concert. I learn that Frank and J.J. are not spending the weekend at Southampton with Larry and Clarice Rivers but, instead, they have gone with Virgil Thomson to Morris Golde's summer place at Water Island, the most remote part of Fire Island.

Sunday morning, about seven. It's J.J. on the phone, calling from what he describes as a "dinky hospital in Mastic Beach." Frank has been injured in a crazy accident at the Pines. "It's serious, Joe." J.J.'s been up all night, now he's waiting for word from the doctor. "I called Morris to let him know what happened, and he said, 'Keep me posted,' like it was no big deal." He explains that the four of them had gone to a bar in the Pines and that he and Frank stayed on to drink while Morris took Virgil back to the house. "So you're there alone." "Yes. I'm exhausted. I'll call back as soon as I know more."

Sunday, late afternoon. I meet Larry at Max's Kansas City; over beers, we're consulting about what to do. Frank is still at Bayview General Hospital, which has inadequate facilities. There is talk about getting him moved to New York by helicopter. Kenneth Koch ambles in, doesn't know what's happened; tears spring to his eyes when we tell him. That evening, J.J. returns to the city with Morris and Virgil. He tells me he thought of staying with Frank but realized there was nothing he could do.

Monday morning, about ten, Larry, Kenneth, J.J., and I drive to Bayview General Hospital, a two-story complex where we meet with the doctor in charge. We're told that Frank has a fifty-fifty chance and that if he lives he'll have to give up alcohol because of the damage to his liver. "Can you imagine Frank not drinking?" I ask J.J. Curiously, it is this prospect that fills us with anxiety about Frank's chances of recovery, not the injuries he sustained.

The doctor tells us we can see him, two at a time and only for a few minutes. J.J. and I go in first. J.J. speaks Frank's name, very softly. I say nothing: I can't find my voice. Seeing him broken and sewn together, with no encouraging sign that he might survive, I hang back as J.J. moves into the room—how admirable he is! "Steve?" Frank says, mistaking J.J. for Stephen Holden, who at that time had a great head of curly, sandy-colored hair like J.J.'s. "No, it's J.J., and Joe's here." I am still unable to speak, nor can I reach out and touch Frank, as J.J. does. A nurse appears: time is up.

Bill and Elaine de Kooning arrive, Bill with a business-size checkbook. He offers a blank check to the hospital: "I vant the best for our friend."

Monday night. I am home alone, waiting. At nine o'clock the phone rings. It is Patsy, who is at the hospital: "Frank died five minutes ago. Tell the people in New York." I call Larry first—"No! No! No! How can I live without him?" he cries—and then J.J., who has already heard.

About forty-five minutes later, people begin arriving at my place, unin-vited—an impromptu wake: J.J., Larry, Mike Goldberg and Karen Edwards, Frank Lima, Camilla McGrath, Ned Rorem, and Joe Adamiak. Mike jokes: "Now Frank will never go completely bald." But when Ned asks Mike how he is, Mike snaps: "What kind of question is that to ask at a time like this?" Larry has a discussion with J.J. about Frank's wallet; it seems he lent Frank several hundred dollars and he won't bring a claim against the estate—"Just give me what's in the wallet." J.J.: "The wallet's at home. I'll see how much there is and send you a check." Alvin Novak, who lives around the corner, phones: "Can I come over?" The phone rings again. It is Patsy, who speaks with Mike and has an argument with him. The phone again: Bill Berkson this time, from Newport or some such place. "Oh, Bill," I say when he identifies himself. "Let me speak to J.J.," he says abruptly, coldly; and when he gets J.J. on the phone, he takes it upon himself to tell him that he shouldn't blame himself for what happened. Next I get a call from Barbara Harris, Arnold Weinstein's girlfriend: "Is Arnold there?" The downstairs buzzer sounds. Kenneth Koch bounds up the five flights of stairs to my place, his two suit-cases in hand. Larry and Frank Lima go to Frank's apartment with Kenneth. Larry removes his sculpture from the place, and Frank Lima takes Frank's passport as a keepsake—I will learn this later. By about one in the morning I am alone with J.J., who spends the night.

Monday morning, at Ned's. For some reason—is it another wake?—a num-ber of us have gathered at his Greenwich Village apartment. Ned is kind, thoughtful, comforting—which does not surprise me. What surprises me is a remark he makes, apparently to explain his calm demeanor: "You must un-derstand, I don't feel things deeply." Harold Brodkey phones, asks to speak to me, says he would like to help; I'm not sure how he can help but I'm struck by his tone of voice, how distraught he sounds. Virgil says two things that I will remember later: "Baby, I hope you kept a journal" and, in reference to Patsy, whom he met at the hospital, "She is a woman of substance."

Tuesday afternoon, East Hampton. J.J., Kynaston, and I have come out together for the funeral and burial, which will take place the next day at Green River Cemetery in Springs. Patsy—stern, determined, incredibly efficient—has made all of the arrangements. J.J., Kynaston, and I end up spending the night at a house rented by Barbara Guest, who feels I should be involved in the service. She fetches Don Allen's *New American Poetry,* turns to Frank's "Ode to Joy," tells me I should read it tomorrow. I practice reading it aloud; she suggests how it should be read; I am up most of the night going over the poem.

Wednesday, around noon. Helen Frankenthaler and Gaby Rodgers hook up with me, drive me to lunch at someone's house. En route Helen says, "Don't be surprised at how calm Bob is—he keeps his feelings to himself." And Robert Motherwell is indeed unemotional, but also cordial. Jerry Lieber is another story. After lunch, he drives me back to Barbara's. As we sit for a moment in front of her house, tears spring to his eyes: "I can only imagine how this is for you. He was an angel."

Wednesday afternoon. With Barbara supporting me on one side and Bob Dash on the other, I feel as if I'm gliding into the crowd of mourners at Green River Cemetery. It is dreamlike, unreal, like being on LSD, except my five or six acid trips had none of the gravity I'm experiencing now: this is another dimension, a brush with death.

The next day—evening, about seven. I am alone, waiting for J.J. We're having drinks and then going to dinner someplace. When I open the door for him, I see that he is holding something, some sort of notebook with a frilly design in orange. "I thought you should have this," he says, and hands it to me. "I think he bought it in Europe, on his last trip. It was with his things." I open it. I read the first page, then flip through the other pages and see that there is only that one page with writing. I turn back to the inscription, read it again—aloud this time: "He falls; but even in falling he is higher than those who fly into the ordinary sun." I close the notebook and look at J.J. for a long moment. "Prophetic, is that what you're thinking?" J.J. says. "He was writing about himself." It is then that I ask if Frank had Mike Kanemitsu's good luck coin with him. J.J. shakes his head. "It figures," I say, and I make our drinks.